SOMETHING

from NOTHING

NEWFIELD

FOUNDING BUSINESS PRINCIPLES

TALENTED EMPLOYEES

FOCUS

BALANCE OF EXPLORATION
AND ACQUISITIONS

EMPHASIS ON TECHNOLOGY
AND TEAMWORK

MINDSET OF AN INDEPENDENT

CONTROL OF OPERATIONS

EMPLOYEE OWNERSHIP

FOUNDER

bright sky press
HOUSTON, TEXAS

2365 Rice Boulevard, Suite 202,
Houston, Texas 77005

Library of Congress Cataloging-in-Publication Data on file with publisher.

10   9   8   7   6   5   4   3   2   1

Creative Direction and cover design, Ellen Cregan; Design, Marla Garcia
Printed in Canada

ARTHUR L. SMITH

SOMETHING
from NOTHING

"There is no greater joy in life than starting with nothing and winding up
with something. That's what parents do when they have children.
That's what poets and artists do when they create something new and different.
And that's what we did when we created and built Newfield."

JOE B. FOSTER
AND THE PEOPLE WHO BUILT
NEWFIELD EXPLORATION COMPANY

TABLE OF CONTENTS

TO MY PARENTS, LILY AND ART—MY CONSTANT, CONSISTENT FANS
WHO ARE STILL DEDICATED TO THE UNREACHABLE GOAL
OF "JUST TRYING TO MAKE YOU PERFECT."

INTRODUCTION

"**Y**ou don't have to be a bastard to be successful in the oil business—but it sure doesn't hurt." So began my first draft.

I began this book with the "snappy" working title: "Gushers and Dusters: Management Lessons from the Toughest Bastards in the Oil Business."

Robert Bryce, my friend and author of *Pipe Dreams, Gusher of Lies* and most recently, *Power Hungry,* encouraged me to collect the wisdom of the top oil industry executives I knew and loved.

I began by interviewing Forrest Hoglund (EOG Resources), Bill Barrett (Barrett Resources), Raymond Plank (Apache), Bob Simpson (XTO Energy), Jon Brumley (Encore Acquisition), and Joe Foster (Newfield Exploration)—all founders or lead executives of their companies. These great oilmen had valuable insights and anecdotes, and some had very bad jokes—but those are my secret!

During my 35 years as an oil analyst and head of my own firm, John S. Herold, Inc., and now, Triple Double Advisors, LLC, I have been fortunate to know many truly inspirational oil and gas executives. One of these, Raymond Plank, provided a memorable interview. Along with some great anecdotes, Raymond also shared a dense cloud of pipe tobacco smoke in his smoke-free office at 2000 Post Oak Blvd. in Houston.

Several common themes emerged from these interviews:

1) *Focus Wins* – **Concentrate on doing a few things very well with first rate geology and well understood geography (and don't allow the organization to be seduced by too many emerging opportunities).**

2) *Practice the "Law of Capture"* – **When a company finds a new drilling area or a new technology that works, "Get all that you can get."**

3) *Practice "Fast Failure"* – **Conversely, if a new initiative is not working (and holds little promise of becoming the next Comstock Lode), "Get the hell out as fast as you can!" Avoid "an increasing commitment to a failing course of action."**

Messrs. Hoglund, Barrett, Plank, Simpson, and Brumley have all had great careers in the oil and gas industry—and their stories need to be told as well. But those are other books.

The story that really grabbed my attention was Joe B. Foster's. ***Something from Nothing*** originated from the first few of those interviews. After some additional fascinating interviews, Joe shared the transcripts of a few speeches he had given over the years to industry trade groups and associations. These were fantastic building-block chapters for this book.

I was familiar with the boardroom crises that led to the dismantlement of Tenneco Oil in 1988; I was at Herold at the time and we did extensive research on the transaction. But I didn't know the inside story of Tenneco and the struggle Joe Foster waged, first to prevent the sale of the Exploration and Production company, then to try to purchase some of its significant assets in a leveraged buyout. Joe's failures with Tenneco led to his quest to launch a new oil and gas company from scratch.

After numerous interviews on Joe's years at Tenneco, I began to flesh out the story of Newfield Exploration Company through interviews with key investors like Howard Newman and Charles Duncan and key associates like Terry Rathert and David Schaible.

New perspectives on Joe and the Newfield story came from Elliott Pew, Bill Schneider, and Bob Waldrup. Finally, I lassoed David Trice and Betty Smith to tell their tales. Later on, I sought out the new guard, which included Gary Packer, Lee Boothby, George Dunn and Steve Campbell. It soon became clear that, while Joe Foster was the lead, this was to be a story about a remarkable group of people who evolved into a close knit clan of energy professionals.

Joe Foster has had—as the Brits would say—a brilliant career. Fellow Texans might be less laudatory and observe that, as a distinguished Texas A&M University (A&M) petroleum engineering grad and a Battalion Commander of the Corps of Cadets, he performed "as expected." But no one in the "oil patch" can challenge the reality: Joe Foster's influence on the exploration and production (E&P) business has been remarkable.

FOREWORD
BY ARTHUR L. SMITH

DO YOU REMEMBER ARTHUR ANDERSEN—THOSE GUYS WITH GREEN EYESHADES WHO SPELLED THEIR LAST NAME WITH AN "E"?

I first met Joe Foster at an Arthur Andersen energy conference in Houston in the early 1990s, hosted by the now-defunct accounting firm whose ship went down with the collapse of Enron.

To this day, I remember being at the Westin Galleria Hotel and shaking Joe's hand. I felt his leadership strength in his comfortable, relaxed style. Joe Foster had a unique, slow, and measured verbal delivery, as he does today.

He knew my company—John S. Herold, Inc.—and he knew we were legitimate oil analysts.

I remember Joe's presentation that day: no slides or overheads, and refreshingly, no PowerPoint®. Joe Foster was humble; he told the energy conference audience the truth. Newfield Exploration was airborne—albeit barely—but he and his comrades had confidence that it would all work out.

NEWFIELD EXPLORATION COMPANY COULD HAVE BEEN STILLBORN

After toiling "flat out" for three decades for one company, in late 1988 Joe found himself in a strange situation. He suddenly went from manning the bridge of Tennessee Gas Transmission and Tenneco Oil, two of the largest oil and gas companies in North America, to unceremoniously being unemployed. Joe Foster could easily have called it quits after an outstanding 31-year career.

Tenneco awarded Joe an ample severance package. However, we are all thankful that the then 54-year-old oil executive didn't grab a new set of golf clubs and head for the country club. As I write these words today, I am 58 and Joe's inspirational story still injects adrenaline into my arteries. There are many more new *Newfields* and *Herolds* to be built: neither of us are ready to call it quits.

In 1989, Joe B. Foster built the foundation that has carried startup Newfield Exploration Company from insignificance to what is today—an $11.6 billion enterprise value energy company that employs more than 1,300 talented professionals. This month Newfield Exploration was recognized among the market's leading public companies and was added to the S&P 500 Index.

I have been truly blessed with the opportunity to help celebrate Joe Foster's remarkable life and business career and to interview the people key to Newfield Exploration Company's success.

Arthur L. Smith
December 2010
Houston, Texas

ACKNOWLEDGMENTS

Although this book lists one author, it is the work of more than a dozen individuals who have played significant roles in telling the Newfield Exploration story. In addition to the top brass at Newfield today—Messrs. Boothby, Rathert, Schneider, Packer, Dunn and Campbell—thanks go to former Newfield executives David Trice, Bob Waldrup, Elliott Pew and Jim Ulm. Also, key Newfield investors Charles Duncan, Howard Newman and Dale Zand gave freely of their time. Special thanks to Betty Smith in her role as top cheerleader for both Joe Foster and Newfield.

Robert Bryce and Mimi Bardagjy, both based in Austin, contributed valuable editorial input, for which I am most appreciative. In addition, Debra Claxton, my executive assistant and Shirley Vaughn, Joe Foster's capable assistant, deserve special recognition for their delicate role in scheduling interviews, editing and re-editing drafts, and general multi-tasking to keep the manuscript moving forward.

I wish to acknowledge the example set by nineteenth-century Victorian author Anthony Trollope for the inspiration to compose a book while holding down a full-time job. Trollope, employed as a postal supervisor, wrote before work each morning between 5:30 and 8:30; the result: 47 novels and 16 miscellaneous books.

FOREWORD
BY JOE B. FOSTER

When Art Smith first interviewed me, it was for a chapter of a book he was writing. I never expected or encouraged it to become a book about me and Newfield. However, this became a real "project" for Art, a labor of love for him, and he would not be deterred. He just kept showing up with his tape recorder. How could I not talk to Art about Newfield? I talk to people in the elevator about Newfield, but none have ever listened as attentively as Art Smith. He infiltrated the organization. How could we not cooperate with him?

Art's original subtitle for this book was *Joe B. Foster and the Exponential Success of Newfield Exploration Company.* I asked him to change it to *Joe B. Foster and the People Who Built Newfield Exploration Company,* for a couple of reasons. First, the story of Newfield is really a people story, a group story, more than a Joe Foster story. Second, as was painfully demonstrated during the stock market rout of 2008-09, Newfield's exponential growth was vulnerable to interruption.

It really was an entire team of people that made Newfield a success. It was by no means Joe Foster alone. I did assemble the group, but those who were there, and those who were watching Newfield in its early days, know it took me awhile to get the right people in the right places. I made as many people mistakes as I did drilling mistakes in the early days. I suppose that is the nature of new beginnings. But, we never gave up; we kept cutting and pasting until we got it right. I am a huge baseball fan. I know that if you get enough at-bats, you'll hit to the average you are capable of. My job during the early days of Newfield was to get the right batting order, and to get enough at-bats for the bright young guys who were good hitters so they could test their ideas adequately. We had some early-season woes, made some line-up changes, and, soon enough, began hitting the cover off the ball before Joe, the manager, got into enough trouble to be fired.

The key figures who made Newfield work in its early days, my "coaches," are highlighted, as are a couple of the franchise players. Every one of them, plus some of our directors, played roles which were, at times, more key than mine. There would be no Newfield today had there not been a Bob Waldrup or David Trice or Bill Schneider during that first year. Bob and Bill held the Lafayette office together when it was in serious danger of unravelling, buying us time to get the staff better positioned under one roof in Houston. David Trice was indefatigable in seeking and finding new investors and in cultivating the ones we had. The influence of Charles Duncan and Mike Patrick in the investment community was enormous. Howard Newman and the potential access of a Warburg Pincus bankroll was a looming presence. Then, there are the ones who grew and assumed real leadership roles later: Terry Rathert, Dave Schaible, George Dunn, Gary Packer, Lee Boothby. There are ones who are now gone: Bryan Nelson, Clay Harmon, Rich Mowrer, Frank Henicke, Todd Stone, Mike Minarovic, Tracy Price, Marion Gray, Elliott Pew. There was my assistant, Betty Smith, our den mother and cheerleader, and brownie baker for Charles Duncan. And this is not to mention the many contributors who came along after I left, some now in very key positions.

Newfield is a people story, all right, but we all recognize it's only getting told because in the end, we were successful. We created value; we created a company of ongoing value. We created nice nest eggs for most of our early employees, and great returns for all our early investors.

Since I retired as chairman of the board in 2005, my sole remaining "duty"—make that "pleasure"—at Newfield has been to attend the monthly birthday luncheons. It has been breathtaking to watch the company continue to grow! My direct influence has been gone from the company since I stepped down as CEO in late 1999. Yet, Newfield continues to grow and prosper at an accelerating rate.

The greatest pride I take in Newfield is that it has not missed a beat without Joe Foster. In those first ten years, the whole group of us created a culture of focus, of paying attention to people, of being open and honest, of doing quality work and lots of it, of peer review, and of keeping costs down—a culture that persists to this day. This tells me we really did create something—something very special—from nothing, other than the talents ideas, and beliefs of a group of kindred souls.

Joe B. Foster
December 2010
Houston, Texas

A NOTE FROM CHARLES DUNCAN

My relationship with Joe Foster began in 1988. I had known of Joe during his days at Tenneco and visited with him while I was Secretary of Energy in the Carter administration. But it was in November 1988 that Joe and I first had a serious face-to-face meeting, when he came to my Houston office in the NationsBank Building (now the Bank of America building). We had been introduced by Evans Attwell, a fellow I had known for my entire career in business and government. Evans was then Managing Partner of Vinson & Elkins, a leading Houston law firm. Vinson & Elkins had worked on spec for Joe in his failed effort to acquire some of the Tenneco Oil properties that were auctioned off in 1988. Evans knew that, with that episode behind him, Joe wanted to gather together a group of talented Tenneco oil finders and operators to form a new startup company. Evans also knew that I was chairman of a private equity fund (they were much rarer then than now) that might have an appetite for investing in such a venture.

Joe got right to the point: "I want to build a Gulf of Mexico independent oil and gas company, taking the best of the best from Tenneco Oil. We will focus on a small area of the Gulf of Mexico that we know extremely well and we will create value. Our mantra is simple: abundant technology, talented people, low costs, and a high degree of focus. We have learned what to do and what not to do at Tenneco." Joe held back no bad news about his failed efforts in the Tenneco bids. Nonetheless, I was impressed that Joe had been able to assemble the backing he had to make the bids he did.

My firm signed on early as one of the lead investors in what was then called "4-D Exploration," before Joe came to his senses and came up with the Newfield Exploration name. Some of the people in my firm introduced Joe and David Trice to the people at the University of Texas Endowment Fund, which decided to invest.

So, with $3 million from us, $3 million from the University of Texas Endowment Fund, and $3 million from Joe and his employees, Newfield was funded in April 1989.

Between January and April 1989, Joe and I would write personal checks into the Newfield account to cover payroll and other expenses. We were repaid in stock at the April closing.

The members of my firm and I invested in Newfield because we trusted Joe Foster, had met the people he brought with him, had seen their track record at Tenneco, and, further, believed that 1989—though not a robust time for the oil and gas business—would be a good time to put private equity into the sector. It helped, also, that they had a guy named David Trice who talked the same financial language some of our analysts did. Also, we liked the idea that David, the only non-Tenneco guy in the group, might break up any potential "group think"!

Both my firm and I made subsequent investments in Newfield Exploration over the years. I did not sell a single share of NFX stock during my entire tenure as a member of its board, which ended in the year 2000. Though I have since sold some for estate-planning purposes, I still hold a sizable stake in Newfield. I still believe in its people and its plan.

I cannot close without mentioning Dave Schaible, the young heir apparent who we lost to cancer in 2007. What a talent! What a tragedy! David Schaible was a go-to guy at Newfield from the very early days. It was a joy to see him progress from a 28-year-old junior engineer to President and COO of the company.

And it was a real pleasure—both psychic and financial—to help Joe Foster create something from nothing.

Charles Duncan
December 2010
Houston, Texas

PROLOGUE
NEWFIELD EXPLORATION BRUSHES WITH BANKRUPTCY

Amarex, Nucorp Energy, Damson Oil, Petro Lewis, GHK Petroleum, Saxon Oil: all independent oil and gas companies and all Chapter 11 bankruptcy victims of the great oil bust of the 1980s. After billions had been lost on bad loans to independent oil and drilling companies and hundreds of Texas and Oklahoma banks were shuttered, an oilman looking for capital was treated by most investors like the proverbial skunk at a picnic. Joe Foster's newly formed oil and gas exploration company was an exception—it was off the ground but traveling at low altitude and high speed.

Originally capitalized on New Year's Day 1989 with $9 million in seed money (18 percent of which was Joe Foster's own retirement stash from his 31-year career with Tenneco), Newfield Exploration Company in the Spring of 1990 was at death's door. It had no oil or natural gas production, no income, no bank facility and only about $100,000 of its original equity capital left in the till.

Newfield had gotten off to a miserable start. The company began operations by drilling three consecutive dry holes—all straight up with its own money. Dry holes are the anathema of exploration and production companies. The only redeeming characteristic of a dry hole—where an executive might derive some economic solace—is the existence of a "farmout" agreement with partners to share the financial pain. Once a well is pronounced a duster all is lost—there will be no oil or gas production or income, and it is standard industry practice to cough up "plug and abandon" dollars to effectively embalm each unsuccessful well. P&A spending in the oilfield is analogous to the receipt of a late and unbudgeted invoice from the undertaker for burial site restoration.

Joe Foster was disappointed, but determined to continue drilling. In his three decades of oil and gas exploration with Tenneco Oil, he had endured many an extended string of dry holes. Lady Luck's beneficence was never a concern for Foster and his Tenneco oil and natural gas explorationists. These gentlemen had a track record and knew that success comes to those who persevere—finding and exploiting commercial oil and natural gas deposits is not influenced by Santería.

"THERE IS NO JOY IN LIFE GREATER THAN STARTING WITH
NOTHING AND ENDING UP WITH SOMETHING. THAT IS
WHAT PARENTS DO WHEN THEY HAVE CHILDREN. IT IS WHAT
ENTREPRENEURS DO WHEN THEY START A BUSINESS.
IT IS WHAT POETS AND ARTISTS DO.

"AND THAT IS WHAT EXPLORERS DO WHEN THEY TAP INTO AN
OIL OR GAS DEPOSIT THAT HAS LAIN THERE, CAREFULLY HIDDEN
BY MOTHER NATURE, UNTOUCHED FOR MILLIONS
OF YEARS. IT IS THE JOY OF DISCOVERY WHICH MAKES
THE EXPLORATION BUSINESS SO SATISFYING."

– JOE B. FOSTER

CHAPTER I
JOE FOSTER'S STORY

FROM ARP TO A&M

It is ironic that Joe Foster grew up in a very dry county in northeast Texas. In the post-Depression 1930s, when Joe was a boy, Hunt County was "doubly dry"—lacking both establishments purveying alcohol and wells producing commercial volumes of petroleum. Over the past 75 years, Hunt has seen some scant production from the several hundred wells drilled in the county, but today Hunt is one of only 36 of the 254 counties in Texas without an economic oil or natural gas well.

In the 1930s and '40s, Hunt County was predominantly an agricultural community, and the Fosters and the Knoxes (Joe's mother's family) had long been farmers and merchants. It was "cotton country," where Joe matured into a Lincolnesque leader—six-foot, stone-chiseled, and soft-spoken. In the '40s, Greenville, Texas (the Hunt County seat) was known for a large sign which hung across Main Street that proclaimed "The Blackest Land—The Whitest People." As a child, Joe was told this simply meant his home in Greenville had the richest soil and the finest people. And he believed it.[1]

Joe's family became involved in oil through an acquaintance of Joe's paternal grand-dad, Bain Foster. Bain, a farmer and justice of the peace, introduced his son William (Joe's father) to Willis Dearing, the owner of R.H. Dearing and Sons, a drilling contractor and independent producer based in Dallas, only 50 miles away. Dearing's company ran several drilling rigs and had oil and gas interests in East Texas and the Fort Worth basin. Willis Dearing was a great friend and regular visitor to Pearl and Bain Foster's home near Greenville. There are several tales about how Dearing and Bain Foster met originally; one story has it that Dearing picked up a traffic ticket and had to appear in Granddad Foster's court; another is that a cousin of Bain's wife married into the Dearing family. In any event, the Dearing and Foster families quickly became fast friends. Willis Dearing took a shine to young William, who had excelled in academics in high school and later at Wesley Junior College in Greenville.

Dearing approached Bain Foster with a surprising proposal: "If your son William will go to Texas A&M College (now University) and get a degree in petroleum engineering, I will pay three-fourths of his way."[2] With this generous sponsor underwriting his college education, William Foster headed off to Texas A&M College Station to study petroleum engineering.

Willis Dearing, true to his word, provided for young William. But William Foster didn't last long at A&M. During William's first semester of his freshman year, Joe was conceived. William Foster and Ruth Knox had secretly married in Fort Worth on October 21, 1933, when William ostensibly came home to take Ruth to a Texas A&M-TCU football game.

The following Spring William Foster returned to Hunt County with his pregnant wife Ruth, the 22-year-old daughter of a Methodist minister, and consulted with Bain Foster. Apparently, Bain Foster and Ruth's preacher father, John Knox, were of the same mind: if William was old enough to have a wife and child, he was plenty old enough to get a job and support his new family. William dropped out of A&M and began a search for gainful employment. He found it as a drilling roughneck. Not long thereafter, the *Caddo Mills Monitor* reported, "Mr. and Mrs. William Foster left to make their home near Overton, Texas where Mr. Foster has employment in the oil fields."[3] Mr. Foster was all of 19 years old. The home near Overton was a very small, white frame house in an oilfield camp at Arp, owned by R. H. Dearing and Sons. William Foster's new employer was his old benefactor, Willis Dearing.

William became a roughneck on a Dearing rig, drilling in the East Texas Oil Field, one of the world's great oilfields.[4] The East Texas Oil Field was discovered in 1930, and by June 15, 1934, there were 13,512 wells in the field, with 390 new wells in the process of being drilled. Producing capacity of the field measured in excess of 100 million barrels per day. By way of contrast, today—more than 75 years later—the whole world produces and consumes some 85 million barrels per day. This was a historic time in the oil business. Fortunes were made and lost. Families were torn apart in disputes over land ownership and the challenge of sharing newly found wealth. Violent deaths from both accidents and murders were commonplace. The Texas Rangers militia was called out to enforce the rationing of oil production. Groundbreaking legislation, which rules the oil industry even today, was passed to ensure conservation of oil resources.

Joe Foster's father may have participated in only a little of Texas oil's early history, but he had the opportunity to observe a great deal of it. He had steady work, advancing from roughneck to derrickman to relief driller. Joe heard him tell stories of working at the derrick station 30-feet above the rig floor and being able to see into the fourth-floor window of a hotel in Kilgore which served mostly as a brothel.

The East Texas Oil Field was a volatile, bustling scene. On July 30, 1930, Columbus Marion "Dad" Joiner drilled the Daisy Bradford A3 discovery well in Rusk County. In November 1930, H. L. Hunt bought out Dad Joiner in one of the most famous oil deals of all time. Hunt acquired all of Joiner's assets for $1.3 million, but only $30,000 of that was cash.

By the spring of 1931, aggressive development of the East Texas Oil Field was in full swing. Oil prices, which had been $1.10 per barrel when Dad Joiner made his discovery, slumped to $0.15 per barrel under the weight of the Depression and a surge in East Texas crude production to 160,000 barrels per day.

Joe Bill Foster was born in the Arp oilfield camp on July 25, 1934 at about 8:00 p.m. For one of the oil industry's most successful wildcatters and businessmen, there was no better place to enter the world. Though called Joe Bill, a typical East Texas double name,

> "Sadly, even after I was in the oil business, I never really questioned him about those heady days. I was only 36 when my Dad passed. I was more interested in my future than his past—and failed to understand that there was a vital link between the two."
>
> **JOE FOSTER**

from childhood through college, he stopped using the moniker some 50 years ago when he vowed to leave the "Bill" permanently parked in College Station when he graduated from Texas A&M.[5]

ANOTHER FOSTER IN AGGIELAND

When young Joe Foster was six and the tumultuous decade of the 1940s had just begun, the Foster family hastily packed up all their belongings and headed due east from Bryson to Greenville. Two years earlier William Foster had been transferred from drilling new wells in east Texas to existing production operations in central Texas in Bryson in the Fort Worth Basin. Still working for Dearing, William had been assigned to field maintenance as a compressor operator.

The cause of the abrupt departure? The two most important men in William Foster's life, Bain Foster and Willis Dearing had died suddenly. William moved the meager family assets to Greenville to help care for Grandma Pearl. Though merely 140 miles, it was at that time a tortuous journey. He left employment in the upstream end of the oil patch permanently, but would later move into the downstream (refining and marketing) side as the bulk plant agent for Cities Service Oil in Greenville.

As World War II moved toward its violent end in 1944, Joe Foster turned 10 and completed fourth grade at Travis Elementary. By then it was increasingly clear that he would be an only child—and thoroughly doted on. Ruth was Joe's Cub Scout den mother and was active in the PTA, and in her spare time she constantly peppered her son with questions.

William had become the distributor for Tom's Toasted Peanut Brand selling nuts and candy to grocery stores, filling stations, and roadside cafes. William Foster's territory radiated out from Greenville to Caddo Mills, Royce City, Rockwell, Garland, Lone Oak, Emory, Alba, Wolfe City, Celeste, Leonard, and Whitewright. As a youth, Joe worked in the Tom's Warehouse in Greenville during the school year. During the summers he rode the distribution circuit with his Dad, and on the road they would "wolf down a lot of 50-cent plate lunches in country cafes."[6]

Though Hunt County was devoid of petroleum, there were always oil people circulating in the county. Perhaps since his arrival on the planet had short-circuited his Dad's academic career at Texas A&M, from Joe Foster's earliest memory his

Joe Foster, age four.

pursuit of a college degree was preordained. Joe briefly considered the Naval Academy in Annapolis and Rice Institute (later Rice University) in Houston. But he had spent hours leafing through his father's A&M yearbook, and been taken to A&M Corps of Cadets parades in Ft. Worth and Dallas and football games at College Station.[7]

His father would occasionally mutter, "Finish what I started."

At Greenville High School, Joe had an inspirational Spanish teacher, Elenita Patton. Joe had gravitated to Spanish as a lesser of evils; a foreign language was required for college admission, and he knew that he did not want to take Latin. Joe credits his success as a high school leader to her: "Elenita Patton, more than anyone else, convinced me that I could not only be smart, I could get things done through other people."[8]

Joe was a good student and a passable athlete throughout grade school and early high school, but by no means had he been a class leader. Miss Patton decided to change that. She used her influence to have him elected president of the Pan American Student Forum. Then she goaded and nagged at Joe, forcing him to get organized, to make speeches and take charge. The next year he was elected Student Body President, which he later claimed gave him confidence that he could handle whatever Texas A&M and its Corps of Cadets could throw at him.[9]

Following the path Willis Dearing and his father had chosen, Joe originally set his sights on a degree in petroleum engineering at A&M. But as he was paging through the A&M catalog in his senior year, he saw that a student could obtain both a Bachelor of Science in petroleum engineering and a Bachelor of Business Administration under a five-year package, and decided to sign up for the dual program. Joe says he had never even heard of an MBA until his third year of college.

Joe's double major at A&M paid huge dividends down the road. He recalls that the third year at A&M Engineering was known as the "meat-grinder" year. Not fully aware of this, students would enroll in thermodynamics, fluid mechanics, and petroleum and electrical engineering during the same semester. Because many of Joe's engineering courses were extremely demanding, and the business courses less so, the chance to dilute the heavy math coursework with a healthy dose of business and economics was a Godsend. Joe excelled and found it easier to handle both disciplines in tandem.[10] Honing skills in petroleum engineering and business at A&M provided Joe the foundation to run a giant integrated oil and gas company and later, to conceive and nurture a successful exploration and production enterprise, Newfield Exploration Company.

> "It was a subtle brainwashing—while I was definitely not *forced* to go there—A&M was in my Foster blood."
>
> **JOE FOSTER**

LESSONS FROM "THE CORPS" AT TEXAS A&M

When Joe Foster entered Texas A&M in 1952, membership in the Corps of Cadets was not only important, it was obligatory. Every student who was not a military veteran had to be in the Corps. College enrollment was controlled through attrition. When Joe Foster arrived in College Station, he was one of 2,200 freshmen who aspired to an A&M degree. At the end of the first year, there were only 800. When he graduated, there were 400. Many young men arrived thinking the Corps would not be too tough, but quickly found that they were not cut out for it; the strict discipline, military regi-

The Corps of Cadets

men, and absence of coeds were not for everyone.

The Corps required underclassmen to introduce themselves to any upperclassman whose names they could not recall by extending a hand and saying their own name. This longstanding A&M tradition is known as "whipping out." Quickly learning the names and faces of his fellow A&M students allowed Joe Foster to avoid torment from his upperclassmen in the Corps. "Since my days on the A&M campus, I have never had a problem walking up to anybody—from lords and ladies to roughnecks and roustabouts on the rig floor—and saying, 'My name is Joe Foster.' That ability to remember names has been important to my business success and in my personal relations all my life."[11]

Joe excelled as a member of the Corps, becoming battalion commander, Editor of *The Engineer* magazine, and senior class secretary. When he graduated in May 1957 among a class of 400 young mostly uniformed men, Joe received his BS in petroleum engineering and his BBA in general business. He was confident of his engineering skills and thought he had a good understanding of business. The Corps of Cadets had toughened Joe up for the real world. When he had arrived at A&M, he wasn't sure he would make it through his first year, but when he left, he was pretty sure he could handle just about anything.[11]

JOE IS SOLD ON TENNECO OVER HUMBLE

In 1954, the first season that legendary football coach Paul "Bear" Bryant coached the Texas A&M Aggies, Joe Foster opened a letter in the lounge of the Student Center. The letter was from Humble Oil and Refining Company—the predecessor of the world's largest public oil enterprise, ExxonMobil. Stunned in disbelief, Joe read Humble's summer job offer of roustabout in Avoca, Texas, at the grand monthly salary of $371. He had earned 40 cents per hour in high school, and $160 per month the previous two summers working a tough job for the Texas Highway Department. Joe could not believe his good fortune.

After that lucrative summer with Humble in Avoca and another in 1956 as an engineering intern in its Tyler, Texas, offices, Joe was set to join the ranks of the giant integrated oil company's upstream operations upon graduation. He had a job with Humble waiting for him in Athens, Texas.

Meanwhile, Core Laboratories, which had provided

> "The business degree helped me understand the financial side of the oil business. When I was a young engineer…at least I knew debits and credits, and the financial people usually came to me with questions. I wound up doing a lot of economic analysis—I gravitated toward that side of the business." **JOE FOSTER**

"I just wanted to get out of there. Don't get me wrong, there were many memorable moments, but graduating was something I was ready for." **JOE FOSTER**

Joe a small scholarship the year before, was enthusiastically recruiting him with a barrage of calls and letters. By accident, Joe arrived an hour early for his final on-campus interview with Core Labs. After Joe was seated, the secretary in the A&M placement office called him over to explain that there were some men there from Tennessee Gas Transmission and no one had talked to them all day. Would he mind going in and meeting with them? Joe felt talking with the Tennessee Gas folks would be a lot better than reading the dog-eared magazines in the placement office. Within the hour, his vision of his employment future had changed.

"I went in and talked to the representatives from Tennessee Gas and I was really impressed. The Tennessee executives knocked my socks off about what a growing, well-funded company it was, with big ambitions. And, I would get a company car! I went back the next day with my suit and tie for a real interview and wound up accepting a job offer from them. I found out later that the guy who really sold me on coming to work for Tennessee had been in his job for only two weeks!"[13]

CHAPTER II
JOE FOSTER – THE TENNECO YEARS

THE FIRST YEARS AT TENNESSEE GAS

After graduation in 1957, Joe spent a year in Tennessee's anchor Mid-Continent upstream office in Oklahoma City. Following a six-month stint in the Army, he returned to "Oke City" in 1958 and resumed his basic training as a greenhorn petroleum engineer. For several months, Joe drove across the dry plains of Oklahoma; he towed a trailer filled with measurement tools to run bottom-hole pressure surveys on flowing oil or gas wells, and dynamometer surveys to assess the efficiency of wells being pumped. Joe came to have a great deal of respect for the pumpers and lease operators. He learned more common sense and oilfield knowledge from them than from many of his professors with their Ph.D.'s.[14]

In 1959, Tennessee Gas acquired a large package of producing oil and gas leases from Phillips Petroleum and established its first offshore operations in the Gulf of Mexico's nascent oil and gas producing fields. Joe found himself in the midst of a major sea change for Tennessee's exploration and production business. To quickly access offshore operational experience, Tennessee Gas hired two senior executives from Phillips and Mobil to head the Gulf's offshore office in New Orleans. A small platoon of relatively experienced offshore personnel was also added. "Relatively experienced" was the operative term at this time. The Gulf of Mexico opened up officially in 1954 when Shell Oil hired Tidewater Inc.'s Mr. Charlie—the first transportable submersible rig—to drill development wells on its East Bay oil discovery, near the mouth of the Mississippi River. Joe's first oilfield exposure to the Gulf of Mexico, a mere five years later, could not have been better timed.

The Tennessee executives in the Houston headquarters appointed Joe Foster and another young engineer to the new Tennessee Gas offshore team. Before heading to their new jobs in Lafayette, they were told that, since they were the ones who knew Tennessee's ways, they were charged with keeping the new Phillips/Mobil offshore guys "in line." The first time he spoke up about "the Tennessee Gas Way," it was made painfully clear to Joe that the big oil guys were the bosses, and he and his partner from Houston were the grunts. Soon enough, they found the best of both ways.[15]

Although originally charged with measuring static, single point bottom-hole pressures, Joe began running bottom-hole pressure build-up surveys, which were not commonly taken at Tennessee Gas in those days. He wrote an internal paper on the use and interpretation of these pressure build-up surveys, which caught the eye of Tennessee's chief engineer in Houston and was then distributed throughout the company.

THE HALCYON DAYS OF THE GULF OF MEXICO

Joe Foster's inadvertent interview in the A&M placement office led to a remarkable career with Tenneco. In his 31 years there, he witnessed some incredible cycles in the oil and natural gas business. The Gulf's early years of development were an extraordinary period when wildcatters—like the Liedtke brothers, Hugh and William, and fellow oilmen like George H. W. Bush, Dean A. McGee, and Robert S. Kerr—were ahead of the curve and amassed huge fortunes.

Leasing in the federal waters of the Gulf of Mexico (GOM) was controlled by the Minerals Management Service (MMS) of the Department of the Interior, one of the few federal agencies, other than the Internal Revenue Service, that actually generates positive cash flows for the Treasury. It was renamed the Bureau of Ocean Energy Management, Regulation and Enforcement (BOEMRE) in June 2010.

Satellite photography and computer-generated images of the GOM available today make it look all too simple. Thousands of giant salt domes are readily visible now, ringed by oil and natural gas wells that exploit their subsea petrotreasures. Seismic "Bright Spot" technology didn't really emerge as an exploration tool until 1973. That was the first true bright-spot lease sale, and it was wild and woolly.

Tenneco devised an innovative—some competitors called it "crazy"—approach to salt dome exploration that was implemented in the early 1960s. The first federal offshore lease sale Tenneco participated in was in 1960, following a long moratorium during which federal leases were not offered. It had some success there, but cranked up its efforts for the 1962 federal sales.

Joe worked full-time on the preparations for the auction from December 1961 through the first quarter of 1962. It was the first lease sale that Joe personally attended in New Orleans. By that time Joe had two years of experience in the Gulf and had established a reputation with management as the engineer who knew the most about economic analysis. This was an outgrowth of his study of C. Jackson Grayson's book, *Decisions Under Uncertainty: Drilling Decisions by Oil and Gas Operators,* a seminal book for many in the industry. It helped differentiate between uncertainty and risk, and gave a framework for better quantification of risk and its impact. Joe had used probability analysis in several of Tenneco's drilling decisions. The analyses seemed to make sense to management and, as a result, he was tapped to do all the statistical and economic analysis for the 1962 sale. Working with rudimentary gravity interpretation, Tenneco gambled on a huge number of lease bids—more than 30—based on their knowledge of salt dome locations.[16]

The sale was actually two sales within three days of each other: March 13 and March 16. The time spread gave bidders the opportunity to see the results of the first sale to get a better sense of what other bidders were offering and how much money they had spent. They could then decide how many dollars to expose in the second sale and alter their bid levels. This is the only time that the Minerals Management Service employed such back-to-back sales in the GOM. The idea was apparently abandoned because the process created too much stress on both the MMS and the large oil companies' chains-of-command.

Tenneco had two basic bidding strategies in that sale. One was what they called a "top block" strategy, where they bid strongly on the highest-quality, lowest-risk blocks with natural gas potential. The second strategy was to place "minimum" bids—per 5,000 acres—on most of the salt dome blocks offered at the sale. Tenneco did not have complete geophysical data sets over these salt domes and had done only a limited amount of geological analysis. The primary indicator they sought was gravity data that indicated where the salt core was and which blocks might have trapping conditions. It was perceived to be a statistical play.[17]

In the first MMS lease sale, Foster's Tenneco team had some modest success, but the majors like Shell Oil, Humble (ExxonMobil), and the California Company (Chevron) were more than a stride ahead, and dollars weren't really an issue for the leasing success of these big boys.

Lacking extensive geophysics at the time, Tenneco decided it was a good gamble to bid on all the salt domes they could identify with some confidence. To their shock, the big oils outbid them on 29 of 30 blocks. So much for statistics![19] The drilling rights that Tenneco won on the one 3-mile by 3-mile tract fetched about $75,000. Although Joe and the Tenneco team were concerned the price was too high, the lease thoroughly proved its worth when oil prices later escalated. "We were stricken with buyer's remorse—if we [had] won, this must be a really bad dome. We learned a valuable lesson from that experience; the lease we acquired more than lived up to expectations. We weren't as successful as we wanted to be, but we were in the game and we were successful. Tenneco learned how to be a player and a highly competitive one to be sure."[20]

Tenneco's "top block" strategy worked also: to go after gas-prone blocks on the premise that leasehold costs and development costs could be capitalized and placed in the rate base of its pipeline affiliate, Tennessee Gas Transmission Company. Over time, this economic approach was discarded as the leases had turned out to be so successful that it was a better deal for Tenneco to include them among its unregulated assets.

TEXAS HOLD 'EM IN THE OIL PATCH

During Joe Foster's tenure at Tenneco from 1959-88, he saw the Arab Oil Embargo of 1973, the fall of the Shah of Iran in 1979 and the oil price crash of 1986.

From 1979-81, insanity plagued the energy markets. After the Shah's fall, oil prices skyrocketed to $40 per barrel ($102 per barrel in 2010 inflation adjusted) and, consequently, Wall Street threw bucket-loads of investment dollars at the sector. Tenneco was extolled by cardigan-resplendent President Jimmy Carter to do its part to solve the Energy Crisis, dubbed MEOW, the Moral Equivalent of War.

Oil companies showered money on offshore leasing and subsequent billion-dollar drilling programs in the Atlantic, California, the Gulf of Alaska, and the Beaufort Sea—with virtually no success. All the while, the most desirable location for leasing was the "sure thing" Gulf of Mexico. In one particularly remarkable lease sale in the Bicentennial year, 1976, Tenneco had teamed up with the big boys, Mobil, Gulf, and Texaco, to craft a bid for a celebrated and highly prospective tract offshore Louisiana in federal waters—South Timbalier 37. Normally a competitor but now a partner in this venture, Tenneco was by far the smallest operator of the group at the bidding table. Joe soon learned that Tenneco was out of its league.[21]

In order to place a joint bid, the bidding partners, in effect, held an auction among themselves prior to the lease sale. The operators' representatives went around the table, each naming a bid they propose for the block. After each round, the highest bid from the round was the starting bid for the next round. In that next round, if any operator thought a higher bid was required to be successful, and was prepared to make that bid if others dropped out, then he would name that number. Others could then elect to join in the bid or to drop out. This process continued until a bid was arrived at which was the highest any of the operators were willing to pay. For very attractive blocks, this is usually an iterative—and tense—process. Eventually, the bid on "South Tim" 37 reached $103 million, with all the players still in. Bidding was for only one 5,000-acre block in the Gulf of Mexico. Texaco was the most aggressive company in the card game and they raised the bid on each round. The other players simply stayed in. Joe represented Tenneco, which, to his relief, had only an 8.33 percent interest in the block; otherwise he would have folded. When Mobil's representative, its executive vice president and head of E&P operations, called time-out and said, "I have to call my supervisor," it was a major stress point. Foster later investigated and discovered that the Mobil "supervisor" who was called was in fact the president of Mobil! The Mobil representative got approval to stay in. Incredibly the escalation did not end there; the partnership wound up bidding $168 million for what turned out to be a marginal lease.

In making joint bids, strict procedure must be followed to ensure that there is no "chilling the bid," which would be an anti-trust violation. A mini-lease sale is conducted among the partners to determine a joint bid. The partners take turns going around the table, with each naming a bid. Afterwards, the next company may raise, stay, or drop out, like poker. This goes on until a bid level is reached where there are no more raises.

It Could Have Been Joe Foster's Tenneco Oil
By Bill Swanston – Petroleum Outlook, November 1988

Tenneco's CEO, James L. Ketelsen was tired of waiting for U.S. natural gas prices to improve—natural gas averaged less than $2.00 per MMbtu in 1988—and he wanted to maintain the $3.04 per share dividend and improve Tenneco's consolidated return on assets. On May 25, 1988, Ketelsen announced that the entire energy portfolio of Tenneco Oil and Gas—its refining and marketing assets, and its prized domestic and overseas producing fields and exploratory properties— would be auctioned off piecemeal. He characterized the Tenneco board's decision as the culmination of the company's "...process of critically reviewing its business strategies and financial alternatives" that had been underway since early 1986. Tenneco had faced downtrending operating profits and cash flow since 1984, along with choking interest costs associated with long-term liabilities that had soared to $6.6 billion at year-end 1987, up 22% from the 1984 debt load. Tenneco's board knew that the company's highly treasured dividend, which was a huge driver of its stock price, was in jeopardy; the Tenneco dividend had been hiked for fourteen consecutive years before being held steady in 1987 and 1988.

It was no secret on Wall Street that Tenneco's finances were failing. Ketelsen's May announcement was triggered when the conglomerate received an undisclosed offer for its entire oil and gas unit from Gulf Financial Resources, a Houston-based investment partnership. Ketelsen quickly turned down the Gulf Financial offer and hired white-shoe investment bankers First Boston and Morgan Stanley, indicating that the board was more interested in receiving top dollar for its energy assets than a fast solution to its debt woes. The Wall Street Journal *noted, "Tenneco should have no trouble finding buyers," and quoted a banker working on the Tenneco offering: "The phone's been ringing off the hook; all the big oil companies are interested."*

Source: Petroleum Outlook[22]
John S. Herold, Inc.

The Tenneco board's decision to divest Tenneco Oil and Gas in 1988 and exit the upstream end of the energy business meant a farewell to the jobs of virtually all senior Tenneco Oil employees. The usual rationale driving consolidation in the oil and gas industry, from ExxonMobil and BP/Amoco/ARCO to Chevron/Texaco and Conoco/Phillips, has been the capture of scale economies and the elimination of redundant overhead costs, known in the industry as "headcount reduction."

Jim Ketelsen's original plan, which he shared with Joe Foster in late 1987, was for Tenneco to package the natural gas pipeline company with the oil company and sell Tenneco Energy Company shares in an initial public offering (IPO). If he could have written the script, that's what Foster would have preferred—but within three months, the strategy had moved from the Tenneco Energy IPO to the outright sale of all the Tenneco oil and gas assets and downstream—the gas pipeline was to be retained.[23]

In April 1988, Joe Foster was stunned when Jim Ketelsen told him what he planned to recommend to the Tenneco board: Divest Tenneco Oil to restore the balance sheet, pay down debt, and, most important, maintain the dividend. Ketelsen said that the attempt to combine Tenneco's oil and pipeline divisions (which both reported to Foster) into an energy company that could be spun off to the public to raise cash, with Tenneco retaining an interest in the spin-off, simply could not be made to work.[24]

The lawyers had dropped a toxic bomb: Since the parent company of Tenneco was its pipeline division (created as a public company in 1943, and the original business unit of what became Tenneco), the spin-off of the pipeline, or parent, would result in a huge taxable event. Further, spinning off just the oil company would result in lost tax benefits and not enough money to remedy Tenneco's cash-flow problems. From a financial standpoint, an outright cash sale of the oil company would provide a much greater benefit to Tenneco. Further, to maximize that benefit, the oil company would be sold in 12 "packages"—five U.S. E&P packages (Gulf of Mexico, Mid-Continent, Gulf Coast-West Texas, Rocky Mountain, and Pacific Coast), three international E&P packages, and four packages consisting of Refining, Marketing, Processing, and Other.

Foster was a director of Tenneco. Within the bounds of those duties, he urged other alternatives on the board, including: a) retention of the U.S. Gulf of Mexico, Rocky Mountain, and Pacific Coast divisions of Tenneco Oil, plus its holdings in the Norwegian North Sea, and b) the sale of the rest of the oil company assets. In addition, to raise the required cash, he proposed the sale of two of Tenneco's industrial companies, Newport News Shipyards and Albright & Wilson Chemicals, neither of which had a strong attachment to Tenneco Inc. nor made significant contributions to it. Plus, he urged that Tenneco announce its intent to sell 20 percent of its perpetually under-performing farm and construction equipment subsidiary, Case-IH, and undertake an aggressive, clearly defined program to reduce annual corporate overhead and

> "I was appalled. Tenneco Oil was a true value-adding organization. Selling it was dumb. Breaking it into parts, casting a very effective organization to the four winds in order to sustain an organization— J.I. Case—which had been a continuing cash drain, was totally illogical, in my opinion." **JOE FOSTER**

CHAPTER II—JOE FOSTER – THE TENNECO YEARS

> "I learned a lesson that is as old as corporate history: In the absence of malfeasance, even in the presence of poor performance, it's virtually impossible for an inside director to win a battle with a sitting chairman of the board. My recommendations were politely heard by the Tenneco Inc. board. Without debate, discussion or vote, it moved to the next item on the agenda." **JOE FOSTER**

general operating expenses to the $60 million to $100 million range—quite achievable, in his opinion.

Having served on a number of boards throughout his career, Foster has learned that most boards approve everything unanimously. But he has been involved in numerous meetings where there have been heated discussions, abstentions, or opposing votes. He knows it takes some guts to disagree "on the record." He has even been in a meeting when a director punted and told the corporate secretary, "Just record me as not present." But the discussion to sell Tenneco Oil was made with little serious debate or discussion of the alternative he presented. In the decision to sell Tenneco Oil, Joe Foster cast the only dissenting vote.[25]

The record clearly shows the sale of Tenneco Oil started a downward spiral for the once-proud enterprise. Later, Ketelsen's successor, Dana Mead, finished off the dirty work that led to Tenneco's decision to leave Houston and relocate its corporate headquarters to back-country Greenwich, Connecticut.

[*Author's Note:* Later Tenneco's massive trunkline natural gas pipeline business was acquired by Houston-based El Paso Company; El Paso amalgamated Coastal States Gas as well. Other Tenneco subsidiaries that have survived and exist as publicly traded enterprises today include Pactiv (the consumer and foodservice packaging giant known for the Hefty brand) as well as Tenneco Automotive and Newport News Shipbuilding.]

Those close to Joe Foster during the periodic cyclical downdrafts in the oil and gas industry have observed his great calm—near stoicism—when confronted with adversity. Faced with the inevitability that Tenneco would soon be dismantled before his eyes, Joe put pen to paper in mid-1988 to communicate to his fellow employees at Tenneco the rationale for embracing an "Alleluia Anyway" attitude. The article which follows is verbatim and was originally released in Tenneco's internal employee magazine, *Tenneco Today.*

> "Jim Ketelsen supported fair and generous sale bonuses and severance payments for Tenneco Oil employees—at all levels in the organization—who were impacted by the sale. Moreover, Ketelsen allowed me to recruit the 'LBO Team' that, albeit unsuccessfully, bid on the Tenneco assets with the support of two major New York banks and two private equity firms. The seeds of Newfield were found in the sale of Tenneco Oil and the creation of the LBO team. And, part of Newfield's early success came from acquiring former Tenneco properties from the successful bidders in the Tenneco auction." **JOE FOSTER**

Alleluia anyway and plans for an LBO
(An article written by Joe B. Foster for Tenneco Today,
the Tenneco employee magazine)

Not long after the announcement of the sale of Tenneco Oil, I was driving along the freeway feeling dejected and frustrated when I came up behind a car with a bumper sticker which said, "Alleluia Anyway!"

Alleluia Anyway! It perked me up. That's about as good a response to trouble and frustration and disappointments we don't understand as any I know.

Once one of those events occurs, what really matters is not "Why?" or "Why me?" but "How shall I respond?"

I want to tell you how proud I am of the way Tenneco Oil E&P has responded to the shocking sale announcement. With professionalism. With pride in the job you have done. With unity and teamwork and realism and humor. With hard work, above and beyond the call of duty. With support for one another. With a focus on the future. It has been an "Alleluia Anyway" kind of response. I appreciate it!

I also appreciate the many expressions of support I have received from so many of you. Cards. Notes. Phone calls. Comments in elevators and hallways and on street corners. I needed them and am grateful for them.

I have been working to secure financial backing to permit an "LBO"—leveraged buyout—bid for E&P. Management and employees would have an ownership position in the resulting company, if its bid is successful. It would permit us to retain much of the culture and character and spirit of Tenneco Oil E&P.

At the present time, it appears we will have the financial support to make a bid. There is no way we could have obtained this backing without the superb reputation and track record of Tenneco Oil E&P's outstanding performance.

Everyone I have talked to in E&P is supportive of this LBO effort and has been helpful wherever possible. I'd like to make sure you understand several points about the LBO group:

First, the bid is being encouraged by Tenneco Inc. and Morgan Stanley, its investment banker. In their view, another bid by a knowledgeable bidder works to increase the value of the asset sale to Tenneco. I have the express consent of Tenneco

Inc. to form such a bidding group, to use designated E&P employees in the evaluation, and to involve selected members of management in the review process.

Second, the outside investors in the LBO group are to receive no data or information that other bidders do not receive. The presence of an LBO group should in no way inhibit the efforts of E&P management or employees to obtain maximum value for the properties. I expect, and expect each of you, to behave in an absolutely ethical manner about this.

Third, the LBO group, which will be using primarily borrowed money, will be competing with some of the richest companies in the world in the bidding process. But I believe our group has a fighting chance to make a winning bid. Obviously, our investors think so or they wouldn't be willing to bear the expense of making a bid. But competition will be intense! There is no assurance we will be a buyer.

Fourth, even if the LBO group makes a winning bid, it will not be "business as usual" for Tenneco Oil E&P. Costs will have to be cut. Properties must be disposed of. Organizations will be changed. We can retain much of the culture and character and spirit which have been responsible for our success. But things will not be the "same." That's just a fact of life.

Whether the LBO group or another group is the buyer, I am optimistic that they will need most of our working-level people. I would not advise jumping ship prematurely.

In any event, I think the kind of people we have in E&P will not be out of work for very long. There are plenty of other companies out there who wish to "build on quality," and our people offer quality. Of that I am sure.

In the meantime, let's do our jobs. Let's continue to behave professionally. Let's sell hard and operate well. If or when we have to turn the key over to someone else, let's do it with our heads held high, with the sure knowledge that we are winners.

Then, collectively or individually—as the Crystal Gayle song says,—"Do it all over again."

Thank you for your efforts in building an absolutely outstanding oil company and thank you for your mature and professional reaction to Tenneco Inc.'s surprising decision to sell it. I count myself fortunate to be "one of you."

"As I read the Offering Memorandum for the total company and geographic packages, I felt a sense of pride in being a part of this organization.

The history of this company is impressive, and I am proud of the accomplishments it has achieved. I am proud of the values by which the company operates. I am proud of the people and their tremendous contributions and loyalty. I have a feeling of sadness when I consider new ownership. Even though I know that the future can still be bright for each of us, I fear that things won't be the same. However, no one can take away our self worth or the record we have completed." **FROM "REFLECTIONS ON E&P" BY WAYNE NANCE,** *TENNECO TODAY* **MAY 1988**

"[During the sale process] our activity level will be high. We have many commitments that we must honor. Many of you have already been working long hours, and there will be many long days ahead. I have not heard any complaints about the work and that speaks volumes about the character of Tenneco employees."

FROM "REFLECTIONS ON E&P" BY WAYNE NANCE, *TENNECO TODAY* **MAY 1988**

JAMES KETELSEN TALKS TO E&P EMPLOYEES

Decision to sell difficult, but necessary
An Article for Tenneco Today *by James Ketelsen*

Tenneco Inc.'s announcement May 25 to sell Tenneco Oil—Exploration & Production and Processing & Marketing—was a decision that "We would have all preferred we not have to make," says James Ketelsen, chairman of the board and chief executive officer.

But he adds that the company's financial status forced the board's decision to sell. A more than $8-billion debt sparked the creation of a task force last year to look at reorganization.

"We reviewed all the options," Ketelsen says about the decision in an interview with E&P Update. He named as factors in the decision-making process Tenneco's financial condition and its need to reduce debt, waning stockholder confidence, the comparison of cash that could be generated by the sale of the oil company versus other divisions, the ongoing threat of unfriendly takeover and the uncertain future of the oil and gas industry.

"All options were studied by our analysts, our investment bankers and, eventually, by the board," he continues.

"Obviously the decision to sell was difficult from an employee standpoint," he adds. "We feel that we have a very, very fine group in E&P. Their record is excellent; the decision wasn't based on anything negative as far as they're concerned."

In pointing out the realities of Tenneco's financial position, Ketelsen says the longer a multi-industry company continues to show weak return on investment, "the more vulnerable" it becomes to takeover.

"We faced the consideration that if we had done nothing," he explains, "we could be going through the same thing, only it would be somebody else doing it. They might not be as concerned with severance and pension and the other employee benefits that we're trying to do a good job on."

Ketelsen says he hopes that E&P will be sold as an intact unit. "It would be terrific if a single company or an LBO group with some of the management involved were the high bidder and life went on," he says. But, he adds, Tenneco cannot show favoritism to one type of bidder over another. "If we expect to get strong competitive bids there isn't a great deal we can do."

But, he continues, if "the price differential is not great" between bids for packages and a bid for the unit, the bid for the entire company would be considered preferable. What that price spread would be, he says, can't be determined ahead of time.

"We have to be realistic. There are going to be many bidders; it's going to be a competitive sale. We have to sell at a price that's fair to our shareholders," he says.

In terms of shareholder value, Tenneco's stock has jumped $6 to $7 per share since the sale announcement, "depending on which day you look at it," Ketelsen says. "You can come to the conclusion that the stock might move further upon consummation of the sale and affirmation of the price level," he says.

Funds from the sale—estimated by outside analysts to range from $5 billion to $7 billion—are tentatively slated to buy-down part of Tenneco's debt, and "there might be consideration of a stock buy-back program depending on the level of the market at that point," Ketelsen says.

Data rooms opened Monday, July 25, 1988 and the evaluation process will continue through August. At the end of that time bidders will be given a few weeks to pull their information together before submitting bids in September. Bids will be messenger-carried to Morgan Stanley offices in New York, but Tenneco representatives will be on hand for the opening and will participate in the bid evaluation process.

Each bid will contain a conformed contract that bidders may have revised. Some bidders may submit qualifications with their bids. In a few instances, further investigation into financial backing may be necessary after bids are submitted. "In the case of a major oil company, we wouldn't have to worry about their capability to come up with the money," Ketelsen says.

Highly leveraged groups, on the other hand, would have their financial backing investigated.

Ketelsen says one potential bidder indicated that he's impressed with the quality of E&P people and that he would keep them on. "I think E&P's culture has *been a plus in this area," he says. "Obviously it has resulted in their doing a better job of presenting E&P than would otherwise be the case—this works to their advantage as well as ours.*

"I think that as the quality of the people comes through in data rooms, there will be recognition of that fact by some bidders who want the whole thing and want the people.

"This is understandably very difficult for all of us," Ketelsen says. "I have a great deal of respect for E&P's employees. But, sometimes you get in a position that you have to make the best of a difficult situation, and make a tough decision."

He concludes by saying, "I regret the necessity of having to sell the oil company. It's unfortunate from a people standpoint. But current returns in the oil industry are unattractive compared with what major companies are willing to pay for properties. This fact made the decision for us."

Tenneco Oil E&P will pass to new ownership 42 years after its origin as The Coast Company. Processing and Marketing dates back to 1955, when Bay Petroleum was acquired, adding refining and marketing operations to Tenneco.

"E&P OPERATIONS: FOCUSED ON VALUE" *TENNECO TODAY* JULY 1988

Within a week of the May 25 bulletin announcing the sale of Tenneco Oil, E&P senior management had finalized plans for interim operations.

The company's driving goal ever since has been "adding value."

"Of course it's business as usual in the sense that adding value to the company isn't a new strategy," says Harold Korell (now executive chairman of the board and former CEO of Southwestern Energy Company, a leading independent oil and gas company), vice president

"As I think about what is happening, there are times that tears come to my eyes. I recognize that the next few months will come and go, and Tenneco Oil will be sold and ownership will pass to new hands. Our world will be changed, but it will not end. We are good and we have a right to be proud of our record. We should let it speak for itself. We built this company together, and we will see it to the end together. I don't know what the future holds for any of us, but I am optimistic that something good will come out of this."

FROM "REFLECTIONS ON E&P" BY WAYNE NANCE, *TENNECO TODAY* MAY 1988

of production. "What is new is that we're more focused on confirming reserves and developing recent discoveries."

This focus has led Production as well as Exploration to place projects that show short-term benefits ahead of projects that will show return years from now. "Proved, developed reserves are the same as money in the bank and brand new discoveries are the next best thing," says Harry Briscoe, vice president of Exploration. "For that reason we're taking some of our better projects and getting them drilled."

Following an accelerated schedule, the Exploration and Production staff had recommendations on capital projects into management by June 6.

For example, two of the many production projects earmarked to add value are development drilling programs in the South Marsh Island 78 Field in the Central Gulf Division and the Mustang Island A-31 Field in the Western Gulf Division.

In addition to this immediate "value adding" category, Production staff is pushing forward on projects that maintain long-term viability.

One such is the Placerita Steamflood Project in the Pacific Coast Division. "We must move forward with the co-generation plant in order to serve the long-term value of the steamflood," explains Korell.

A third category of capital projects in production involves competitive drainage. "When we have drilling locations in the same reservoirs as offset operators we must pursue our opportunity to remain competitive," Korell continues.

In terms of Tenneco Oil's exploration program, the mixture of short-, medium-, and long-term projects has narrowed to short-term with intensified effort placed on those wells expected to be drilled and evaluated by the end of September—before bids are due, says Briscoe.

When this year's $380 million E&P budget was allocated at the first of June, division Exploration staff set to work on a schedule that includes twenty-five more exploration wells than were originally targeted.

As successes mounted, updates were added to the data rooms so that potential buyers could assess new reserves. Companies will also have updates mailed to them after they've visited the data rooms.

While acknowledging that employees have re-focused on short-term drilling, Briscoe says they haven't turned their backs on the future. "Primary exploration work—generating ideas, confirming leads and prospects and documenting work—continues," he says. "We have a responsibility to Tenneco and to potential purchasers to earn our salaries by continuing to do our best work."

The group's best work is an asset, he continues. "Our value comes from our people as well as our reserves. It's our people who put our operations together," he adds. "As long as we continue putting forth our best efforts, we demonstrate our collective and individual value to buyers."

Teamwork is what Korell calls E&P's "hidden asset." "Our integrated exploration and production teams have the unique ability to put together long-term opportunities for the company," he says. Both VPs agree that teamwork is one strategy that E&P won't change.

CHAPTER III
THE CATALYST FOR NEWFIELD – THE FAILED LBO EFFORT

The business environment facing the American economy and Joe Foster in the late 1980s featured "LBO Levitation"—in which immense funds were borrowed for "go private" transactions. The most celebrated LBO of that time was the $25 billion buyout of RJR Nabisco. In *Barbarians at the Gate*, authors Bryan Burrough and John Helyar recount the power struggle that led to the dismantling of the cookie and cigarette conglomerate. Many of the same cast of characters in Barbarians— Henry Kravis of KKR, Peter Cohen of Shearson Lehman, Eric Gleacher of Morgan Stanley—were solicited by Joe Foster and his Tenneco LBO Team. **ART SMITH**

ENCORE OIL AND GAS

Immediately after the sale of Tenneco Oil was announced, Morgan Stanley, Tenneco's representative in selling the properties, quietly put out the word that Joe Foster was putting together an LBO team to evaluate the properties. Foster was looking for financing to bid on individual packages and, if possible, to bid on the entire company.

Joe made a number of calls and several visits to LBO firms and smaller oil companies to discuss this concept. The firm that seemed to fit best was United Meridian, a private company headquartered in Dallas headed by Ralph Bailey, retired CEO of Conoco. Joseph D. Mahaffey, a former Gulf Oil executive, was CFO and Elvis Mason, retired CEO of InterFirst Bank, was a lead investor. Walter Wriston, the legendary CEO of Citicorp (deceased since 2005), was also a director. Joe Mahaffey had good contacts within the firm then known as Shearson Lehman Hutton, a subsidiary of American Express. The Chairman and CEO of Shearson Lehman was Peter Cohen, and Mike McMahon was one of the senior executives on its energy side.

In addition, Mahaffey had contacts with both Chase Bank and J.P. Morgan, then separate entities. Fairly quickly, Bailey and Mahaffey found that all three firms were interested in joining Joe's LBO effort to bid on some—or all—of the Tenneco Oil properties. Shearson would provide or raise the equity and Chase and Morgan would be the lenders.

Joe decided that this group had the most resources and the most interest, the greatest financial strength, and the best knowledge of how the oil and gas business works. He agreed to work with them. In his deal with Ketelsen, one condition was that the LBO Team had to secure its own funding for legal, financial, and other outside help. Joe could use Tenneco Oil people who agreed to accept assignment to the team for evaluating reserves, running economics models, and the like, but Tenneco would pay no invoices for outside services provided to the LBO Team. Vinson & Elkins on the legal side and Arthur Andersen on the financial side worked "on spec"—they would only collect their regular fees if and when a successful transaction was concluded. United Meridian paid the other miscellaneous bills that were incurred in the LBO effort.

Peter Cohen, the Shearson Lehman chairman and CEO, was at first quite interested in a bid on the whole company. However, Cohen's enthusiasm waned quickly when he realized that the new company's very high percentage of probable and proved undeveloped reserves would require substantially more than the 10 to 20 percent equity Shearson—or any other firm—might be willing to commit.

By mid-summer, it became clear to Joe and company that only the Mid-Continent and the Gulf Coast packages had enough proved reserve content to adequately finance an LBO-type bid with a high ratio of debt to equity.

However, the package that Joe knew the best and had the most interest in, the Gulf of Mexico, had a lot of warts: a dismantlement obligation for offshore platforms, a short reserve life, and many undrilled locations that would require a large reinvestment of up-stream capital. Although the LBO Team got little feedback about what was going on in the data rooms, the word about Tenneco's Gulf of Mexico package was that the majors were "salivating."

By September, Foster's bidding entity for the LBO had been named Encore Oil and Gas. This was, of course, well before Jon Brumley, formerly of Southland Royalty Company and Cross Timbers Oil Co., formed his Encore Acquisition Company in April 1998.

> "The fact that we had a vision for growth gave us the courage to push our bids a bit on the two packages we bid on."
> **JOE FOSTER**

The Encore Oil and Gas team resigned themselves to making only two bids in the auction, for the Mid-Continent and the Gulf Coast packages. United Meridian was their lead equity investor and Mike McMahon had introduced them to some other possible participants, including Warburg Pincus. Joe recalls that they had very informal agreements about how the equity would be divided up if they were successful. They knew how much Morgan and Chase would lend on the properties and they bid at levels where they were confident equity investors would join.[26]

Even though each package would be profitable at the levels bid, Joe was concerned that it would be difficult early on to reinvest the proceeds in either the Mid-Continent or the Gulf Coast to provide attractive growth to investors.

He asked the Gulf of Mexico team for a model, which was labeled "Operation Coldstart." For years, Tenneco had been a dominant player in the Gulf of Mexico. It had a proven track record and it had achieved exceptional success in the Pliocene trend of the Central Gulf. Using historical probabilities of success, reserve sizes, and productivities based on Tenneco's experience in the Gulf, an analysis was made of the capital requirements in the

Central Gulf to provide growth if Encore Oil & Gas was successful on either or both of the onshore packages. The economics of Coldstart were quite attractive, based upon replicating Tenneco Oil's performance record in the Gulf of Mexico. Coldstart would be a solid complement to either acquisition package.

To no one's surprise, however, both bids failed. Fina bought the Gulf Coast packages and Mesa bought the Mid-Continent assets.

Tenneco received high bids totaling $7.4 billion for the 12 packages.

Nobody, not even Joe Foster, could argue that Tenneco failed to realize a good value from the auction process. He had fought the sale of the properties and lost. He had bid on them and lost.

It was time to think about what to do next.

LBO TEAM MEMO

> TO: *MEMBERS OF THE LBO TEAM*
> DATE: *OCTOBER 6, 1988*
> FOR:
> FROM: *JOE B. FOSTER*
> RE: *PROJECT ENCORE*
>
> *As you have heard or guessed by now, Encore Oil and Gas—our LBO effort—was not successful.*
>
> *The headline in the paper the day we submitted our bid said, "Oil Prices Lowest Since '86—OPEC Leader Says May Go to $5/BBl." There is no question falling oil prices and rising interest rates, with the fear and uncertainty they created on Wall Street, hurt us more than the better funded major companies we were competing with.*
>
> *There were other factors, however:*
>
> *The discrepancy between our reserve estimates and those of reservoir engineers DeGolyer & MacNaughton (D&M) resulted in inadequate lending values. The banks had great difficulty taking their reserve estimates much beyond D&M's.*
>
> *The bank gave no upside to natural gas, holding the oil/gas price ratio at 10:1 throughout the life of the properties.*

The need for a capital structure to "live through" a two- to three-year period of low prices reduced our bid and did not permit us to give proper value to some probable and long-life reserves.

As oil prices fell, "junk bond" financing ranged from inordinately expensive to unavailable.

We gave it 110 percent effort. So did our bankers and LBO sponsors. It was not due to lack of work or lack of trying that we were unsuccessful. I have replayed the sequence of events in my mind many times, and, although there are clearly some things we should have done differently, I find none that were possible which would have made us winners.

I said early on that we were going against long odds. I was right; I just didn't know how long the odds were. I also said, "The worst that can happen is we will learn a lot." I don't know about you, but I learned more than I bargained for.

I was guided by the maxim, "The only sure way to fail is not to try." We tried. We failed. We did our best. We should have no regrets about our effort.

I appreciate the hard work, extra hours, and creative thought each of you put into Project Encore. I appreciate also the sacrifices your spouses and families made during the extra hours you were involved in the project. It was a worthwhile endeavor to try to salvage something from a group of people and a set of properties that we cared about very much.

Now it is time to deal with what comes next. Whatever it is, I am confident that you will handle it well.

I'll see you before closing. Thanks again.

Sincerely,
Joe B. Foster

/bs

Chevron weighed in with the highest bid ($2.6 billion) and walked away with Tenneco's offshore properties in the Gulf of Mexico. With the benefit of 20/20 hindsight, there is little doubt that Mesa grossly overpaid for Tenneco's MidContinent assets; T. Boone Pickens will even concede that his timing was wrong. Later, Atlantic Richfield, in a mea culpa executive statement, admitted that it too had grossly overvalued Tenneco's California assets.

Joe Foster's view today is that Chevron paid full value for Tenneco's core Gulf of Mexico asset package – but received full value over time. However, Amoco got a great deal on Tenneco's Rockies package. Joe remembers, "I went to a Potential Gas Committee meeting a while back and an Amoco engineer made a presentation about how much reserve appreciation had been documented in the San Juan Basin. I knew that he was talking specifically about Tenneco's Rockies divestiture properties. While he didn't crow about the great performance of the Tenneco assets in his presentation, I talked to him later. He said, 'We got you on that one!'"

To be fair, Amoco (now owned by BP) had long ago determined (as did Burlington Resources, now merged into ConocoPhillips) that the San Juan Basin was a core producing area. It is clear that a good strategy in E&P is, "When you find something good, you get as much of it as you can." Once an oil and gas company figures out that it is on to a "sweet spot" and it is working—don't look up, just keep concentrating on the law of capture.

JOE FOSTER'S NOTES ON "THE TRANSITION"
A compilation of notes from Joe's Yellow Legal Pads

October 1, 1988
The bids were submitted yesterday. Ours was but a whimper; I always suspected that we had no chance.

By late-afternoon I had heard that Jim [Ketelsen] was "satisfied" with the bids, that the company would be sold in packages, and that the total price was north of $7 billion—not far from what we had expected. I did my "duty" yesterday. I spent time with my LBO team workers. With the "review" team, we performed an autopsy of the deal—what happened and why we failed.

I know that I will unwind over time, but, as of now, I have not put it behind me. I do believe it is probably best that we did not win; the valuation required was excessive and the risks of low prices for oil and gas are simply too great. The struggle would have been too much. A reasonable and realistic buying opportunity is just not here yet.

October 29, 1988
Our last Awards Dinner at Tenneco was not as maudlin or sentimental as it could have been. Sure we were emotional—but relieved to have closure. I stressed in my final Tenneco speech the following thoughts:

> *"A year from now it will be October 1989 and we will all have gone our separate ways. We will be in new situations often with new people, doing new things. We will be making new friends. But let's not forget this classic toast: 'Make new friends, but keep the old; the new ones are silver, but these are gold.'"*

November 20, 1988
Breakfast Friday a.m. with Charles Duncan. I'm seriously thinking of teaming up with them in my startup venture. I like 'em. I followed up with lunch with Wayne Nance. Wayne was very helpful with comments and suggestions on the offering memo for the new company.

December 3, 1988
I have been pleased with the way this idea has been received by investors.

Charles Duncan and his guys are ready to back me, sort of sight unseen, insofar as the people and prospects are concerned.

The people I want to recruit in Lafayette are ready to sign on and are sure this will work. I hope they are right, since it is a leap of faith for all of us. They just "know" we can do it. More importantly, they know the drilling prospects are there and are sure they can find them. That gives me a ton of confidence.

There is a different feeling about this effort than the LBO effort. There is no skepticism here; there is pure enthusiasm. We are in control now. Had we persevered with the LBO acquisition, the Arabs, the bankers, and the guys in the WTI oil trading pit would have been in control of our destiny. Moreover, it was risky and everything had to break right for that deal to work. Here, if we do our jobs right, only as well as we have already done them in the past, it will work. We know we can do this, because we have already done it. That's very important.

December 30, 1988
Yesterday, I went through the experience of packing, of keeping some stuff and throwing away more, as I wound up a 31-year career.

The pile of stuff I discarded was immense and the material I left on shelves and in drawers, was tremendous. Mountains of memos, volumes of reports, pages and pages of published information. Most of it had once had value to me, but a great deal of it had never even been read. Those pristine reports and memos had been saved, "just in case."

When you see all that typed material you realize why bureaucracy is so inefficient and expensive. Weekly reports, monthly reports, quarterly reports, big-think annual reports—all started out with a good use and purpose when originally conceived. Many, however, were no longer the means to the end of effective operations, but the end itself.

Those reports have become the "product," the reader, some level of "management" (and not a high one at that), had become the customer. The focus of the effort had been divorced from effective business ends; instead the focus had morphed into the process itself.

On the eve of launching a new business I thought to myself, "How do you stop all that?" The answer was obvious: By starting over. Certainly, by huge cutbacks in people, in supervisors, in layers of management. Most likely you stop it by revolution. It is the rare organization with the discipline to police itself and evolve correctly.

I helped create a lot of those reports. I stood by and let them perpetuate themselves. I asked for more data and more detail. I did things, e.g., wrote detailed memos, that were easy for me, but which led others to staff up to get them done or to reply to mine.

I must keep all that in mind in our new business. I must keep the focus on the business, on the objective, on the product—not on the process.

Well, that's one useful and positive aspect of cleaning out the office.

Another was to find old handwritten notes and notebooks in a folder that represented only a fraction of the effort and thought which went into solving the problem or dealing with each situation. Each was a humongous problem requiring gargantuan effort. It has now been dealt with. And this is all there is to show for it. At least all I have, of my own, to show for it.

Then there's the aspect of "So what?" It's done now. Here's the paper and here's the record, but who cares? The company has been sold. Times have changed. The facts in these documents no longer apply. Why save this? When did it cease to be relevant? Did I need it in the first place?

January 13, 1989

Good trip to Lafayette. The University of Texas Endowment Fund confirmed they would invest in our company. The offices look good. The people seem happy. And excited. They have some prospects they are pursuing.

I put the name issue to rest; we are going with Newfield Exploration.

It's interesting how the decision process works for me. I just keep moving along, listening and thinking, leaning one way, then the other, eliminating this option, then that one, narrowing it down, feeling ambivalent, and then finally making a choice. Then I start to feel good about the choice, to accept it, and very soon, to wonder why I was ever ambivalent. Or why I ever even agonized over the matter.

January 19, 1989

What are some of the things I might say to "the troops," two weeks into the effort?

1. These "startup pains" are normal.

2. Controlling costs is essential—but not at the expense of missing opportunities or managing risk.

3. Some companies are deal-driven. Some dollar-driven. We want to be data-driven.

4. External contacts are more important to an independent than to a major. There is a ton of information out there and more people are willing to help than you'd believe. But be careful—it can take a lot of time and you can give more than you get. Networking and exposure are important.

5. Use of pay-as-you-go services is important and necessary. Quality vendors with integrity are available. We mustn't let the obligatory overhead of this company get out of hand.

6. We have to make fair trades, not necessarily the best trades. We need property. But we must not let our eagerness for property cause us to do dumb things.

7. To obtain early cash flow, we must do some small deals that won't be attractive to a major. In fact, we will for a long time want to do those deals because they will be economic for us. But we must not abandon the search for bigger targets. We must have both kinds of efforts.

8. We must generate options and exposure to ideas. We must allow an adequate gestation time. We must encourage open and candid discussion. We must be prepared to live with failure and obtain sufficient exposure.

9. Finally, when we achieve success we must not let it go to our heads.

"When oil prices were in the pits in the late 1980s, I never hesitated to start a new oil company. I didn't know whether we would make it or not, but I was very sure that the opportunity would be there for us to do well." **JOE FOSTER**

THE BEGINNING OF THE NEWFIELD STORY

After more than 30 years at Tenneco, Joe B. Foster saw his empire carved up and unceremoniously carted off by a host of large oil companies from Shell to Chevron. Joe's severance package was ample and he didn't fear the poorhouse. But Foster found himself suddenly unemployed at the age of 54, still with plenty of fire in his belly. Foster was at that critical period in life when retirement was not yet tempting: when you're too old to rush the tennis net, but too young to take up serious golf. Moreover, Joe Foster had always had a love affair with the oil and gas exploration and production business, and he needed a new vehicle.

RAISED OR REINVESTED, THE DOLLARS ARE THE SAME

Following the news that Encore Oil and Gas' bids were not acceptable, Joe was in Lafayette, visiting with the Gulf of Mexico team that had worked on Encore's LBO. Rich Mowrer, a petroleum engineer on the team, asked Joe why they needed to have existing production to do "Operation Coldstart." It seemed to Mowrer that it didn't matter where the money came from, whether it was raised or whether it was reinvested from production. The same results would be achieved, without $500 million or $600 million worth of debt to worry about while doing it.[27]

Joe responded that there are a lot of people willing to finance acquiring production, but not that many willing to finance buying seismic data and drilling wildcat wells. Mowrer emphatically countered, "Our new team could raise a lot less money and use our funds to make smaller, bite-size acquisitions." Joe realized that Mowrer had a point. Tenneco did have a compelling track record in the Gulf, and, to a large extent, it was Foster's.

Not long after, Joe began putting together his thoughts about an E&P IPO. He incorporated data generated in the Operation Coldstart exercise. He began studying how other smaller entities had succeeded as Gulf of Mexico operators. He listed the "business principles" that his years of experience told him were requisites for success. He reviewed the roster of employees in Tenneco's Lafayette office to determine who could help him get an offshore exploration company up and running.

In the late 1960s, Joe had headed the first Planning and Economic Analysis group for the E&P side of Tenneco Oil. In Tenneco's corporate office, he had for a time overseen its strategic planning effort. This experience would prove quite valuable: Foster had 20 years to reflect on the correct course for pursuing "big plans for a small company."

The people at United Meridian Corporation (UMC) were interested in backing Joe and other Tenneco-exes for a Gulf of Mexico venture. On Halloween 1988, just a few weeks after the LBO team learned of its shortfall, Joe Foster composed a five-page letter to Ralph Bailey, Chairman & CEO of United Meridian and former Chairman of Conoco. Foster would make a similar proposal to Charles Duncan on November 23 (see page 58). However, the UMC business plan contained several areas of significant concern to Joe.

After serious discussions, the deal with Bailey was not "simple" enough for Joe. It would have required assuming an existing operations staff, dealing with UMC's 55 percent interest in Ensoure, a small publicly-traded E&P company headed by John Brock, integrating or affiliating with Joe Mahaffey's unit directed at corporate mergers and acquisitions, and accommodating Ralph Bailey's desire to make international deals.

The deal that UMC presented did not allow Joe Foster to become nearly enough focused.

START FROM SCRATCH, AND CREATE MY OWN PROBLEMS

While there were several fine, seasoned executives at United Meridian, the firm was relatively small. Moreover, Joe was concerned that there would be too many cooks in the kitchen, which could lead to conflicting agendas and stress in the boardroom. After several meetings, discussions with UMC tailed off.

Then at a lunch several weeks later in November 1988, Evans Attwell, Managing Partner of Vinson & Elkins law firm in Houston, asked Joe about his plans for the future. They talked some about the Gulf of Mexico company.

"I'd been approached about several opportunities to go into existing companies and solve problems created by others. What I wanted to do was start a new company, from scratch, and create my own problems and I succeeded." **JOE FOSTER**

Next day, Attwell called Joe to say he should meet with Charles Duncan to discuss the possibility of his private equity firm investing in Joe's proposed E&P company. Joe took Attwell's advice and scheduled a breakfast meeting for November 20.

Charles Duncan, Jr. was well known to Joe. He was chairman of the board of governors at Rice University and partner in a small Houston LBO investment firm, Duncan & Cook, which had participated in several LBOs involving grocery stores and retail and mail-order outlets. However, Duncan was concerned the LBO boom had run its course and felt that it was time to consider putting "straight up" money into the energy business. Duncan was Secretary of Energy under President Carter from 1979-81, and had been Deputy Secretary of Defense and president of the Coca-Cola Company, his most visible public role. Clearly, Duncan was well respected in Houston and Joe knew he could open doors to investors and help bring credibility to the new venture.

Though they had previously met, they had never exchanged much more than pleasantries. It was clear in the initial discussions that there was genuine interest on both sides. And each man left the meeting confident he could trust the other.

Joe's initial reaction was quite positive. Apparently, Duncan's was also. Within days they began working together to form a new company. The name "Newfield" did not yet exist. But thus began a strong business relationship and, in short time, the concept was clearly articulated. Joe says, "A strong business relationship had begun the concept. We both left the table thinking, 'This is going to work'."

New Business Proposal
Oil And Gas Start-Up Company

November 23, 1988

The object of this memorandum is to describe the concept, strategy, and plans for a start-up company in the oil and gas exploration and production business to be headed by Joe B. Foster, former executive vice president of Tenneco Inc. The company will focus on exploration in the Gulf of Mexico and will be staffed by high-quality personnel available as a result of Tenneco's sale of its oil and gas properties.

The concept: *Form a new company composed of management and employees who have worked together and established a superior track record in oil and gas exploration/production. Focus on an area of high potential in the Gulf of Mexico which is gas prone, where the group has knowledge and has had success. Fund the operation so that it can conduct a data-intense, team-oriented, technically strong exploration effort on a scale, in the focus area, equal to that previously conducted by Tenneco and clearly superior to that conducted by most* "independents." Operate, however, with the economics, incentives, and flexibility of an independent. In addition, have a selective acquisition effort in the Gulf of Mexico, consider a small venture in Colombia, and utilize a "network" of former Tenneco employees to generate high-graded acquisition opportunities outside the focus area.

Premises about the business environment. The strategies and business plan outlined herein are based upon a very conservative outlook with respect to oil and gas pricing, as follows:

1. The transaction prices of oil and gas reserves in place have not reached their bottom.

2. Oil prices will remain low and will be so volatile in the next two to three years that more properties will be offered for sale, institutional buyers (e.g., Graham, American Gas and Oil, others) will become skittish, and the strategic acquirers (e.g., the major oil companies) will revise their price projections.

3. Gas prices will increase somewhat. There may be shortages soon and a perception that the "gas bubble" has ended. The result may be an industry wide emphasis on infill drilling, recompletions, development of mothballed discoveries, reemergence of a mini bubble, lower than expected prices, and a downward revision of price expectations.

4. Hence, the proper time for a strong reserve acquisition effort is expected to be two to three years from now rather than now. Current acquisition efforts should not bet on large price increases, but should be directed where definable reserve upsides and/or achievable cost reductions are present.

5. However, now is a good time to be exploring. Drilling costs are low. Acreage is available. Seismic and other data are relatively inexpensive. Production from discoveries should be commencing at a time when both oil and gas supplies are tightening and prices may be improving.

Business Strategy – Exploration. This would be a very focused effort in a 3,000- to 4,000-square-mile area of the Gulf of Mexico. Elements of the strategy would be those which have worked for Tenneco:

1. Focus on a relatively small area with good geologic and economic potential and which is gas prone.

2. Develop a superior data base. As a newcomer, do this with 3-D geophysics. Use 3-D as a regional exploration tool as well as an exploitation tool.

3. *Apply all technical disciplines in a team approach. Supplement the heavy emphasis on geophysics with plenty of geology, engineering, and economics.*

4. *Make hands-on data processing tools and analytical systems available to every worker.*

5. *Have the patience to wait for the good buys and to stay through some early failures without cutting and running.*

6. *Don't clutter up the place with a lot of people, but have good ones, good pay, and a very flat organization structure.*

7. *Use industry leverage (i.e. bring in others on a promoted basis) to get more exposure.*

Business Strategy – Acquisitions. *This would be a very selective effort, directed primarily at properties rather than companies. It would seek undervalued properties and be driven by reserve upsides and cost reductions, not by price upsides. A very conservative price deck would be used. Elements of this strategy would be as follows:*

1. *Define a focus area for acquisitions in the Gulf of Mexico. This is appropriate for the following reasons:*
   a. *Many offshore properties are now becoming marginal and major companies will be willing to sell them to avoid the P&A and platform salvage liabilities.*
   b. *Marginal properties of majors are usually handled by the youngest of least competent engineers. The new company should be able to cut costs or increase revenues on many of these.*
   c. *There is much less competition for acquisitions in the Gulf. The institutional players do not know the game. The strategic acquirers are not after marginal properties.*
   d. *3-D seismic can be used to evaluate additional potential in these marginal fields. Few old fields have been 3-D'd.*
   e. *The new company can conduct plugging and salvage operations less expensively than most majors, thereby making its offer more competitive.*
   f. *Some acquired reservoirs can be used as gas storage reservoirs to earn a return.*

> 2. *Utilize a network of independents and consultants in the producing community to help find these undervalued situations.*
>> a. *A "Tenneco network" would exist immediately and could possibly be used to "scavenge" Tenneco properties being sold by the package buyers. It could also be used for other acquisitions.*
>> b. *There are others in the industry who could be part of this network.*
>> c. *In some instances, retainers would be necessary and/or helpful.*
>> d. *An in-house staff would screen and recommend opportunities generated and presented by the network.*
> 3. *Acquisitions, after an initial screening period, would be focused in selected areas of highest potential profitability.*

THE PRESENCE OF WARBURG PINCUS

After a dozen years in energy banking with the prestigious investment banking firm of Morgan Stanley and Company, Howard Herman Newman changed stripes in 1987 and joined the "buy side" at E. M. Warburg Pincus & Co., Inc. Few address Howard as Dr. Newman, but he sports an impressive academic pedigree, having tacked on a Ph.D. in business economics from Harvard following B.A. and M.A. degrees from Yale. Lanky and grey-eyed, Newman often appears professorially disheveled and in serious need of a haircut.

Howard Newman likes to remind us that his investment success was abetted by the low expectations he assumed when he took his place behind the roll-top desk at the venerable investment firm's office at 466 Lexington Avenue in Manhattan. "At the time, Warburg had a perfect record: we had lost all our money in every investment in the energy sector."

As far as Bob Waldrup is concerned, Howard Newman provided the real backbone for Newfield's growth. "Howard believed in us. He asked the right questions at the right time. He pushed us to do the right things. When the Portfolio B deal with Chevron imploded, it was Howard's push that made us consider going public."

In early 1988, during the LBO effort, Michael McMahon had introduced Warburg Pincus and Howard Newman to Joe Foster. McMahon was well known to Newman—he was another "Haahvahd" man and acting senior managing director for the energy group at Shearson Lehman Brothers. Joe and United Meridian, with the blessing of Tenneco's board of directors, selected McMahon to be Foster's Wall Street rainmaker—charged to pursue and capture the fresh investment capital required to anchor Joe's "slice of Tenneco Oil" bid.

Knowing the extremely competitive nature of the auction process for quality oil and gas assets, Newman had immediately sized up the Mergers and Acquisitions (M&A)

transaction landscape and concluded that the Tenneco properties would likely be valued at a single-digit (six percent to eight percent) capitalization, or discount, rate. Here, Joe Foster's team had a real problem—among private equity firms, the going rate for financing a risky buyout with junk or high yield debt was, at a minimum, twelve percent to fifteen percent. When Newman confronted him with this irrefutable financing conundrum, the senior Tenneco executive's reaction was classic Joe Foster: "So, where's the leverage in this leveraged buyout?"

Newman was well aware of the low probability of success surrounding Foster's initiative to slice off a wedge of the Tenneco Oil asset pie. But he saw merit in Joe's team—the top-flight Tenneco personnel, their collective knowledge base, and the assets creamed for acquisition. In the end, Warburg's multi-million dollar commitment was never drawn down; Newman had a hunch from the outset that the Foster-led team would be hopelessly outbid. As Newman had feared, when the offering envelopes were sliced opened at Morgan Stanley's Manhattan headquarters, Foster's bid was well short of success.

CARVING UP TENNECO
A LOOK AT LOUISIANA
A BRITISH INVESTMENT HOUSE
THE LATEST PROPERTIES

PLS News October 1988*

While deeply dispirited by the failed offer, Joe Foster also realized that he had developed some exceptional contacts in the investment community which might prove useful. He was correct. His contact with Warburg's Howard Newman would prove instrumental to the future success of Newfield Exploration Company.

Newman made it clear that Warburg wanted no part of a startup E&P company, which he perceived as capital "E" and lower-case "p." He had had all the "E" he—or his partners—could stand.

Howard Newman befriended David Trice once he joined the Newfield team in early 1989, and Trice made it point to stay in touch with Howard. He realized that if he had made the right decision in joining Newfield, a second round of financing would be required.

The Warburg Pincus investment in Newfield went from a gleam in the eye to a possibility to a likelihood, with a few strings attached.

Warburg Pincus and Howard Newman were not founding shareholders in Newfield, but whether they knew it or not, they were a constant presence. David Trice made sure of that.

---

* Courtesy of Ronyld Wise

In large part, Warburg disdained program investments, given the dismal track record. David Trice noted, "Investing in common stock worked for them because such an investment structure avoids the unrelated business income tax feature that could wreak havoc on their endowment and pension fund investors. I really saw Newman's perspective as a positive because it meant we were going to infuse enough capital in Newfield that Newfield could take its own working interests to build value and not be entirely dependent on the maturation of back-ins."

CHAPTER IV
NEWFIELD EXPLORATION – THE EARLY DAYS

"Nobody—I mean nobody—liked the "4-D" name but me. My wife gave me that 'Are you crazy?' look. My secretary simply said, 'Oh!' The potential employees were less than impressed. Charles Duncan said, 'Joe, you have one bad break, and they'll be calling you Quad(ruple) Dog! You can do better than that!'" **JOE FOSTER**

FROM 4-D TO NEWFIELD

On December 8, 1988, Joe incorporated his new firm in the corporation-friendly state of Delaware under the name 4-D Exploration Company. Foster hadn't taken the time to discuss the name with anyone else. He needed a corporate vehicle to commence business, and he needed a name for it.

Foster's notion was that the new company would make much use of 3D geophysical data, and would have people, imagination, teamwork, creativity, or whatever anyone else could think of as the additional fourth dimension. When the important people in Joe's life reacted negatively to the name, he decided to get some expert help in the branding process.

A week earlier, he had read a brief piece in *Texas Monthly* magazine about Lee Ballard, a public relations specialist in Dallas who created names for new products and new companies. Joe's mother then lived near Dallas and he owed her a visit, so he arranged to see Ballard.

Ballard described the naming process very simply. Joe would write a one-page description of the company's activities, mission, values, and objectives. Ballard would send that description to a hundred or so people he worked with in the Dallas area—teachers, housewives, other advertising people, former colleagues, all with some aptitude for originating names. Ballard would then select the 100 of those he received. He put each name on an 11 by 14 inch card. Ballard, Joe and a couple of others in the company would then narrow the choice to five names. Then, after some gestation time, pick the winning one.

When Joe asked Ballard what his fee was, Ballard pointed out the window at a building across the street that had a big Oryx Energy sign on it. Oryx had changed its name from Sun Exploration and Development (XP) a few years earlier. Ballard had used the identical naming process and received a fee of $25,000. Startled, Foster explained there was no way his startup company could afford that. The most he would consider was $10,000. Without batting an eye, Ballard said, "That's fine. It's a deal."

"I knew then I had left our first money on the table," Joe winced. In a couple of weeks, Lee Ballard was in Joe Foster's Houston office with 100 cards, each containing a name in bold black letters. It was pretty easy to get rid of the first ninety and it took another hour to narrow it to five. Then Joe showed those five to family, friends, future employees, and the cleaning lady. "Newfield" was always the first or second choice. It dawned on him that that's what his team was all about—finding new fields. A few months later, they realized they also needed a logo, for which they paid Ballard's firm another $10,000. (It goes without saying that Oryx paid Ballard a lot more for their logo!) Joe remarks, "Although I winced when I signed both checks, both the name and the logo have served Newfield well. I still like 'em!"

In the initial days of forming the enterprise there was an inordinate amount of discussion about naming the new Company—not unlike a garage band whose members focus greater energies on naming their troupe than on mastering their instruments. "Joe came up with another name, despite the fact that everybody else on the initial team had been in agreement—all of us wanted to name it Foster Oil and Gas Company. We originally formed the company under another name— 4-D Exploration. Yeah. None of us liked it. We didn't like it at all and so we kept moaning about it. Finally, Joe relented and called someone in Dallas and he put together some ideas for names and logos. We debated the color of the logo and got to share input…and in the end, we all selected Newfield Exploration Company and were very happy." **BETTY SMITH**

Former Tenneco exec forms exploration firm

By John Ira Petty – *The Houston Post*   January 19, 1989

Joe B. Foster, former executive vice president of Tenneco Inc., said Monday a new company has been formed under his leadership to explore for oil and natural gas in the Gulf of Mexico.

The venture is called Newfield Exploration Co. Foster is its chairman and chief executive officer.

Foster, 54, said the company would focus on an area of the Gulf of Mexico that is gas-prone, where members of the group have knowledge and where they have had good success.

"I think a small company can be very competitive in the Gulf," he said.

One difference between Newfield Exploration and most smaller concerns will be a strong technical effort.

"We'll approach it in many respects like a major company from a technical standpoint, but still have the cost advantage, flexibility and the incentives an independent can offer," he said.

The new company will focus on a portion of offshore Louisiana generally ranging from the Vermilion area eastward through the South Timbalier area in water depths to about 300 feet.

Newfield Exploration has about twenty-five former employees of Tenneco, twenty of them in Lafayette, LA.

Foster said the first year's budget is in the range of $10 million.

Foster, who will remain in Houston, had corporate level responsibility for Tenneco's oil and gas operations and its pipeline companies. He resigned as Tenneco's top oil man and as director effective December 31, when Tenneco completed the $7.5 billion sale of its oil and gas properties.

Duncan, Cook & Co., a Houston-based investment firm is providing initial funding and investment advice for this new venture.

Newfield Initial Funding

> *Charles W. Duncan, Jr., former U.S. secretary of energy, and chairman of Duncan, Cook & Co., said, "We were attracted by the team, the timing, and the focus of this investment. These people have proven they can find oil and gas, they have participated in discoveries containing over a trillion cubic feet of gas in the past three years."*
>
> *A.A. Wilkinson, vice president and general manager of Tenneco's Eastern Gulf Division, will become managing partner in Newfield's Lafayette office.*
>
> *Newfield's Houston offices are in the 1100 Milam Building, Suite 2711.*

LESS THAN 10 PERCENT OF JOE'S ORIGINAL BUSINESS PLAN

Joe's original business plan was to raise $100 million of equity for his new oil and gas company. That amount of funding would provide the staying power for the new company to drill enough wells to avoid gamblers' ruin and to insure its success."[28]

He quickly discovered that those kinds of dollars were not available in the private equity markets that existed in late 1988 and early 1989. The 1986 oil price collapse was still fresh in everyone's mind and natural gas prices were in the doldrums. The LBO craze, which relied on high ratios of debt to equity, was in full swing, and Joe was not about to ask for—or get—debt financing to drill wildcat wells. And good acquisitions were few and far between: the majors had not yet aggressively reviewed their portfolios and implemented marginal upstream asset dispositions.

Joe settled for $9 million of equity, which he referred to as seed money: $3 million from himself and the other Newfield employees, $3 million from the Duncan group, and $3 million from the University of Texas (UT) Endowment Fund, plus an agreement from UT to loan the new company an additional $3 million—at the going annual interest rate of 15 percent.

Key to the investment were the strong contacts of John and Charles Duncan and Ed Randall of the Duncan Group to Mike Patrick and Thomas Ricks of the University of Texas Endowment System. Today, Ricks and Duncan retain their close Newfield connections. Ricks continues to serve on its board of directors and Duncan retired from the board in 2005. Remember, fully one-third of Newfield's original $9 million was sponsored by the UT Endowment Fund. Foster is greatly pleased (and proud to relate) that the financial backing of University of Texas Longhorns helped launch an Aggie's second career.

Private equity investments in petroleum companies were hardly in vogue in the late 1980s, but a number of investors reasoned that the University of Texas was in, and it should know something about the oil business. The affirmative from Austin lent Foster and Trice much-needed credibility within the endowment fund circle. Mike Patrick was much more than an important and influential money man at UT. From his earlier career in the oil-patch as Chief Financial Officer of large independent Superior Oil (sold to Mobil in 1984), Patrick knew that Tenneco was a top flight oil and gas competitor. Patrick was interested in hearing the business plan from Foster's startup because he was predisposed to the Tenneco lineage. Mike introduced Foster and Trice to Duke University, where Trice had gone to school. Mike was close to Duke's head of endowment, and he also recommended them to Dartmouth's investment managers, some of whom Trice knew from his Huffco days.[29]

Given tough petroleum industry fundamentals and a shaky capital market on Wall Street, Joe was forced to downsize his original business plan. Roughly one-third of the overhead was squeezed out, reflecting the urging of legendary investor Gordon Cain, and the decision was made to seek "participants" or program investors to finance half of every exploration well Newfield drilled. Each program investor would take a 12.5 percent interest in each well Newfield drilled, with a maximum of four participants per well. Together they would pay half of Newfield's overhead. After each participant had recovered its investment in a given program, Newfield would then (and only then) "back in" to twenty percent to twenty-five percent of each participant's interest. Furthermore, a two percent overriding royalty interest would be retained for the Newfield employees' bonus pool.

The presence of these quality, seasoned investors helped Newfield spread its risks more broadly, reduce its net overhead, and, with the reversionary interest, improve the economics in each drilling program. As a result, substantially less equity would be required to achieve the desired outcome.

A CONVENIENT COINCIDENCE

John Duncan and Ed Randall, Charles Duncan's associates in his private equity firm, took Joe and David to see Mike Patrick and Tom Ricks, the top two investment managers for the University of Texas Endowment Fund. (The Fund has been enlarged and is now called UTIMCO, University of Texas Investment Management Company.)

As Joe recalls, "David and I did not think it was a total long shot. After all, John and Ed were on the advisory board for the Endowment, and a lot of its revenue was from state oil and gas lands. But this was an *endowment* for Pete's sake, and our name was Newfield *Exploration*. Plus, I was an Aggie. That was before I even knew that one-third of the proceeds from the oil and gas lands portion (of the UT Endowment Fund) went to Texas A&M."

It did not happen overnight, but by April, UT was in the fold. "Tom Ricks came to our initial Founders' Dinner in Lafayette, and we were elated!"

Only later, did Mike Patrick (now chief investment officer for the Meadows Foundation in Dallas), tell Joe Foster the "rest of the story."

Before joining the University of Texas Endowment Fund, Mike Patrick's team at Superior Oil Company, had performed a competitor review focusing on offshore Louisiana and Texas bidding performance in Federal Lease Sales in the '70s and '80s. As Joe remembers Mike telling him, the conclusion was that in terms of both bidding efficiency (i.e., least dollars left on the table) and bidding results (reserves added per bonus dollar spent), Shell and Tenneco were the two companies at the top of each list.

Mike remembered that. That was the main, if not the only, reason he decided to meet with Joe and David.

What a convenient coincidence for Newfield!

POSITIVE REJECTION

A point often forgotten in the Newfield story is how many Houston investors "passed" on the investment opportunity.

Charles Duncan hosted a lunch for wealthy investors in Houston, seeking investment either through his fund or directly in Newfield. None bit. These were not heady days in the oil and gas business, and private equity was not the darling it has become in recent years. However, Gordon Cain showed the most interest and did the most due diligence. Cain, deceased in 2002, was a superstar investor and very knowledgeable about private equity.

After a couple of weeks, Cain's emissary, Gene Graham, let Joe know that Gordon had decided to pass. "Why?" Joe asked.

"Why don't you ask Gordon, Joe," replied Gene.

Gordon was to the point with Joe. "Two things," he said. "I don't do exploration. It is not my bag, but I wanted to see if you had any low-risk stuff. None now. Not enough planned.

"Second, you've got too damn much overhead for a startup. That's the biggest mistake startups make. That's what I wanted to tell you. I wouldn't invest in your company even if your overhead was lower, but you should look at reducing it."

Joe took his advice. He cut one-third of the company's originally planned overhead.

"And I should have taken more out, in hindsight. We damned near didn't make it with the overhead we had. It would have been fatal had we not decided to bring [in] fewer employees and scuttled our thoughts about 'possible selected international ventures.'

"That's the most positive rejection I've ever had," Joe says. "I had the good fortune to take Gordon and his wife, Mary to lunch at Tony's…after Newfield was a success, to thank him for the great advice he gave me."

Who says blind hogs don't find acorns?[124]

A PIECE OF THE UPSIDE

Joe came out of Tenneco with the view that employee and management bonuses should be structured to permit them to participate in so-called "windfall profits."

He had seen oil prices increase from $3 per barrel in 1973 to over $30 per barrel in 1980, while Tenneco bonuses were held at roughly the same percentage of salary during that period.

"As oil prices increased, income targets at Tenneco for bonus purposes were stepped up in concert. Tenneco's income may have doubled or tripled from one year to the next, but so did the targets to exceed expectations and earn a bonus."

Joe saw that it was different with the independent operator. They—and many of their employees—got much fatter paychecks as prices soared. When he established Newfield, Joe was determined that management and employees would share more of the upside—and be at greater risk on the downside.

That, to him, was the appeal in basing the bonus pool on an overriding royalty. The two percent override for the Newfield employee bonus pool was originally intended to apply to the Newfield interest and to the participants' interest in each well.

Overrides—royalties paid to prospect generators—are controversial. Geologists love them; investors hate them. Enter Howard Newman at the beginning of the second round of financing in late 1989, who thought that the two percent ORRI for a bonus pool was inappropriate.

As it turned out, Newman had no objection to the employees capturing some super-charged bonuses in their performance remuneration. Rather, he did not want to see bonuses awarded when the company was losing money. "An override may pay off on a bad deal. I don't want you guys getting bonuses when you are, in fact, destroying value. I don't want you or your geologists or geophysicists to even be tempted to drill a well for an override."

Joe had no quarrel with that. When Warburg Pincus came in as an investor, the two percent ORRI bonus pool portion from the Newfield working interest was capped at five percent of the company's pre-tax profits, after all charges, including overhead and non-cash charges.

Interestingly enough, through the years at Newfield, the five percent of profits target has been very close to the two percent ORRI figure—usually slightly less.

ANOTHER CONVENIENT COINCIDENCE

Another coincidence occurred when Newfield approached Princeton's endowment group about the possibility of investing. Joe recalled, "After our success with UT and Yale in the second round, David and I got on an endowment kick, calling all the big ones we could think of. We called Princeton's endowment in New York City. We visited with a retired financial guy named John Beck who was, effectively, their chief investment officer. Beck was a partner in the highly regarded investment firm, Beck, Mack and Oliver LLC, which was founded in 1931 by his father. He politely heard our pitch, which by that time had become pretty efficient, and replied, 'We don't buy equity in oil and gas companies. We invest in wells. We are working interest investors.'"

Although he and David were surprised by this, Joe remembers that "David piped up immediately saying, 'We offer that too,' and proceeded to explain our program participation model through which an investor could take a 12.5 percent participation in all the wells we drilled, subject to paying his share of our overhead, plus a two percent override and a twenty-five percent back-in after payout."

Joe remembered that "after David finished his explanation, Beck said 'These terms sound familiar, but the guy you must convince to invest is located in Houston. He knows oil and gas. I'll give you his name if you'd like.'"

After assuring Beck that they would be happy to talk to anyone necessary. Joe remembers being pleasantly surprised to hear who they would need to meet with. "John Beck said, 'He is Billy Pete (B.P.) Huddleston. B.P. has a consulting and engineering firm there. His firm handles our working interest investments. I'll give you his number, and tell him you'll call.' I said, 'No need. I have it.' And then I explained that Pete Huddleston was a classmate of mine through all five years of college. 'It won't take him long to decide if he wants to invest with us," I said. "Just let him know I'll be calling."

Joe remembers not being sure how Pete would feel about that. "I knew I would welcome him as the manager of Princeton's money ensconced at Newfield. Pete is a first-class guy. I knew him well enough to know that our being classmates would not have been the cause for him to invest Princeton's money with us. But, it sure made the communication a lot easier. Long story short, Princeton invested.

"Another convenient coincidence!"

SOMETIMES YOU HAVE TO RECUT THE DEAL

When Joe Foster and David Trice came seeking funding in 1989, Howard Newman made it very clear that Warburg would not be a player with Newfield as a drilling participant. Newman studied the dismal track record in energy investment at his new firm and concluded that Warburg Pincus had learned one very hard lesson from the millions it lost in oil and gas ventures in the '70s and early '80s: all had been drilling fund investments and all had been complete dusters. He was, however, interested in making an equity investment in Newfield under terms that Joe did not like—the purchase of common stock.

David Trice had proposed several different equity structures using preferred stock for Warburg's entry. Preferred equity would permit the original investors, including management and employees, to retain a bigger portion of the upside after Warburg had earned an above-average senior return. Joe was reluctant to retrade the common stock deal with his founding investors and said as much to Howard: "This is my deal and I can't go back to my investors with something different." Trice knew Joe was not that interested, but he persevered with a strong entreaty: "This fellow Newman wants to give us $20 million—maybe we should listen to him."[30]

Joe Foster's negotiations in the spring of 1990, during Newfield's second round of equity financing, were very difficult. Warburg Pincus and Yale and Duke Universities were willing to make a common equity investment in Newfield, and America Express appeared

It's been said that no one should observe how politicians make law or how butchers make sausage; the same can be said of how private equity investments are fashioned. When Howard Newman and Yale Chief Investment Officer David Swenson were through, the UT Endowment Fund and most of the original investors had agreed to amend its original deal structure and to join with Warburg, Yale, and Duke to purchase new shares in the company. In a series of private placements in April and May 1990, Newfield sold an aggregate of 29.6 million new common shares to the investor group at a split-adjusted $1.25 per share. By 1993—less than three years later—the stock held by Warburg, Yale, UT, and Duke had appreciated by a fabulous 350 percent . At the time of Newfield's IPO in November 1993, the four lead steer investors held 74.7 percent of the outstanding shares: Warburg Pincus had 34.2 percent; Yale had 21 percent; the University of Texas had 13.5 percent, and Duke had six percent.

Today these same Newfield shares trade at $70 per share. This remarkable forty-fold increase has caused the value of the roughly 75 percent ownership of Newfield to explode to some $7.5 billion today!

to be on the verge but Joe thought that scenario would unduly dilute the holdings of his original investors and employees.

When Joe expressed his honorable unwillingness to renege on his original understanding with his backers, Newman took charge, receiving Joe's blessing to recut the deal with the founding investors. He broke out his textbook on Corporate Finance 101 and fashioned an all common-stock deal, with additional options for employees and some concessions to the founding investors that melded their interests with those of new investors.[31]

"It was a long, wrenching saga, raising that first round of institutional investment. Howard was very committed to doing something with Newfield because he immensely liked (and believed in) Joe—but he was meeting resistance from his Warburg partners. We had Shearson/American Express effectively committed as an investor, but then Shearson backed out at the last minute because there was a corporate train wreck—Amex had to provide a $2 billion transfusion into the ailing Shearson. We had the backing of the exuberant American Express executive who invested the financial giant's huge float of cash. Then he was handcuffed.

"When you boil it down, however, these sophisticated investors came into our deal because of Joe Foster; people invested on the shoulders of Joe Foster, plain and simple. They thought: 'This is a guy who can do great things. If anybody can make it work, Joe Foster will be able to make it work.'" **DAVID TRICE**

A LONG, WRENCHING SAGA – SECOND ROUND OF FINANCING

As David Trice recalls, "Howard Newman became the key guy for us in one second round of equity financing. But even Howard went through a waffling period. We had a period of six weeks where we were fast running out of money, and Joe and I were wondering if any investors would step up to the plate. Warburg appeared to be craw-fishing, and then came the blow when American Express backed out overnight. I remember making the pitch to Duke and Dartmouth while Joe really courted Yale. Joe held a critical two-hour conversation with Joe Williams, head of the endowment investment committee at Yale. Yale was going to be a 'no,' and somehow Joe got him turned around and Yale invested $10 million. The others then came along. When the funds all came together in March of 1990 we had raised $37 million; without those funds Newfield Exploration was effectively out of money and out of time."[32]

There are numerous investment professionals who turned Foster and Trice down—and of course regret it. For example, Trice's Duke classmate John McNabb was at Prudential Insurance—but John didn't pull the investment trigger for the company.

"We didn't make any cold calls. Every call was either a contact that I had developed from my days raising money for Huffco, [or] one that came to us through Charles Duncan's firm or UT's Mike Patrick, or [from] Joe's Rolodex. Warburg was the lead institutional investor joined by the blue-ribbon Four Horsemen of [the] Academe—UT, Yale, Duke, and Dartmouth."

MEMO TO NEWFIELD EMPLOYEES

TO: *ALL EMPLOYEES*
DATE: *JUNE 1, 1990*
FROM: *JOE B. FOSTER*
RE: *THIS WEEK*

I cannot let the week of May 28, 1990 pass without reflecting on it.

Monday, we logged Newfield's first discovery: It has about 100 feet of pay with more hole to be logged and drilled. A nice Memorial Day!

Wednesday, we closed out our equity offering, receiving $17 million to go with the $20 million we received on April 20.

Thursday, we closed on our first producing property acquisition and took over operations.

Friday, we are moving in a rig to drill in West Cameron, adding to the operations where we are already participating in Eugene Island and West Delta.

Little old Newfield, with three rigs running, a producing platform (and a non-producing one on Vermilion 241), seventeen prospects, and a full crew of motivated employees! Not to mention a prestigious group of investors and partners and over $30 million in the bank.

Wednesday and Thursday, we met with representatives of MDU Resources of Bismarck, North Dakota, who are considering joining our program. The presentations were enthusiastic, and they were well received. I am optimistic MDU will join.

It has been a good week!

But, good as it has been, it, like life, has more than one perspective.

Our discovery now has stuck drill pipe.

The newly acquired producing property is off production.

Our three operations consist of the rig with stuck pipe, a rig listing forty-five degrees, and a rig under tow.

MDU has not yet committed, we are still 15 percent short of bringing in all the partners we want, and we must get "up" for a presentation to Berry Petroleum next week.

It has been a long trip down the runway. We are finally airborne. As Chief Pilot, I am ready to declare "wheels up." It is more important than ever not to slow down now. The journey is just beginning.

Nevertheless, for a brief moment, on our own time, over the weekend, let's pause and be proud of ourselves. We've done a helluva job.

> Sincerely,
> Joe B. Foster

/bs

[*Author's Note:* Thanks to a few pack-rats like Joe's long-time assistant, Betty Smith (note her secretarial signature at the bottom left: /bs), the following memorandum to employees dated June 1, 1990 has survived to chronicle that major first moment of uplift at Newfield. Good CEOs are good commemorators: Joe says it all in this memo titled, *This Week.*]

DEFECTIONS WERE RAMPANT

At the time he wrote that June memo to the staff, Joe's steadfast resolve and optimism were not equally felt by the remaining handful of original Newfield employees. Defections had been rampant.

In the first eighteen months of Newfield's existence, ten of the company's original starting team—fully 40 percent—had left. Several employees were not up to a small company's uncertainty and lack of infrastructure, and were lured back to larger, more secure companies; one decided to go to business school; and several left "by mutual agreement" because they did not adapt to the ways of an independent operator.

Joe's long-time assistant, Betty Smith, remembers the first few months of 1989: "Mr. Duncan was in another building downtown. When we first started and we didn't have any real money in the bank, we ran on Joe's and Mr. Duncan's money. On paydays or crisis dates for paying vendors, I would call Mr. Duncan's office and his secretary would send a check over and Joe would take money from his personal account, and that's what Newfield survived on. It was a real trusting situation." In Betty Smith's view, Charles Duncan is "a really fine gentleman." And the feeling is mutual. Duncan recalls, "I remember our early board meetings; Betty would stop and buy Cokes at K-Mart on the way to the office. I can still taste those delicious brownies Betty used to make at home and bring to the board meetings."

Joe Foster was not partial to corporate spending on walnut-trimmed paneling or deep plush

"The question was: What kind of investment vehicle did we want to have? When I worked for Huffington, we had no outside shareholders. The Huffington family owned it all, and everything else was managed through an investment program. Outside corporations and institutional types effectively invested alongside Roy, and Huffco would earn back-ins on successful drilling ventures plus management fees for running the enterprise. The problem with that business model was that you never could develop any substance; it takes a long time for back-ins to reach fruition. Moreover, if you had one bad drilling year, many investors would not re-up and would just disappear. I worked to sell Joe on the concept that we really needed permanent equity capital in the company. It was music to my ears when we saw Howard Newman; I can remember that first meeting at Warburg Pincus— Howard said bluntly, 'We don't do programs. We will invest with you. We will not invest in programs.' Investing with Howard meant investing in the stock of the company." **DAVID TRICE**

"It was a bet on a very effective and proven CEO, on an experienced and competent management team, and on a solid business plan. Moreover, all of the founding employees had made a significant investment—roughly one-third of their net worth—and all our interests were aligned." **HOWARD NEWMAN**

"The day we got the money into Newfield's bank account was the day we drilled our third dry hole, our third consecutive dry hole. But right after that we made our first discovery, followed up by our first successful acquisition. Then we had a run from the middle of 1990 through the end of '91 where Newfield really hit its stride. What a difference! When we got ready to seek another round of capital investment at the end of '91, we literally had people knocking down the door. Our original lead investors didn't want to let anybody else in, so they took it all themselves." **DAVID TRICE**

> "I want the record to be clear that I am not a geologist or geophysicist. I have never generated a prospect. I have never drawn a geologic map—and I've never selected a wildcat drilling location. I have spent most of my career trying to create an environment where good explorationists have had the technology and the incentives to generate prospects, and have the funding to drill the really good ones."
>
> **JOE FOSTER,** "Legends in Wildcatting," presentation to the Houston Geological Society, January 10, 2000.

carpeting. In founding Newfield, Foster's goal was to utilize the essentials that made the major oils successful—namely technology and vision—while leaving the frills behind. That meant no fancy office equipment, much less corporate aircraft or country club memberships. Newfield's original 1989 Lafayette office was kindly described as Spartan, with

The early days: Ron Lege, David Schaible, Rich Mowrer, Mike Sewell and Bob Waldrup

bare walls and offices furnished with surplus items from its founding employees' homes, such as patio chairs and folding card tables. Joe says, "With respect to Newfield's furniture… we talked about that when we were first setting up offices. We agreed that we needed to look like we were substantial enough that people would be willing to want to invest in us, but we also wanted to convey an image that stated 'we're not going to waste a damn penny.'" In the upstream business of profitably finding and producing oil and natural gas, success has nothing to do with mahogany desks and leather-backed chairs. One truism of the oilpatch is the caveat, "You'll never find any oil at the Petroleum Club."

WALL STREET JOURNAL ARTICLE FROM 1992

After its keystone 1990 equity financing led by Warburg Pincus, Newfield's first four years in business were bootstrapped with a series of private placements and the use of an institutional drilling program. Angel investors Warburg Pincus, Yale Investments, the University of Texas Endowment Fund, and Duke University purchased Newfield common stock at split adjusted prices between $1.25 and $1.75 per share. Charles Duncan invested $1 million in 1991, acquiring new equity at $1.75 per share.

By the fall of 1992, Newfield Exploration Company was beginning to show up on the

> Joe Foster is an engineer and businessman, and not a geologist. Joe states, "Exploration—wildcatting—is a lot more risky than the statisticians tell us it is. Even with all the new and exotic technology, the probability of success we assume for a wildcat is nearly always too high."

radar screen for its aggressive yet parsimonious up-stream growth activities. Caleb Solomon, a journalist with the *Wall Street Journal,* spent a week with Newfield's executives. Solomon's article, "Oil Firm's Best Find: Penny-Pinching" ran on September 30, 1992.

Early in the building years at Newfield, Joe Foster was often interviewed by the financial press. He diligently expressed his goals of constantly challenging costs and "drill[ing] the cheapest dry holes" in the oilpatch. He continued with this advice: "Pay as much attention to the downside as the upside. Don't avoid all high-risk wells, but manage your resources so that you can drill more and less expensive dry holes and still have the capability to keep going."[126]

Newfield acquired virgin leases and doggy old producing properties with full knowledge of the abandonment liabilities that ultimately went with them. The company sought "planned serendipity" that comes from "farm-ins," or incremental acquisitions in which the real driver is a novel geological interpretation that indicates an exploration test is warranted and promising.

Oil Firm's Best Find:
Penny-Pinching

By Caleb Solomon, staff reporter of The Wall Street Journal

September 30, 1992

A helicopter whirs across forty miles of mottled gray sea, leaving the Louisiana coast for an oil and gas platform in the Gulf of Mexico.

The Bell 206-B hovers a moment, then eases down on the heliport of a garish, multicolored oil-production platform cobbled from a mishmash of used parts. With red pads and gray pipes, yellow stairs and white tanks, the refurbished decks seem downright circus-like. This is a jalopy of a platform in an industry partial to stretch limos.

It may also be the future of U.S. energy exploration.

In 1990 Joe stated, "About one-third of our proved reserve adds have come from producing property acquisition at the time of acquisition, about one-third have come from the conversion of possible and probable reserves generally associated with those acquisitions, and one-third of the reserve adds have come from exploration."

Many industry players are abandoning the U.S., rushing overseas to more plentiful reserves and lower exploration and production costs. Since 1986, nearly half of the nation's 15,000 independent oil companies have gone belly-up. But penny-pinching Newfield Exploration Co., which owns this bargain-basement platform, was born into the industry's maelstrom and is designed to cope with hard times.

"It's independents like Newfield that will keep the American oil industry alive," says Jack Mullins, a supervisor at a drilling rig leased by Newfield.

Joe B. Foster, 57 years old, is betting his considerable reputation as an oil man and more that $1 million of his own money that they will. The former Tenneco Inc. executive founded Newfield four years ago—just as sliding prices and rising costs decimated oil and gas exploration in the Gulf of Mexico.

Newfield's 18 wells last year made the company one of the gulf's most active drillers. The closely held company says it is profitable and that its annual revenue is approaching $40 million.

Much of the oil and natural gas that remains in the Gulf of Mexico is in scattered pockets, tough to locate for small independents without the seismic and engineering know-how and not worth the trouble now for large companies. With low overhead and high technology, tiny Newfield makes main courses of the scraps that have been missed or left behind in these well-worked waters.

"One of the things we do best is to plan for failure," Mr. Foster says. "We assume every well we're going to drill is a dry hole, so we drill the cheapest dry holes out there." Newfield, which is based in Houston, spends an average of $2 million a well, while others often spend twice that.

"We are better explorers because we are acquirers, and we are far better acquirers because we are explorers." **JOE FOSTER**

That explains the decidedly tacky but utilitarian platform here at Ship Shoal 157, off the coast of Terrebonne Parish. It is a 157-foot-high structure that resembles construction scaffolding and serves as a base of operations for production. Newfield's operations manager, Robert Waldrup, drove his blue Ford Taurus from one Gulf Coast shipyard to another finding the pieces and getting the platform built in seven months for $7.5 million.

Prodigal oil companies would have spent about $11 million and taken four months longer. By shaving construction time, Newfield pumps crude faster than competitors, Mr. Foster says. This boosts returns on investment to the 20% to 25% range from the 10% to 15% that could be expected otherwise, he says.

Newfield's fortunes—and those of other industry players—have benefited immensely from a recent sharp rise in natural gas prices. But Mr. Foster maintains that the jump in prices won't affect Newfield's way of doing business. "We said all along we're not betting on prices; we're betting on our ability to find and acquire reserves," Mr. Foster says.

Newfield's penurious ways extend to personnel. Each of the company's first 25 employees—24 of them former Tenneco workers and all investors in Newfield— took big pay cuts to sign on.

"We just thought Joe could do it again," says Steve King, a lease negotiator who turned down a better-paying job elsewhere to join Mr. Foster at Newfield. Bryan Nelson, a geologist, voices the most common reason people signed on: "If everything works, everyone could become a millionaire."

Mr. Foster is already one. He left Tenneco in late 1988 with a severance package valued at several million dollars, after the oil and gas operations he built during 30 years there were sold off in pieces for $7.5 billion. That sale also made the 300 people in Tenneco's Lafayette, La. division available. Mr. Foster chose two dozen top oil prospectors from those ranks, and they invested their Tenneco severance pay in Newfield.

Newfield set up shop in January 1989, three miles from Tenneco's old Lafayette office. Ronald Lege, Newfield's controller, administrative manager and purchasing agent, paid Tenneco 25 cents on the dollar for desks and chairs he had been in charge of buying new for that company in 1980.

Though Mr. Foster pinches the pennies, his company doesn't stint on explo-

ration technology. Other small companies use shoestring systems; Newfield bought $3.5 million of seismic data on 30,000 acres of the Gulf for its whiz kids to interpret with high-powered computers. Prospects such as Ship Shoal 157 wouldn't have been discovered without that database.

The company started out with $9.1 million, raised equally from employees, the University of Texas endowment fund and Duncan, Cook & Co., a Houston investment firm. Mr. Foster, who had kicked in $1.3 million, paid the payroll from his own bank account in the first lean months.

From August 1989 until February 1990, Newfield drilled three wells, all dry holes. On the fourth, slippery currents ate away the foundation below the rig, and it capsized. Redrilled later, that well was also a dud. By late March 1990, the $9.1 million had dwindled to $100,000. A big investment bank considered dropping plans to buy Newfield stock. One by one, nine Newfield founders, including a geological engineer and a geophysicist, left.

But Mr. Foster persuaded the investment bank to stick to its plans, and in April 1990, Newfield placed $37 million of equity. Filling job vacancies at least gave Mr. Foster a chance to infuse Newfield with some non-Tenneco blood.

Memorial Day weekend 1990 marked the first discovery—20 billion cubic feet of gas and 300,000 barrels of oil in West Delta 20. A week later, Newfield completed its first acquisition and picked up an additional 24 billion cubic feet of gas and 250,000 barrels of oil.

On a roll, Newfield soon erased the red ink. The company acquired more leases—and discovered a further 39 billion cubic feet of natural gas.

Those successes have given Newfield the cushion and confidence it needed to weather dry spells—including a recent string of nine wells that yielded nothing. But nobody is relaxing. "In a small company, you're always on the edge," Mr. Foster says.

"Even when we were down to our last $100,000, and I knew that's all we had in the bank, we were at the stage with the second-stage investors that I was sure the money was going to come through. I mean, I was very disappointed in some of the things that had happened, but I never ever had the feeling that Newfield was not going to make it." **JOE FOSTER, NEWFIELD'S 20TH ANNUAL FOUNDERS' DINNER – MAY 1, 2008**

> "Newfield has resisted the seduction to have the Newfield Exploration Tower at North Belt – or as it used to be, 363 North Sam Houston Parkway East....Newfield relocated there in the beginning of 1991 and has 18-plus years at the same location. As by far the lead tenant at 363, [we have] the privilege of naming rights. No! That doesn't fit the Newfield culture and, Heaven forbid, we don't want people to think we own it! Another reason [is], lease terms are always negotiable, but a lot less so if a 25-foot corporate logo adorns the building. Look at it this way: if somebody comes in and gives me a really good deal on a cheaper, better lease, we might move. We don't have an anchor down here." **TERRY RATHERT**

THE GREENSPOINT LOCATION

Joe Foster had an incredibly demanding travel schedule in the early months of 1988. Newfield had had the tough start with its string of dry wells. Meanwhile, Joe was making trip after trip to New York to talk to people like Howard Newman and David Swenson—taking him away from the business, but a necessary step.

"Then there were many long days at the wheel in car trips to Lafayette," says Betty Smith. Southwest Airlines still hasn't annexed Lafayette, so Joe "decided to move the fellows over here" to Houston in late 1989.[127]

Betty remembers that Joe was, as always, diplomatic but forceful about the corporate relocation. "He listened very carefully to everybody…and the consensus [was they] did not want to move back to the congestion of downtown Houston." This meant finding a different Houston location. However, Smith was not ready to concede, since she loved downtown Houston—it was a straight-shot commute for her that she had down pat. But Joe had another card to play. He told Betty, "I promise that we'll move closer to your grandchildren. That's a big positive"—and one that Betty could not rebut.[128]

The location chosen for Newfield's Houston HQ was 363 N. Sam Houston Parkway East. This 19-story atrium building in the Greenspoint area is convenient to Bush Intercontinental Airport. It proved to be an excellent choice despite a slightly higher than average base rent—acceptable to Rathert and Trice, though they knew it bothered Foster. Betty Smith sums it up: "It worked out well—a lot better than most corporate relocations. Most of the Lafayette contingent were happy and moved to the Woodlands and Kingwood, both north of the new HQ and offering quality affordable housing, good schools, and trees, amenities, and country clubs."[129] Later in the 1990s, the creation of the Hardy Toll Road, linking downtown Houston with the Woodlands, made the Newfield location even better.

OFFICE DÉCOR DOESN'T MATTER MUCH

As any visitor today will attest, Newfield's office furniture and fixtures remain plain, simple, and fully depreciated. Its Houston headquarters are still in the same

> "Pennzoil was our Lee Harvey Oswald. The Portfolio B deal died before the ER ambulance left the curb for the hospital."
> **JOE FOSTER**

barely Class-A office building. Newfield's frugality is deliberate and is not due to corporate inertia; its occupancy cost is well under $30 per square foot per annum, a 30 percent or more discount from a slick downtown office tower on Houston's Smith or Louisiana Streets.

With 275 Houston-based employees occupying 158,000 square feet, surely Newfield could justify its own named Class-A custom office complex.

From his office window, Newfield's then-current CEO, David Trice, scanned the Houston skyline and thought about the two nearly vacant Enron towers as well as the underutilized skyscrapers of Anadarko, Calpine, Dynegy, El Paso and Williams. Call it the fear of bad Karma—Newfield sees no benefit in having naming rights for its headquarters' building. In fact, the company has twice turned down such an offer from its leasing company.

As Joe puts it, "My observation has been that corporate signage has been a negative thing. Enron Field is now Minute Maid Field. The Tenneco Building where I worked for 20 plus years is, for the time being, the El Paso Building."

CHEVRON (WITH THE HELP OF PENNZOIL) THROWS NEWFIELD A WICKED CURVE BALL

In late 1992, Chevron assembled a billion-dollar divestiture package of mature "harvest" domestic properties—what was widely known among Wall Street energy investment bankers as Portfolio B. At that point, Chevron came to Newfield and proposed that Newfield acquire the package for some cash but mostly for new Newfield Exploration shares. Apache Corporation had blazed this trail with a highly successful landmark deal with Amoco, in which Amoco took mostly cash and some APA stock for its MW Petroleum unit.

Under the Portfolio B initiative, Newfield would acquire the assets and Chevron might wind up owning anywhere from 60 percent to 80 percent of a "new Newfield," which would be ten times larger than it had been. Chevron ostensibly sought a deal in which the San Francisco-based integrated giant would own 80 percent and could consolidate its interest in Newfield for tax purposes. The Newfield team had worked for a giant oil and gas bureaucracy before and, to put it bluntly, Joe felt they were not excited about Chevron being in control.[130]

Notwithstanding those reservations, the Newfield executive team was seduced by the prospect of a mega-deal that would instantly catapult the tiny private E&P to the billion-dollar-market asset tier. Negotiations with Chevron ran all day and all night, and then the pendulum governing the transaction suddenly came to a standstill. Substantial progress on the key issues had been made and a deal was close when Pennzoil stepped into the picture.

To recap some oil and gas merger history, in 1989 Pennzoil had received $3 billion in cash from the humbled but previously imperious Texaco, based in White Plains, New York. Flamboyant Houston attorney Joe Jamail, a close friend of Pennzoil's chairman Hugh Liedtke, had found a treasure trove for Pennzoil. In a case that still haunts the Texas legal system, a Texas civil jury awarded Pennzoil an outrageous $11 billion for "tortious interference" related to Pennzoil's purported loss (to Texaco) in its overture to purchase Getty Oil in 1984. In its late 1980s attempt to shelter from taxation the $3 billion of windfall proceeds, Pennzoil had acquired 32.9 million shares of Chevron stock (9.4 percent of total outstanding), and then claimed to the IRS that its CHV ownership constituted a "like-kind exchange" for the assets it would have acquired had the Getty deal materialized.

How could the merits of Pennzoil's case with the IRS be challenged if it were able to swap its Chevron shares for Portfolio B? More important, it was common knowledge on Wall Street that the Chevron board of directors was extremely uncomfortable with the large stake that Pennzoil controlled in the Bush Street SanFran Seven-Sister. Who blinked first? Chevron.

From a business standpoint, Joe couldn't fault the Chevron folks. They negotiated in good faith, but at the end of the road, Pennzoil had a superior deal. Newfield kept its "game face" but they were more than a little bit disappointed. On the plus side, the Portfolio B exercise caused Newfield to focus on the steps they would eventually need to pursue in taking the company to the public market.[131]

In the end, the IRS prevailed and Pennzoil paid its taxes due. Later, Pennzoil management fought tooth and nail against a cash tender offer of $84 per share from Union Pacific for the company (a large part of Pennzoil's value was Portfolio B). Management won; shareholders lost.

Five years later PennzEnergy and QuakerState Pennzoil (the residual entities of Pennzoil Corporation) were sold to Devon Energy and Royal Dutch/Shell, respectively, for an aggregate value of $42 per share—one-half the "unacceptable" value turned down half a decade earlier!

KEY MAN INSURANCE – AN EARLY ISSUE

Betty Smith and Bob Waldrup shared a deep-seated concern that Joe Foster would be run over by the proverbial truck. Waldrup had personally placed a huge financial bet on the company and he was adamant that the new Newfield take out a so-called "key man" insurance policy on Joe B. Foster—that is, insurance on Joe's life. Betty was caught in the middle. "Joe, in his own modesty, would reply, 'You know, we've got a good group of people here…this company will survive, you know, even without me.'" But Betty countered, "However great a team it is, Bob is right, they wouldn't have my money without Joe Foster." So Bob Waldrup prevailed and Newfield bought the insurance. It was a necessary financial outflow for the new company that fortunately proved unnecessary.

JOE'S NEWFIELD – THE COURAGE TO INVEST

Joe Foster's values are Newfield Exploration's values. In Howard Newman's view, its bedrock competitive strength stemmed from Joe Foster's communication and managerial skills. Foster established a high-performance "work hard, play hard" culture from the get-go. Newfield was a no-frills organization whose people have always been viewed as the company's key asset, treated with honor and dignity. Joe Foster always sought the best

"It's not just Joe Foster. He put together an organization of people that were really very noteworthy and very good—people [who] sold themselves when they had contact with others. So we may have had meager financial resources, but we have tremendous people resources. And people is what built the business to the tremendous success it's become."

CHARLES W. DUNCAN, JR., CHAIRMAN, DUNCAN INTERESTS

people to screen opportunities "a mile wide and an inch thick"; having unearthed a promising prospect or deal, he would put his top people against it.

In the early 1990s, Newfield did raise capital from both permanent equity issuance and drilling investment programs. The alongside drilling programs were structured such that Newfield would take half of each venture and the program investors the other half. Princeton was a participant in the drilling investment programs along with Fidelity Oil, a subsidiary of Montana Dakota Utilities. The other three significant program investors included institutional energy investor, Resource Investors Management Company (RIMCO), based in Hartford, Connecticut; a Iowa Illinois Electric; and Houston private independent, Continental Land & Fur.

David Trice opines, "That's how we started. The benefit of having the alongside drilling program investors was that when we took a deal—we were not big enough at that time to take 100 percent of anything—everything was pre-marketed. Our people could focus on finding good exploration prospects and not on spinning their wheels marketing those prospects to joint venture partners. We stopped worrying about selling prospects and accelerated our drilling efforts; the program investors provided Newfield with major momentum."[132]

CHAPTER V
THE FOUNDERS

BOB WALDRUP – ONE TOUGH HOMBRE

Offshore with Dad Waldrup

It was preordained that Robert Waldo Waldrup would become an oilman. In the early 1950s, his family moved from Quitman, Mississippi to New Orleans. After several jobs in the construction industry, primarily as a welder, Waldrup's father, Ben found an excellent gig with Shell Oil working "seven and seven" offshore, first as a roustabout and then as a lease operator, boat mechanic, welder and, finally, instrument tech. He could do anything with his hands.

Waldrup recalls, "I graduated from Murrah High School in Jackson, Mississippi in 1962, and enrolled at Mississippi State as an engineering student. Shell had a program where they would allow sons in their junior year of high school to go offshore a week with their dads. After a week offshore on Shell's platforms, I was certain I wanted to be a petroleum engineer.

"Shell was gracious and gave some modest scholarship money, the latitude to complete course-work in five years and valuable work offshore during the summers. A lot of people say college is the greatest time of their lives. College was not fun for me. My father and mother had almost no money, and during my freshman year, my dad came down with cancer."[33]

Bob Waldrup's father struggled off and on with cancer the whole time Bob was going through college. And so he struggled, too. Scratching to cover expenses through his years at Mississippi State, Waldrup worked as a dorm daddy, a soda jerk, and bussed tables in the cafeteria. It was not glamorous employment, but he sure enjoyed the cafeteria work, where he got free meals. Waldrup married his wife Judy in February 1967 and graduated from Mississippi State with a BS in petroleum engineering that June, when he went directly to work for Freeport Sulphur. His first assignment was Grand Isle Frasch sulphur mine in the Gulf of Mexico offshore from Grand Isle, Louisiana.

Tough Decisions!

On a new assignment with Freeport in 1970, Bob and Judy moved to Houma, Louisiana. His usual routine was to go offshore from Monday morning to Tuesday night, Wednesday morning to Thursday night, and Friday morning to late Friday. That was the drill, unless there was an operational breakdown. Then, of course, Waldrup was stuck offshore until it was fixed. In addition, Bob was taking business classes on Tuesday and Thursday evenings at Nicholls State University working on an MBA. Bob Waldrup had aspirations to be more than just another petroleum engineer.

When Freeport transferred him to the Lake Pelto Mine, Louisiana, the sulphur market was in a horrible state. New incremental sulphur supplies were being produced from sour gas wells and huge mounds of golden elemental sulphur were stacking up throughout the Gulf Coast. Frasch sulphur (produced from hot water injected into sulphur reservoirs) had stiff competition from the byproduct sour gas supplies. At Lake Pelto, Waldrup was named superintendent of drilling and production, and he thought he would focus on day-to-day operations. Instead, he was told the grim news upon arrival: "We have to shut down the entire operation in six months."

Waldrup reported directly to two Freeport hands who were twenty and thirty-five years older than him. Nonetheless, the twenty-five year old Mississippi State engineer was given the unpleasant role of firing half of the Lake Pelto staff. His boss, Fred Osterloh, had deferred to him, exclaiming, "I'm not laying these people off. I've worked with them all my life."

Waldrup took a firm tack: "Okay, so and so, you're a tool pusher right now. I don't have any driller's jobs open because you are not physically capable of doing active drilling any more. The only thing I've got left for you is a pumping job. Do you want it or not? Here's your layoff package if you don't." Waldrup quickly pared forty seasoned Freeport employees, favoring seniority as instructed, and immediately gained respect for being a very tough hombre. He recalls that despite the sulphur price collapse, Freeport managed to keep that mine open until he moved on to Lafayette to join Tenneco in October 1972.

Bob Waldrup joined the Tennessee Gas Transmission company in 1972 and bled "Tenneco blood" until the end. In Joe Foster's view, it was Waldrup who "put the teeth in" Newfield Exploration's commitment to becoming a leading low-cost operator in the Gulf of Mexico. Now retired from Newfield, Waldrup is a burly tough guy who played an instrumental role in seeing that every precious dollar of capital was well spent—especially in the early white-knuckle days of the company's drilling and operating history.

In the Tenneco hierarchy, each geographic division unit had a general manager, a production manager, an exploration manager, and an administrative manager. Under a reassignment, Ron Lege became the Eastern Division administrative manager and Waldrup its production manager. With an ample amount of pride, Waldrup recollects, "When Tenneco Oil was sold in 1988, our Eastern Division had the most production of oil, the most production of natural gas, the lowest operating costs, and the best safety records; we were rated the best in the company."

Foster was fully aware of the Eastern Division's outstanding performance; it had built a great young team. Many of those hands formed the nucleus of Newfield.

Bad News and Brews

Waldrup clearly remembers learning about the Tenneco sale. He recalls, "We were working on a deal with Tennessee Gas pipeline group for the development of a gas storage operation at a Tenneco Oil field we operated, Eugene Island 198 in the Gulf of Mexico. We were in the middle of a major negotiation with the pipeline people. Mike McGonagill, who had worked for me and then worked as an executive assistant to Joe Foster, was head of the team for Tennessee Gas."

About halfway through the negotiations, Waldrup noticed an unusual volume of activity in the conference room with people coming and going constantly. "Finally, Mike called me off to the side saying, 'Let's go out and talk.' McGonagill asked me, 'Did you hear that Tenneco just announced that they were selling the entire oil and gas company?' After a few minutes of discussion, McGonagill and I went back in and announced, 'Guys, there's no use continuing these discussions and we might as well leave. This meeting's over and adjourned as of right now.'"

Waldrup and his team had come to Houston that morning on a Tenneco plane that shuttled personnel back and forth from Lafayette. Before he boarded the plane with his five-man team, Waldrup made a stop at a convenience store and bought several six-packs of beer. Waldrup recalls, "We drank beer all the way back to Lafayette on that plane. We probably were not authorized to imbibe on the company plane, but this was a shock to us all. When I arrived in Lafayette, I told my wife, 'That's life in the oilfield, and you accept it.'"

After the divestiture was announced, Waldrup had another challenge. "The next big hurdle that came at us fast was: What do we do between now and when the new owner comes in? Tenneco had a bunch of wells that needed to be drilled, and we went out and got 'em drilled, got 'em drilled right, helped arrange the data rooms and worked with Joe Foster on the LBO project."

Waldrup's most distasteful assignment while finishing out his tenure with Tenneco was as a member of the transition team after Chevron purchased Tenneco's offshore properties in the Gulf of Mexico. "[Even though I was never on the Chevron payroll] every time there was somebody in the offshore division who the new Chevron team figured out didn't fit, I was the one who ended up having to tell 'em they were being let go. I probably knew more of the guys in Tenneco's offshore operations, in all three divisions, than just about anybody. When I first joined the offshore division in '72, there were about sixty of us. When we shut it down, we had close to 300 operation-side engineers. And I knew most of those guys. I had trained many of them and they had worked closely with me over the years."[34]

[*Author's Note:* Few senior operators and field hands were offered jobs with Chevron at their pay scale and took a step back if they elected to stay; as a result, only 250 of 1,100 employees moved on with the California major oil.[35a]]

At the time Tenneco Oil was auctioned off in 1988, Bob Waldrup held a senior position in its upstream business: Division Production Manager for the Eastern Gulf of Mexico Offshore Division. Waldrup was proud of his tenure in the Tenneco Gulf of Mexico operations. When he first arrived, Tenneco was producing 400 million cubic feet (MMcf) of gas a day and maybe 30,000 barrels of oil per day—from the entire Gulf. When Tenneco sold to Chevron, the Eastern Gulf Division—one-third of offshore—was producing close to one billion cubic feet (Bcf) of gas a day (1,000 million cubic feet) and about 50,000 barrels of liquids per day.[35]

After Chevron acquired the Tenneco assets that Waldrup managed, Carney Block, a Chevron operations manager, told him that "Momma Chevron" wanted to send Waldrup over to West Africa to be production manager on their big Angola program, a two- to three-year assignment. When Waldrup asked how long the current manager had been there, Block came clean with Waldrup and replied that a Gulf Oil man had been there since '83. Block told him that they had had a hard time getting a strong production manager to replace him.[36]

Waldrup was intrigued. This was a very senior job in the Chevron organization, but it required a work schedule of 28 days on and 28 days off, reporting back to San Francisco at the end of the 28 on in Angola. He could live wherever he wanted to, which was appealing; but still, Angola was a long haul—a little too long for Waldrup.[37]

At the time, Bob Waldrup didn't really know Joe Foster very well. In his mind, Joe was one of those high, lofty figures housed in a grand office at Tenneco's headquarters. Waldrup's initial meeting with Foster to discuss joining Newfield was the week before Thanksgiving 1988 at the Lafayette Hilton in Room 711. When Bob Waldrup greeted Foster he remarked, "Joe, you've got a lucky room here. Seven come eleven." Waldrup felt it was a fantastic omen.[38]

> "Our objective was not to cobble together some petroleum assets and flog them to the highest bidder in two, three, or five years. Hell, if we did that I would later find myself out looking for a job at 55 years of age."
>
> **BOB WALDRUP**

Waldrup told Foster that three essential things were necessary for him to sign on with Newfield. First on his list was autonomy. He wanted to run operations in a manner that made him happy—which to Waldrup meant that they would not take shortcuts. Things would be done properly. Second, they would always be in compliance with standards. Waldrup had a good reputation in the oil and gas industry and he was strongly against tarnishing it. He had seen a lot of little independents operate on a shoestring, and he didn't want to do that. And third, they would be in it to build a great, lasting company.[39]

Joe Foster assured Waldrup that all three issues would be addressed head on: first, Waldrup would be empowered to run operations; second, Newfield would not just be run according to the letter of the law, but in the spirit of operations that are always managed the correct way; and third, they would be in it to build a company of enduring value.

At the same time, Waldrup got another tempting offer to join another ex-Tenneco hand, Jack Gregory. Gregory had been persuaded to join British Gas to run the portion of Tenneco's international assets that the United Kingdom (UK) gas behemoth had acquired. (Conoco had gotten the bulk of Tenneco's overseas assets.) Gregory wanted Waldrup to move from Lafayette to Houston to be his vice president of production for British Gas. Waldrup had a real dilemma. Did he take his severance nest egg from Tenneco and put it in Newfield, or did he take the British Gas position, which would pay a bit more than he had made at Tenneco? If he took the British Gas position, he could keep all his retirement savings from Tenneco.[40]

Waldrup recalls the difficult decision. "We talked it over really hard, and with my wife Judy's blessing, I took Joe's offer. The reasons? I could run my own show and I was energized by the challenge of something new and different. I knew if I went to Chevron, or if I joined British Gas, I wouldn't be running my own show. I would always be the operations guy—stuck in the middle of some organization chart."

Given his experience and seniority, Waldrup was never concerned about job security when Tenneco Oil was divvied up. Waldrup chose Newfield and "decided to gamble on the new deal with Joe Foster." Aside from Joe Foster and Charles Duncan, Bob Waldrup was the most significant investor among the 22 founders who put up seed money for the company's launch in late 1988. Waldrup humbly notes that his investment in Newfield "…has stood very well by me…I not only had major stakes from options and grants that I received during my working tenure, but also because I put a very sizable personal investment into Newfield when we first cranked up." A lesson from Bob Waldrup to any of us who have a chance to invest in a quality startup company at the outset: "I struggled really hard to push the sophisticated investor limits to be able to put as much of my savings into the company as I did…and it paid off handsomely."[41]

Cheap Dry Holes and a Capsized Rig

When Newfield was getting off the ground in 1989, the company participated in an MMS lease sale and acquired rights to several offshore Gulf of Mexico blocks. It had a number of prospects to drill, and although Bob Waldrup, as a senior Tenneco manager, hadn't been directly responsible for drilling a well in fifteen years, he quickly got back to basics and geared up. Waldrup was a fan of "turnkey" drilling arrangements, in which the drilling contractor is paid a fixed fee to drill and complete a well. However, his first Newfield turnkey well estimate was "off the charts" at $750,000. It was a little 3,500-foot well that was easy to drill. Waldrup told Joe Foster, "We can drill it for a lot less than that," and managed to complete that well—unfortunately a duster—for about $500,000.[42]

Around the Newfield office in Lafayette, one of the sayings was, "We can drill as cheap a dry hole as anyone in the industry." But the joke about low-cost dry holes began to wear thin when the company's next two wells were also dry. Although the second and third wells were drilled for less than the amounts estimated, Newfield was "crunching money" and seven original employees had defected.[43]

"In those tumultuous first twelve months of Newfield's existence, Bob Waldrup's experience as a manager was put to the test repeatedly. He recalls a very important conversation with Dave Schaible in September. "Dave walked in my office in Lafayette and questioned whether he should stay, or whether he should go. Where were we going with this Newfield Exploration thing? I told him, 'Dave, I can't tell you what you should do. But I'll tell you what you need to do. You need to make a decision and stick to it. Whatever you do, you need to do it 100 percent . We can't do it half way. We've got to have 100 percent on board and we've got to be united in our belief that we can make this thing work.'" **BOB WALDRUP**

Things were getting tough by the time Newfield was ready to spud its fourth well. Bob Waldrup had negotiated a turnkey contract, his first. The drilling contractor was operating a shallow water barge rig in south Louisiana and had just reached surface casing point at about 3,000 feet. Waldrup was over at Kerr-McGee's office when Foster called to let him know the rig had capsized. Foster asked, "How do we stand?" Waldrup replied, "They've got all the liability; the contract says that it's their problem."[44]

Waldrup returned to Newfield's office to find Joe Foster, David Trice, Terry Rathert, and Wendell Bares (a lawyer who had come from Tenneco to negotiate the contract) all sequestered in different offices feverishly reading the contract. Waldrup was duly relieved when his Newfield colleagues concurred that the liability rested with the drilling contractor. Further relief came when Waldrup got on the phone with A&P, the turnkey operator out of Houma, and they agreed that they had the liability. A&P ended up taking care of all the barge rig problems at no charge to Newfield. Then Waldrup negotiated a slightly modified turnkey contract to drill a replacement.[45] This was about the same time, Memorial Day 1989, that Newfield had its first discovery in the Forest Oil Corporation operated well, West Delta 21.

Foster and Bill Schneider confronted Waldrup, "We've lost seven of our original guys in Lafayette; we need somebody to step up and be a leader." Waldrup replied, "Well, I'm an operations engineer and I admit that I don't know a lot about exploration." They replied, "That's not what we need. We need leadership." So Waldrup assumed day-to-day management of the Louisiana office, with Bill Schneider having responsibility for guiding the exploration process and exerting technical quality control.

It was Waldrup's job to coordinate; he could make sure that the division met deadlines, checked the right boxes, and kept integrity and safety at the fore. After that, they only lost one person, but for an entirely different reason—he chose not to relocate to Houston when the company closed the Lafayette office.

After Waldrup closed down the Lafayette office for Newfield at year-end 1989, he moved to Houston; the decision had been made to consolidate and put everyone under one roof. On January 2, 1990, Waldrup walked into the Houston Newfield office and sat down with David Trice and Joe Foster. Foster asked, "Well, Bob what's going to be your role in Houston?"

Waldrup didn't hesitate: "Joe, I'm going to run operations. You can have those explorationists. I have been babysitting these geoscience guys for six months now." Waldrup continued, "I'm a real good operations guy, but I'm not a good babysitter."

Joe Foster took over direct management of exploration and Waldrup was kept in the "prospect generation" loop and consulted on quality control.

"We always dealt with the top operators. We didn't deal with the shiftless guys you see every day on the corner and down the street. We had all been burned by those types; the next thing [you know], that lease that used to be yours is now theirs. We didn't suffer any low-end talent. Joe brought morality and character, and looked for outstanding people—and I like to think I'm one of them—who had that same philosophy, that same mentality, that we're not going to cut corners just to cut corners, or we're not going to go out and try to stiff anybody. We're going to deal hard, we're going to deal with Newfield's best interest foremost, but we're going to be fair; that's our reputation around the industry. If you go around and talk to different people outside in the service business or in the land business, Newfield has an excellent reputation. They deal hard. They deal fairly. They carry out what they say they're going to do…Newfield people worked long hours. People say, 'Well, Bob Waldrup walked away with a lot of money from Newfield.' I feel that I earned every penny. All of us put in our time, put in great effort, whatever it took to get the job done. Some of our families probably suffered a little bit, but even with a hard-work culture, the Newfield management group all have very strong family ties." **BOB WALDRUP**

Turn of the Turnkeys – West Delta, Eugene Island, and Vermilion

Waldrup was livid and infuriated if he learned that some of his team was "tight-holing" key information. If a geologist or engineer was hiding adverse information for a recommendation or key prospect, that person was gone from Newfield by the end of the day. It was important to the company that all information be on the table. If a well was going to be budgeted for $2.5 million, everyone had to believe that it could be drilled for $2.5 million, or else they would be unable to properly assess whether to turnkey it, drill it themselves, or not drill it at all.[46]

Waldrup was a one-man operations and engineering department during Newfield's early years, relying on outside consultants to assist him in carrying out the operations. They used third parties and they outsourced permitting, too. Waldrup also preferred to employ outside contract labor for Newfield's infrastructure requirements, leaning on a key construction expert, Mike Lowe. David Trice had recommended Lowe as a result of his top-notch work experience at Huffco. Lowe ran an excellent construction group that also believed that platforms could be reused and equipment could be built to the right size. Newfield's platforms were often built for 50 percent or even less of the costs incurred by the major oils. And all of Newfield's facilities were fully compliant; they built the simplest platform possible that would work safely.

Thirty days before a Newfield platform, new or reworked, went offshore, Waldrup would take the platform's two head operators to the construction site. They spent those days looking at the platform and identifying changes. *Where did they want steps? Could they reach this valve? Could Newfield change or repipe it? Could Newfield change this? Could they do that?* As a result, when the platform went offshore, the operators knew that platform, and they knew how it was going to work. Newfield and Waldrup did this every time. By 1995, Newfield got to the point where there were 250 people working offshore on their platforms. They worked for Danos & Curole, Island Operating or Grasso Operating, the three main contractors that supplied personnel, all out of south Louisiana. Newfield was one of the first independents in the Gulf of Mexico to operate extensively using third-party operators, and they still use those same three contractors today.

Newfield has always pushed open, honest communication. Waldrup feels that the working relationship between their drilling group and their exploration team was the best of any group of oil and gas professionals he ever worked with. There was mutual trust. The drilling group would work to get the best possible price and the exploration team would do its best to drill and successfully complete each and every well.[47]

From the early discussions in the Fall of 1988 until the company went public in November 1993, one drilling engineer, Frank Henicke, worked for Waldrup. Henicke was Newfield's first drilling guy. He came from Lafayette to work full-time for Newfield when the company moved to Houston. Frank was Waldrup's drilling superintendent in the Eastern Division, and in Waldrup's estimation Henicke is the best drilling operations guy he ever worked with. Henicke was in charge of the wildcat well Tenneco drilled off the Bahamas, off the Cuban coast. He also managed Tenneco's lone exploration test drilled on the North Slope of Alaska. Henicke always did a phenomenal job because he only knew one approach to success: he was there every day with a "hands on" approach on every well.

Henicke had the skill-set to work with the contractors and the guys in the field. He also learned how to manage turnkey projects. There were no production engineers until 1994. They still had no construction engineers. Frank Henicke resisted turnkey when Newfield first started, but he quickly converted when he realized they would lack the staff they had had at Tenneco. Waldrup notes, "Newfield used turnkeys like insurance, not to make money. Newfield used the turnkey approach to ensure that the investment budget established by Newfield to drill and complete a well would not be exceeded."[48] Newfield probably used turnkeys on 60 percent of its drilling projects. Using turnkeys ensured that Newfield controlled their capital exposure. Waldrup never wanted to make money on turnkeys; he just didn't want to lose money because Newfield had made a mistake. However, Newfield personnel were there to manage the completion process and all workovers.

If you go back and look at those first five years, Newfield was one of the most active operators in the Gulf of Mexico. Some statistics show that Newfield's cost to drill, when you combine the turnkey and the operating expenses, was the most competitive of any company in the Gulf of Mexico. Waldrup achieved this impressive feat by using independent operators, an approach the MMS did not like at all. The MMS was totally opposed to using contract labor to outsource operating activities. But Newfield held the line, established its own operating procedure manual and its own rules, and ended up winning annual safety awards. With its team of ex-Tenneco hands, Newfield's philosophy was that they would do it right. "And if you do it right, it ends up invariably costing you less money all the time." Waldrup recalls, "We wrote our own safety program. We treated the contractors like they were our own people and, therefore, those people believed in Newfield. We didn't lose a whole lot of operators."[49]

Newfield was also one of the first independent operators to initiate a cash bonus program for its contract offshore operators; in decreasing importance, the awards are based on HSE (health/safety/environmental), MMS compliance, attaining production goals, and controlling operating expenses. They awarded bonuses every six months, and yet those payouts cost far less than having all the contract labor on the Newfield payroll. The MMS could see evidence of Newfield's top performance and that it was related to its people and to the way it regularly and consistently rewarded safety and performance. The bonus was not just lip service, it was a way to pay for results, because if the contractors didn't hit all the targets, they didn't get a bonus.[50]

"We put a bonus program in effect for our operations contractors—the first time that had ever been done in the Gulf of Mexico. We stressed the base bonus standards on safety and on MMS compliance. But we also looked at online performance—[the amount of] time that wells capable of flowing were on production or …shut in."[51]

Newfield and Waldrup never lost sight of the importance of lean operations. If outside operators could stay within Waldrup's budget on the jobs that they controlled, then they shared in bonuses. Newfield did this within the first year after offshore operations started up. Waldrup still strongly believes that the bonuses created employee loyalty. "We'd go to the platform, and I'd say, 'Guys, this is your platform. It's not anybody else's platform. You're gonna run this platform, and this is yours. You take care of it like it's yours.' And when I hit that platform, they knew that I was going to be walking around and looking. And

U.S. DEPARTMENT OF THE INTERIOR

MINERALS MANAGEMENT SERVICE

1997

NATIONAL OFFSHORE
SAFETY AWARD FOR EXCELLENCE

IS PRESENTED TO

NEWFIELD EXPLORATION COMPANY

SECRETARY OF THE INTERIOR

One of many Safety Awards earned by Newfield Exploration from the Minerals Management Service

[within] five minutes …I could tell you whether they were taking care of that platform or not. And they took care of the platforms like they were their own."

Bob Waldrup recalls each and every significant Newfield property in the Gulf of Mexico with excitement and a twinkle in his eye; a casual observer might overhear the conversation and think he's boasting about his grandchildren.

According to Waldrup, Newfield learned a great deal drilling the company's first discovery well. A deep exploration well, the West Delta 21, was being drilled by Forest Oil Corporation, and Forest was having real problems. Waldrup had numerous meetings with the folks from Forest trying to resolve the delays. Forest finally got the well down, and it was a discovery; Newfield's first discovery was outside operated and it took a painful two years to finally bring on production. Out of that experience came the Newfield philosophy that, in order to control costs and timing, the company wanted to operate its own wells.

"Newfield suffered with the West Delta 21 well that was over budget. It was painful and costing the company precious dollars. Newfield had drilled two dry holes and had basically run out of money. Joe Foster and David Trice had been trying to find another source of capital. They had American Express lined up, but that fell through. They closed a loan with some of the ex-partners at the University of Texas, a group of universities which had included Dartmouth and Princeton. Warburg Pincus was the leader on the group. They raised $35 million. That allowed Newfield to go buy an ex-Tenneco property called Eugene Island 172 for $7.5 million. David Schaible was the guy that really pushed Newfield to buy that property in 1990. Eugene Island 172 had four wells that were shut in at the time of acquisition. Three of the wells had failed subsurface safety valves and two also had casing pressure problems due to leaks in the tubing."[52]

The property was producing nothing, but with it came a lease for Vermilion 241, a subsea well right next to Vermilion 241 and Eugene Island 172. Eugene Island 172 came with abandonment liability; Eugene Island 172 had four shut-in wells with sixty days to go on the lease, which meant that if there wasn't production in sixty days, the company was going to lose title to the block. Three of the wells had casing pressure. Two of those three had failed downhole safety valves. Waldrup went out with a wireline crew that included Chris Mabee, their first offshore operator. They played with the safety valve, got it locked open, and then put in an insert valve. Waldrup recalls, "So, the first thing we did after we took it over, we put people on the problem; I went out to the EI 172 platform in June of 1990 that had been shut in for sixty days. We played with the safety valve on the A1 well. I tell you,

Another one of Waldrup's favorite fields is Eugene Island 62. This was a lease bought from Exxon where Newfield drilled four discovery wells in 1993. Within a short eight months a platform was installed and production began at about 90 MMcf of gas a day. When Newfield made the original discovery total reserves were estimated at 80 to 90 Bcf. Waldrup notes, "Now Newfield thinks EI 62 will be close to 200 Bcf. It's been a big-time money generator for the company and it's still making 25 million [cubic feet] a day." **BOB WALDRUP**

we played with it: bled it down, ran a wireline in it, slid it open and closed. We played with the seals and got the valve operating properly and then we got the well flowing again." With that one well Newfield began producing 1.5 to 2 MMcf of gas per day. That basically paid the operating expenses of the Lafayette office. It was Newfield's first production and the company was allowed to hold title to the lease.

About forty days later, Waldrup mobilized, got all the equipment rounded up, and wrote the program strategy to workover the wells. He took Chris to run the operation offshore, a long stroke snubbing unit, which is essentially a small workover rig. The two of them pulled the tubing on all three of the other wells over the next three months and repaired the casing damage and downhole safety valves. By the end of the year, Newfield had 20 MMcf of gas per day, and about 1,000 barrels of condensate per day coming out of those wells. They were supposed to be depleted, but, in reality, they were just orphans needing some TLC and attention. Newfield got a lot more production out of the wells than Chevron ever thought there would be; even Newfield's expectations were exceeded.

That was Newfield's first true workover, as Waldrup would call it: going back into an old property to work on existing wells, looking at the geology for missed opportunities, cutting costs and maximizing the remaining life of the property. From about 1991 to 1996, workovers accounted for much of Newfield's production. Newfield would go back into the properties that the company had bought from the majors, and either drill new wells, work on the existing wells, or somehow enhance the production. Significant production came from improving existing wells on those prospects.

We Did Not Waste Money Anywhere, Anyhow

Ship Shoal 157, a.k.a. "the kaleidoscope of colors," is an especially memorable field in Newfield's history. When Newfield originally made the deal on Eugene Island 172 with Chevron, they had assumed the obligation to abandon the Vermilion 241 platform, where the lease had already expired. Waldrup went to the other four Newfield partners, who together held a 50 percent working interest, with the offer to participate in the abandonment costs of the Vermilion 241 platform for ownership in the equipment. He knew that Newfield could reuse whatever they could salvage for the new discovery at Ship Shoal 157. He gave each partner the same cost estimate: what it would cost to plug, abandon, and dismantle the existing Gulf of Mexico platform. One partner consented, the other three declined. The estimate to abandon all of that was about $1.25 million. The AFE [author-

"The heliport has a good coat of yellow paint on it. The platform needed some touching up, so we touched it up—a little bit of grey, a little bit of yellow, some blue. The production equipment was all grey, but it didn't get repainted, either, because it had a good paint coat on it. And as long as you've got good paint, you don't have to make it beautiful. It's only got to work for you. Newfield did things that needed to be done. We didn't do things to make it pretty." **BOB WALDRUP**

ity for expenditure] was $1.5 million, and that's what they charged out to the Vermilion 241 owners. Then Newfield started reusing the platform: the deck, all of the production equipment, the generators, and the cranes on Ship Shoal 157. By employing suitable used equipment and charging it back, they got more than the $1.25 million. Newfield used the platform jacket and the other equipment on two other fields and ended up making real money on that abandonment.

Waldrup recalls, "We took the subsea well manifold out. We cut the pilings and lifted off the platform jacket and put it on the beach. We pulled the deck and put it on the beach. We pulled all the production equipment and abandoned the pipeline. We took the deck and reused it at Ship Shoal 157. We used the crane at Ship Shoal 157. We used some of the production equipment. I bought a used heliport and used that heliport somewhere else. Later, we used the jacket at South Timbalier 193. When we got through with the accounting of that field, it had cost us about $1 million dollars to take the platform out and abandon it. We had credited that account with something like $1.8 million because that was the going price for a used jacket, deck and production equipment. So the people who participated in that made about an 80 percent return on their money. We were able to reuse the majority of the equipment."[53]

Waldrup continues, "There's a story about that, too. Early on, before we went public, the *Wall Street Journal* did a story on Newfield. It was my assignment to accompany the *Wall Street Journal* reporter, Caleb Solomon, to South Louisiana—Ship Shoal 157 then here comes the *Wall Street Journal* article about the kaleidoscope of colors on the platform topsides. I caught more ribbing about that from all of the guys that I had worked with all my life. We were always cost-conscious and when we looked at the paint job, [it] did not need to be redone. So we ended up with a yellow jacket. We ended up with gray production equipment, a different yellow on the heliport, and a white living quarters building. The generators were already painted blue, and the paint was good; so why would I paint them a different color? There were a whole bunch of different colors on the platform, but it worked. We did it very economically. We kept our cost down very well; it's the Newfield culture.

Newfield wasn't unique—there were a lot of small independents buying and installing used parts of platforms. In Waldrup's view, the oil industry was overpopulated with "constructionists" who want to build the biggest, most impressive platforms. Waldrup felt the objective was to engineer something that would serve throughout its life, not simply for the peak moment when you get 10,000 barrels a day and then it is over-designed for the life of the project.[54]

In turn, Ship Shoal 157 worked out exceptionally well. When Newfield brought it online it was that rare "on time, under budget" project and it made its projected production volumes. Waldrup reckons that Ship Shoal 157 was exploited at half the costs Chevron or another major operator would have incurred. In the early 1990s, natural gas prices were in the tank and wellhead prices plunged to less than a dollar per thousand cubic feet (Mcf). At the time, if you weren't a low-cost operator, you weren't an operator at all. Waldrup notes that Newfield reused platforms, building new only when there were no better economic options. They built tripods, they learned to use caissons. Newfield did not waste money, anywhere, anyhow.

The Newfield Sprint

Waldrup says, "We did things rapidly, compared to major oil companies. Eugene Island 262 is an example of this rapidity. We made a discovery there, and it was a good discovery, and it was off of a property that we had bought: Eugene Island 251 and Eugene Island 262, from Exxon. The Eugene Island 251 had a big old junky platform, but it had a little bit of production coming off of it. Eugene Island 262 was to the south of it. Exxon had drilled a well down on 262, and it was uneconomic. Too far a reach from the platform to hit paydirt sands and Exxon lost the well. Newfield came in and drilled a nice discovery at a location requiring a new platform. While we were drilling the second and third wells, and the fourth well with the rig, a jacket was put in place and wells were tied back—at the time no topsides, just the jacket. Then we drilled second, third, and fourth wells, through the jacket. And while they were drilling those wells, we began construction on the topside deck and production equipment to handle up to 90 MMcf of daily gas production.

"The wells were all completed when we stabbed the jacket, and it took only two months to hook it up and get it online. From start to finish, we probably had Eugene Island 251 online in nine months, producing sixty million a day. The majors would not even think about doing that…even Tenneco was not doing that. We did that kind of innovative operation. And that, to me, made a large difference in the value that we added to the company."[55]

Another big difference between Newfield and many of the major oil companies is that the majors move at their own pace. At Newfield, there was a definite "We've gotta get this done," or "We've gotta get this finished. We've got to move on. If it's no good, let's put it aside and stop working on it. If it's good, let's finish it." From the beginning, Newfield had the "push to closure" meeting every week. It was basically a weekly summary meeting, to talk about where we were on active projects and what it would take to complete them.

Waldrup says, "I think Tenneco's philosophy was the best philosophy to train young engineers of any company that I've ever seen. They put people to work. They gave them responsibility, and they gave them authority. And they expected them to fail. You are going to fail if you get into any situation. My job, and the manager's job, is to keep you from having an ultimate failure, to keep the failures small. That was the way Joe approached this, to some extent. You know, we're not always going to be right, but as long as we gave it our best effort, then that's okay. My job was to keep it from being a catastrophe. If you got a failure, that's fine. But a catastrophe is not fine."[56]

> "My job was to keep it from being a catastrophe. If you got a failure, that's fine. But a catastrophe is not fine."
> **BOB WALDRUP**

Waldrup saw many of his employees grow, moving from their first jobs as area engineers into positions as managers. He could watch their progress. He is proudest that he had a hand in their lives and had something to do with their success.

"When I look back at all the kids that I've had work for me, and I've had a bunch, Dave Schaible probably ranked up in the top two or three of all the kids I ever had to train. A guy named Mike McGonagill was another one. Mike is now manager of the northern pipeline that goes into Canada. Right now, he manages that whole pipeline system. Lee Boothby was another one—smart, intelligent, smooth. Those three are three of the best that I've ever seen."

Geologist Bryan Nelson was one of the originals at Newfield, a talented ex-Tenneco explorationist who was the inspiration behind the discovery of the important Broussard Field onshore Louisiana. He came out of South Dakota School of Mines and had worked for Waldrup in the Tenneco Eastern Division. Todd Stone, who was probably the best development geologist Bob Waldrup recalls working with, was a young PE who also was a Waldrup protégé from Tenneco's Eastern Division. Nelson and Stone, along with Dave Schaible, were involved in finding 70 percent of the oil and gas that Newfield discovered with the drillbit between 1993 and 1996.
BOB WALDRUP

Waldrup is fond of the book series The One-Minute Manager, which stresses the importance of MBWA—managing by walking around. Waldrup had a new twist: MBDA—managing by driving around. "How many employees get to spend six uninterrupted hours in a car with their manager, discussing what they're trying to do and how they're trying to do it, developing a solid trust? When we get back to the office, I don't have to ask any more questions. I know what he's going to do, I don't need to baby-sit him. I can turn him loose because we've already got the fire drill down. That's one of the failures of the big oil companies—managers are on such a pedestal. They've got all this experience, but they never get it down into the ranks. It never gets communicated." **BOB WALDRUP**

When asked how it was to work for Waldrup, Dave Schaible replied, "Well, as long as you're trying, Bob's not bad to work for. He's good to work for. But if you don't try, you might as well leave right now."[57]

Newfield's management leads by wandering around—and it works. Waldrup believes that you have to get out of the office to accomplish your job. "You have to go and talk to these people. You've got to go offshore and walk on that platform. The operator shows you around, and he is proud of it. That platform's going to be like that six months from now. If you never go out there, [if] he never shows it to anybody, that platform's going to look like heck. I tried twice a year to hit every platform in the Gulf of Mexico with every operator, to give them a chance to see me, to ask me questions, and for me to see what they were doing and how they were performing."[58]

Waldrup says, "I would try at least once to get to every rig where we were drilling a well, and see those consultants that are actually running the job for us. They can make the difference in whether the well is going to be a duster or a gusher. For every turnkey project that Newfield undertook, I made an effort to visit the site as often as possible. It meant a lot of travel in a lot of helicopters; I visited every platform that Newfield built, from about 1991 until about 1995, at least two or three times.[59]

"Gary Gonzales and Mike McGonagill and I would drive out of Houston at roughly four o'clock in the morning. At seven o'clock, we would be sitting in Lafayette; then it was often on to Morgan City and Houma. And then turn around, start back, hitting yards as we went. We'd get back into Houston at midnight, one o'clock in the morning. We'd do that trip about once a month. Or, if we were going to make a two-day trip of it, we'd end up in Lafayette usually that afternoon. We'd go hit two or three platforms under construction or two or three wells turning to the right. Maybe we would visit and have lunch [or] supper with a foreman, senior foreman or whomever. Some trips involved overseeing operating facilities offshore; we might go offshore for two or three days, and then come back and hit the yards. You cannot do your job sitting in the office. You have got to get out and mix with the operations people, the construction people, the drilling people, and know what's going on. You sit in that office all day long, it isn't going to happen—not the way you want it to, anyway."[60]

Even though Newfield's stock price took a downturn during the 2008-2009 market crash, Waldrup remained a long-time believer: "It'll come back. I have no doubt myself. I know the people, and I know what's going on, and I know the business … every oil and gas stock got beat severely in the downturn; I've seen it before."

The Original Tenneco Team is the Current Newfield Team

Bob Waldrup left an indelible imprint on the Newfield organization. He recalls, "Terry Rathert worked for me as a production engineer after he was hired directly from A&M to join Tenneco. Lee Boothby, now Newfield's CEO, worked for me as reservoir engineer after being hired out of LSU. George Dunn worked for me as a drilling engineer before being moved to reservoir. Jim Metcalf worked for me. Dave Schaible worked for me as a reservoir engineer after being hired out of Marietta. I either hired 'em out of school, or they [had] worked for me at Tenneco. Mike Sewell worked with me…you can go down the list of a

"Up until the time he retired, Bob Waldrup enjoyed going over to Lafayette, taking one of his production engineers or drilling engineers. One of the guys who regularly used make the Lafayette trek with Bob was Mike Lowe, the consultant who performed all of our platform designs. Waldrup would spend all of the time driving over to Lafayette grilling these guys. 'Why don't you do this? Why don't you do that?' I recall Mike Lowe returning to the office and saying, 'Gosh, I'm just exhausted.' Can you imagine spending twelve hours in one day in a car with Bob Waldrup?" **JOE FOSTER**

core group of Newfield top professionals—the guys who are managing the organization—a ton of them came from Tenneco. Gary Parker, Jim Zernell, Chris Nelson all came from Tenneco. And Tenneco was an excellent trainer.

"We carried the Tenneco philosophy over to Newfield—that you didn't have to have done everything fourteen times before you were allowed to manage it. Tenneco had the program of working triple-seven in the drilling group [*Author's Note:* seven days in the office, seven days on the rig, and seven days off] and letting the young engineers go out and drill wells. So, they learned how to do it. At Tenneco, the m.o. was not to have the trainees sit in the office until some foreman with forty years of experience showed them what to do. We were trial-and-error committed. You have to go run it on site, in the field. If workovers needed to be done, you did the workovers. If production equipment needed to be inspected, you checked the production equipment. If compressors needed to be set, you designed and put those compressors out there.

"You can't always be there to manage every decision that's made. If you do, you've only got one guy running the team. What's essential is to have a bunch of people who think the way you do…as a manager, with a belief that they're not going to carry you over the edge of the cliff with them. We built that type of organization at Newfield—not only on the production side, but on the exploration side. One of the things that we always did with the exploration group was to evaluate every prospect in laborious detail; then when we got through, we asked those guys, would you drill this? Would you drill this with your money, dollars [from] your pocket? It was their money, because if it was a dry hole, they didn't get credit on their bonus.[61]

"Every guy had to stand up there and [answer the question], 'What do you think?' And we didn't tolerate wishy-washy answers like, 'Oh, yeah, we ought to think about drilling that thing.' What we wanted were answers such as, 'I think this has an excellent chance to be successful and these are the good points and these are the shortcomings,' or 'I don't think we should drill the well and this is why.' When you let people express both sides of the equation, good and bad, they are much more likely to tell you what they really think about something."[62]

Waldrup's Successors

Who really does Bob Waldrup's job now? Waldrup reels off the names: "Jim Metcalf has drilling. Jim Zernell has production. Tony Comeaux [no longer at Newfield] has all the operations to manage; international activities are run by Jim Eisterhold." During his last years with Newfield, Waldrup was on contract, working closely with the Australian operations. He states emphatically, "From mid-1998 to 2001, I made thirteen trips to Australia."

In Waldrup's view, Newfield's success was aided by one of Joe Foster's key attributes: plain old persistence. "Joe always believed that he could do what he needed to do, and he wouldn't take no for an answer. If we had problems drilling dry holes, he would go out and find a way to solve that problem. And we did have a problem. We once experienced a painful string of eleven dry holes. When we were really struggling with the application of technology, it was Joe's persistence that brought us through.

> "Newfield went [for] a decade ... without a major lawsuit. And that first lawsuit, over a well blowout, was one it ended up winning easily. Newfield resolved its differences. It acted in good faith. People acted in good faith with them. Right? Because they knew that was what we expected. We dealt with only top-flight vendors. We didn't deal with the fly-by-nights." **BOB WALDRUP**

"Joe's exceptional Rolodex of contacts was absolutely invaluable to Newfield's startup. There was nobody in the oil and gas industry they couldn't get in to talk to or negotiate with, and it was all because of Joe's knowledge and reputation. He brought a presence that filtered down to the rest of the team. Foster made them believe they were going to be a solid oil company, not another fly-by-night. If Newfield tells you they're going to do something, they're going to do it."[63]

When Joe Foster stepped down as Newfield CEO at the end of 1999, the company had 107 employees; it now has more than a thousand, housed in offices in London, Kuala Lumpur, Malaysia and Beijing, China and, in addition to its Houston headquarters, it has domestic offices in Tulsa and Denver. [*Author's Note:* Newfield's Australian operations were divested in 1999.]

> When he was informed that there was some apparent tension in the current Newfield Exploration executive suite about continuing to fly coach class and not first-class, Foster commented, "Well, let 'em struggle. I made two or three overseas trips—one, only a couple of months before I retired, was to Australia—and I always flew tourist—coach. I remember Bill Schneider, who was making that trip to Down Under on a regular basis, say, 'Are you going to fly business class, Joe?' I said, 'No. You don't fly business class, do you?' And he said, 'Well, no, but I thought maybe you might and we might get a precedent going.' And I said, 'No, no, no. Not on my watch.'" **JOE FOSTER**

BILL SCHNEIDER – CRUSTY OLD ORIGINAL

After acquiring Bachelor's and Master's degrees in geology from Boston University, William David Schneider moved west to Denver, spending five years doing uranium and base metal exploration with the German company UG (formerly referred to as Urangesellschaft.) He remembers that period as not unlike the recent commodity boom: "It was during…the inflationary '70s, and metal prices had gone wild. It was boom and bust: metals exploration had gotten red hot and, just as quickly, went stone cold."[64] Schneider left Denver for Tenneco in 1981, moving southeast to Lafayette, where he toiled as Division Geologist in the Western Division—focused on offshore Texas but including the productive West Cameron area of Louisiana.

Now a twenty-one-year Newfield veteran, Bill Schneider was a key member of the original team that was recruited along with stalwarts Bob Waldrup, Terry Rathert, and Dave Schaible. Schneider notes, "Yes, I am one of the crusty old originals—one of the few still around today who was there on day one.

"It was a very interesting time back in 1988. Like everyone in the oil patch, I was shocked when Tenneco announced the sale of the oil company. It was a fire drill from day one as we didn't have long to prepare the data rooms; then there was the ordeal of 'show and tell' before the many prospective buyers. I was very involved…the sales part of the process. Some people were involved with Joe and his leveraged buyout team…I was a 'Company man' on the data room team."[65]

Schneider had a terrific vantage point while running the data room at Lafayette—from his crow's nest, he had the opportunity to see all the potential purchasers who came through the data room. "My team and I were elbow to elbow and picked up the sense of how…the management and the technical staff interacted. SoCal [Standard Oil of California, now Chevron] was one of the giant oils, with four different technical teams poring through the data room, that I was personally managing. So I had a pretty good sense of the paternalistic behavior of the Chevron organization." Schneider states diplomatically, "When CHV turned out to be the successful bidder, it didn't take me long to determine that that was not the type of organization that particularly appealed to me."[66]

Schneider was direct. "I made it known that I wasn't interested, that I did not want an offer from Chevron, that I wanted to get the Tenneco severance package." Nonetheless, Chevron had a position in their San Francisco headquarters that they wanted to offer him; they were just trying to get things organized. But in ponderous big-oil fashion, Chevron never did get organized.

Recalls Schneider, "I said to myself, 'I need a break from big oil.' So I was proactive, and before the purchaser of Tenneco's Gulf of Mexico assets was even announced, I wrote a letter to Joe Foster." The letter was plain and straightforward: "I didn't know what he was doing, I didn't know what I was doing, but if he was gonna do something new, I'd like to work with him."[67]

Schneider Is Not Risk Averse

At the time of Newfield's formation, Bill Schneider, with a wife and three children (the youngest less than a year old) demonstrated remarkable determination. He wasn't concerned over the great risks inherent in a new startup. "I was thirty-seven at the end of 1988, when we had to make decisions on where we were going to go and what we were going to do. I didn't view Newfield as a great risk. In my view, if I put my money in and this organization wasn't successful, I could still get another job. It was a great opportunity to try a startup. But none of us had any idea how difficult it was going to be."[68]

Schneider tapped his Tenneco severance, in his case his 401(k), for his contribution to Newfield's "seed capital." "There was a blue sky law that affected us since we weren't considered sophisticated investors. We were required to hire an investment advisor to inform us of the risks. In the end, most of the initial Newfield 'tribe' just anted up the minimum, which was $10,000. I put up as much as I could—$35,000—that was as much as they would let me invest."[69]

An Interesting Social Experiment

Schneider notes that for the first year and a half, Ad Wilkinson ran the Lafayette office –until Joe Foster terminated him. Schneider recollects, "It was a very interesting social experiment, to take people who had been at four or five different levels within Tenneco and throw them in the same cauldron. Ad had been a general manager. Waldrup and Carleton Sheffield were the next level down, senior managers. I was among five or six division-level geologists and geophysicists. And then there were senior geologists and project geophysicists. There were all these different people from Tenneco who were accustomed to a reporting hierarchy—reporting up this well-established Tenneco chain of command. And, all of the sudden, boom! We're all equals![70]

"At Tenneco they graded people as A's, B's, and C's under a performance valuation model. At Newfield we began with a roomful of A's and the sorting-out process was very painful. Unfortunately Ad Wilkinson wasn't able to knock the heads together. Don't get me wrong—he had a lot of qualities that served him well in an organization like Tenneco, and Ad advanced to be manager of one of the biggest upstream divisions within Tenneco. But he wasn't the guy to crack the whip and say, 'Let's all act like adults here.'"

The dysfunction was readily apparent when key people abruptly quit at Newfield—five technical people left within three months. That's when Joe decided it was time for a change: Foster dismissed several people and put Bob Waldrup in charge in Lafayette, with the understanding that at the end of the year, the entire Lafayette staff was moving to Houston. Foster's message was clear: If you don't want to go to Houston, well … that's where the company is going, so you can find the exit door yourself.

"It all happened one Sunday evening," says Schneider. "David and Joe drove over from Houston to Lafayette and I got a phone call at home: 'Meet me at the Hilton.' It was me and Bob and David and Joe. We all bought in on the plan, which was delivered succinctly: 'This is what's gotta happen. And, this is how are we gonna get it done.'"[71]

Schneider harkens back to 1990 as the real turning point for Newfield. "The mass exodus of the technical staff was odd to me. We'd finally raised the money. We'd gotten the Warburg commitment. We [had] bought a producing property. We were covering our overhead and we had a drilling calendar with some good-looking prospects, one of which, West Delta 27, was our first discovery, logged over the 1990 Memorial Day weekend.[72]

The move to Houston was as much of a commitment as joining the company had been in the first place. It meant leaving everything behind and starting over again. Foster addressed the troops: "I'm gonna give everybody $20,000. You can spend it however you want." Schneider observes, "No, it didn't cover much."

"Few people remember how the move from Lafayette to Houston was a great financial burden to almost everybody. I had moved to Lafayette at the height of the boom and paid a ton of money for my house. I paid the mortgage for nine years and put a lot of money into it. Then I went to closing with a check to pay off that mortgage. We had no home equity."[73]

Superior Information Leads To Superior Results

"From day one at Newfield, we were prospecting with a data set that was superior to the data used by most of our competition," notes Schneider. "We made the commitment to buy a multi-million dollar regional seismic data set as opposed to postage-stamp parcels, and that set us apart from a lot of the small companies that we were competing with at the time. The smaller E&P outfits would be willing to take farm-ins, to go into a company's office and look at the data and analysis their prospective partner had accumulated. Since we had our own data, we could evaluate the quality of the farm-in potential. That investment in the new seismic really set us apart. The other technology that was so successful was the addition of 3-D surveys over fields and discoveries. 3-D surveys were very expensive, so a lot of operators didn't buy 3-D. But when we'd acquire property, if there wasn't a 3-D on it, we'd conduct our own 3-D survey."[74]

"For the most part, these 3-D surveys weren't proprietary; we would work with the seismic vendors, and have them shoot spec data. We would underwrite the shooting at a reduced cost to us because they could sell the data to anyone. We'd get 3-D over all of the properties that we bought. And the difference in what you could see on the 3-D, versus what you could see on the 2-D data, was just night and day. With 3-D, Newfield found all sorts of low-hanging fruit that was always there, but you just couldn't image it before."[75]

"The lesson is, to be successful, you must be willing to use the most current technical tools available, and pay what you need to get them. Nonetheless, these tools more than offset their costs because of the improved accuracy and improved visualization qualities. It's a pretty good management lesson all around. If you don't have the expertise, you'd better go out and get it somehow and somewhere."

The Technical Reviews Were Bloody

Schneider describes Newfield's process for selecting drilling prospects. "It was with the mindset that it's your own money that you're investing, and, therefore, those technical reviews were bloody, very bloody. Am I going to invest my money in your prospect? It took

Bill Schneider stresses that Joe Foster had a lot of patience, and enough experience to know that you must persevere. One of his lines was, "Success is never final and failure is rarely fatal." Schneider remembers, "Joe was willing to tolerate a higher degree of uncertainty—chaos isn't the right word, but disorder… so that lessons could be learned…Like a parent comes to realize, 'Well, the kids are going to have to learn it on their own. Even though I know how to—I know what the answer is, I know the outcome—they're gonna have to learn it on their own.' And Joe would allow for dissent and discord. But in his mind, he knew what the outcome would be."

a while for that process to evolve…and [it] became a very good process, a very important part of our technical control. That was our technical quality control."[76]

"One of the interesting things we did, early on, was to take people who had worked the Central Gulf for Tenneco and put them into the Eastern Gulf. Then, we moved the people who had worked the Eastern Gulf, and put them into the Central Gulf—swapped areas. There wasn't much information in the Eastern Gulf areas that I didn't know. And vice versa. So I'm…the audience, the jury, for a technical review, and [if] somebody doesn't bring up something over there, well, I'm gonna bring it up. If I'm presenting a new prospect, the guys who used to work in the Central Gulf Division…know all those wells. The early group had so much expertise in the areas they had worked in. That focus was outstanding—we weren't going to pull anything over anybody's eyes."[77]

BETTY SMITH – ASSISTANT TO THE CEO, DEN MOTHER, CHEERLEADER

Betty Jo Smith is testament to the axiom that "age is a state of mind." She is a dynamo—a bright, articulate woman who hitched herself to a rising star at Tenneco and never had the slightest inclination to let him go. But in 1998, a reluctant Betty Smith finally did let go of Joe Foster after a memorable 24 years together, when she retired coincident with her husband, Buddy.

Betty Smith continues to be welcome at all Newfield functions. "I still go back every chance I get. My husband and I went over there when the company dedicated its big new conference room—the Joe Foster Conference Room. And they called me and asked me to come over, and they had lunch and a big function. Yeah, you know that Joe's retiring from the board. I have to say that it isn't my choice." Betty recalls a conversation with longstanding director Charles Schultz—another Tenneco alum and former CEO of Gulf Canada. Betty bent Schultz's ear back in 1998 when she retired, "Now, Chuck, don't let Joe ever leave Newfield, because I still have a lot of my retirement savings tied up in Newfield…as long as his name is associated, I feel very comfortable."[78]

"Joe knew that, in the end, Newfield would be a stronger organization. These people will be a little smarter, a little wiser, and preventing a few mistakes through management intervention isn't healthy. We can tolerate a little short-term pain."

Today, with her quick wit and easy chuckle, Betty Smith is as vivacious as ever. It was easy to get her to reminisce about her Joe Foster/Tenneco/Newfield experiences, but difficult to schedule an appointment with her; Betty has an extremely active social calendar around Houston. Does Betty Smith find that the scheduling demands of the Internet, cell phones, DVRs, and e-mails still raise her blood pressure? You bet! She confides that she really misses Newfield's quality IT support.

Trading Johnson for Foster

Betty's brother-in-law had worked for Tenneco for about 20 years when he abruptly got crossways with his manager and quit. Says Smith, "I can remember my mother being in a state of shock—this was when they were building the new…Tenneco Building [*Author's Note:* now the El Paso Building at 1001 Louisiana St.] My mother just thought my poor sister and her family were going to starve, because until then they had been so secure working for Tenneco." Shortly thereafter, Betty accompanied her daughter, a college graduate, when she [Betty's daughter] went downtown to apply for a new opening at Texaco. Betty recollects, "Here I was in downtown Houston. My brother-in-law had worked for Tennessee Gas and I thought, well, they're a good company. On a whim, I walked in and filled out an application. To my surprise, they hired me immediately and I went to work the next week. For the first two years, I worked for everybody in the Production Department—at the ground floor—filing and doing everything and anything."[79]

Betty first became aware of Joe Foster when she overheard a conversation in the hallway of the Production Department. A memo had caused a considerable stir: "What? A petroleum engineer—at the head of Exploration?" And Betty thought, well, what's the big deal here? "Why are they saying, 'Can you believe they made Joe Foster head of Exploration?' He's an Aggie petroleum engineer!"[80]

Once she learned the ropes in Production, Betty was promoted to assistant for Dan Johnson, Tenneco's Vice President of Production. Then she was asked to interview for a promotion to become Joe Foster's secretary. In Betty's words, "So one day, Joe needed a secretary and he called me over for an interview. I was direct with him and inquired, 'Well, does Dan Johnson know that you're talking with me?'"[81]

The following response was priceless. Joe's answer was "Oh, yes, Betty. You wouldn't…you don't fool with another man's secretary."

Joe offered Betty the job and a raise, which she accepted. But then the Tenneco bureaucracy intervened. "You had copies to complete in triplicate, you know, all this paperwork. When you'd get the blue copy back, that meant everything was approved. But the blue copy never arrived." Although Joe was a high-ranking Senior Vice President at the time, Betty Smith's salary boost was turned down. "This was one of the most embarrassing moments I ever shared with Joe, and at the time I didn't even know him well, but I could feel his stress.

"Joe called me into his office and said 'Betty, I really don't know how to tell you this, but your raise wasn't approved.'" Later Betty learned the whole truth: Tenneco's President had turned it down because it meant Smith would be making as much as his secretary did, and that was not going to fly. With a twinkle in her eye Betty recalls her reply to Joe: "I said, 'Well, that's okay. It'll work out.' And, of course, I had a husband who worked, or maybe I wouldn't have been so big-hearted." Betty was fortunate to have other means, but she recalls that Tenneco always treated her well. "I will tell you this. The first day Joe was promoted to President of Tenneco, I was given a very nice raise. Joe didn't forget that embarrassing moment."[82]

"For all the years I was with Joe Foster, the oil and gas producing company was always very special—a big happy family. Even though Joe and I were based in Houston and we had to keep up with the ten or so divisions, we still felt in touch with all of them." Like all big corporations at the time, you had to earn "transfer stripes" if you wished to advance at Tenneco. "Every month would be a new list of transfers. Some of them would bounce between regional offices and the Houston headquarters repeatedly. Joe and I saw these quality Tenneco hands and got to know them—and a little (but never enough) about their families and outside interests. When the Tenneco oil business was divested, it was agony—real agony—to cut the ties

A magazine journalist asked Betty, "How is it that Joe Foster has such a…good reputation in the oil and gas business?" Smith did not hesitate to answer. "It's simple: because he's one of the last few corporate men with whom you can make an agreement or a contract on the shake of a hand." She continued, "With Joe Foster you never need a whole stack of legal papers—that is the way he is." Betty reminisces that Joe's mom shaped his reputation: "Whenever Joe would leave his home in Greenville and head out into the world at large, Mom Foster would always say, 'Remember whose boy you are.' And it stuck with him forever." **BETTY SMITH**

with this great pool of quality people whom we had grown to know and love."

"When I first started working with Joe, he was Senior Vice President of Tenneco Oil E&P and on a roll. [During] all the years at Tenneco, I thought something was wrong with the oil business if Joe didn't get promoted every eighteen or twenty-four months. There were very few disappointments, and Joe climbed the corporate ladder very fast. That is, until 1988, when all hell broke loose at the corporation."

By then, Betty had a laundry list of titles to manage for her boss: Joe Foster was Executive Vice President of Tenneco Inc., Chairman of the Tenneco Oil & Gas Company, and Chairman of the Tennessee Gas Gas Transmission Company. Plus, on the top floor of corporate headquarters, Foster served on the board of directors of parent Tenneco Inc., the apex enterprise holding company.

When Tenneco E&P and R&M were sold off by the fall of 1988, Betty Smith elected to move on with Joe Foster. "I chose to go with him. I really wasn't out of a job. Bob Waldrup and Ron Lege and Dave Schaible, they were out of a job, but I could have chosen to stay with Tenneco Inc. But I chose to stay with Joe Foster."[83]

Sheet Rock All Around Us

When Newfield opened its doors on January 1, 1989, Joe Foster and Betty Smith were the only survivors to migrate over from Tenneco Oil E&P in Houston. "Actually, Joe and I were at Tenneco Inc., and Terry Rathert still worked for the oil company, and then we hired David Trice and then he hired our first landman—Tracy Price. We set up offices across the street in the 1100 Milam Building, on McKinney and Milam." In the beginning, it was a small staff at the Houston headquarters, with only Joe and Betty. "We had sheetrock all around us while they remodeled the offices. We bought some used furniture from Tenneco. We didn't have computers. We bought my typewriter…then Terry Rathert joined us. After Rathert and Trice moved in, a young lady came in to help support the team; her name was Kayleen Dahmes."[84]

To this day, Betty Smith still bristles over the mistaken assumption that Newfield was spun off by its well-heeled and generous predecessor, Tenneco, with a treasure trove of startup capital. "The truth is, we didn't have squat. We didn't have a stick of furniture or even a copier. We didn't own a coffee pot. I brought in a coffee pot from home and Joe brought in a little microwave." In fact, the Newfield Lafayette office had more amenities than Houston's HQ." Betty Smith saw a full refrigerator in the Lafayette office and thought, "Something's wrong here; the head of Newfield—the president of this company and chairman—doesn't have a college-dorm sized refrigerator!"[85]

Meetings and Yellow Tablets

Betty Smith confirms one of Joe Foster's lasting managerial legacies: "He really did listen to you. When Joe held morning meetings, he really did listen. A lot of people would attend and look interested but never really listen and retain information. Not Joe—he was always jotting down notes in his yellow pads…We never ran out of them. That was one of my key jobs at both Tenneco and Newfield—to keep a good supply of yellow tablets. [At] every meeting Joe Foster attended, he wrote everything down."[86]

There was one drawback to Joe's scratchings: "We had files and files of these yellow tablets—and the legal department at Tenneco would beg him not to save those records. But he did anyway. And a couple of times, the legal department really wished he hadn't done it…but Joe Foster carried a yellow tablet with him to every meeting he attended until the day he retired."[87]

Betty Smith and her husband Buddy recognized a great investment opportunity when Newfield was first hatched. They spent a crucial night in discussion. Betty Smith recalls only the good: "Without a doubt it was a wise decision…The night before we invested our money, my husband said, 'I think we ought to put in a lot more… than what we originally talked about.' And we put [in] twice as much, and…it's been great for retirement."

Joe worried about people like Betty risking so much of their hard-earned savings; all of the original twenty-two Newfielders invested money (i.e., their retirement savings) from their Tenneco severance packages. Betty recalls a particularly tense moment when she accompanied Joe to the headquarters, then in Lafayette.

Joe made it clear that the startup Newfield "was a risky proposition and that there was downside—great downside—like losing it all in a bad bet at the gaming table."

First off, with no infrastructure, producing assets or exploration prospects ready to be drilled, the technical issues were daunting, if not downright depressing. Joe wanted to make sure that all Newfield investors had done adequate "due diligence"—and no question about the company was left unanswered.

Smith vividly recalls Joe Foster's soft-sell "buy-in" to Newfield; Joe brought in an outsider to help explain everything. And Betty remembers the look in Joe's eyes when the "Newfield West" contingent reconvened in Houston. "Joe really looked worried, and confided to me: 'You know, I kind of worry about these people putting in their money.' I said, 'I want to tell you, you have done everything legally and even personally…that you could do for us.' And I said, 'You cannot tuck us in bed every night.'" **BETTY SMITH**

DAVID TRICE – LAWYER TURNED OILMAN

David Alan Trice graduated from Duke in 1970 with a B.A. in Business, and then moved to Manhattan to enroll at Columbia Law School. After graduating in 1973 with his Juris Doctorate, Trice went to work as an attorney in Atlanta. At that time, the country was in a major economic recession brought on by the first Oil Shock, which ironically had stemmed from the Arab Oil

> "David was the only non-Tenneco hand to join Newfield—he didn't bleed blue the day he signed on."
>
> **TERRY RATHERT**

Embargo. The law practice in Atlanta was dull and Trice felt unchallenged. When approached by a headhunter, Trice was easily convinced to emigrate to Texas to work for a tax specialty firm in Corpus Christi.

Trice recalls, "After growing up in Virginia and living in North Carolina and Manhattan for my university years, Texas was certainly viewed by my wife and family as a great adventure. We were immediately disappointed!"[88]

The South Texas beaches were strewn with rust-colored seaweed over a fine, brown sand and tepid waves of silty water lapped against the shore. It looked nothing like the mile-wide white dunes of North Carolina's Outer Banks where Orville and Wilbur had first glided off the globe. Nor was there any resemblance to the familiar pristine shores of Cape Cod and Nantucket, where huge azure breakers crash with bracing cold foam.

David Trice reported to work in the center of modern downtown Corpus Christi. The city hugged the shoreline with a necklace of 20 story modern buildings that enjoyed a wide-angle harbor view of the Gulf of Mexico, with waters sloshing against the fleet of shrimpers and yachts anchored in the boat basin. North and south offered nothing but more shoreline; due west from Corpus are several large refineries and acres and acres of oil tank farms; another fifty miles farther west is the Tom O'Connor oilfield—once one of the most prolific of all time, but waning by the time Trice arrived. Corpus offers a wonderful 100-mile spit of preserved beaches and protected wildlife at Padre Island, but otherwise it was extremely uninspiring to the Trice family.

At the law office, things were no better. "I knew within thirty-six hours that I had made a big mistake. I loved the people in the Corpus Christi law firm, but the job was not right for me and the family."[89] Trice tried hard to make a go of it, but in the end he did an about-face; after six months, the Trice clan returned to Atlanta.

David Trice was on the cusp of grabbing the "golden ring" at his Atlanta law firm when he was approached with another challenge. "I was about to make partner but I still wasn't sure I wanted to spend the rest of my life practicing law. Then, out of the blue, I took a call from a former colleague in Corpus Christi who had subsequently become the general counsel for Roy Huffington in Houston. I knew from a business trip I had made to Houston that Huffco—Roy Huffington's business—was blowing and going in the late 1970s."[90] Trice's former Corpus associate wanted to know if David would be interested in the oil business. Reluctant

> Lee Boothby has succeeded David Trice as CEO of Newfield, but as Howard Newman remarked, "The Joe Foster culture has survived though the people have changed."

to relocate his family again, in addition to taking a new career direction, Trice resisted: "No, no, I'm not going to—I don't want to do that." But three more times he was contacted with the entreaty, "Why don't you come down to Houston and meet Roy Huffington and learn a little bit about the opportunity?"

In the end, David made the trip to Houston and he was impressed: "Huffco's business was fascinating." Roy Huffington was a pioneer in the fast-growing worldwide liquefied natural gas (LNG) business, and with soaring global petroleum prices, Huffco's interest in the Bontang Indonesia LNG plant was minting money.

Trice reflects on his thinking at the time: "If you don't take a few chances in your career, what fun is life? So I took that chance in 1980—left the private practice of law and got in the oil business. I have had a blast for the last 30 years and I wouldn't change that decision for anything."[91]

Trice started out in Huffco's legal department and, within a year, moved into the financial arena. While he had no business training beyond his years at Duke and no prior management experience, he naturally gravitated to finance and leadership: "I learned it on the fly." During his four and a half years at Huffco, David was active with the company's domestic Exploration and Production group. Huffco's U.S. upstream assets were eventually sold to Elf Aquitaine (now TOTAL) in the summer of 1988, just prior to the Tenneco Oil sale. Trice recalls, "My job there had been great—I worked for a guy named Clyde Metz, who was one of the greatest oil finders I have ever met. Clyde ran all the oil- and gas-finding part of the business and delegated management of all the commercial side of the business [to me]."[92]

To fund Huffco's U.S. exploration and production activity, Trice and Metz were also charged with continually raising new money. "We had some established Huffco co-investors but we had to go out and raise additional funds constantly. We had some Saudi investors, Gillette, some Dutch investors, and a couple of insurance companies."[93] Trice promoted other special Huffco drilling programs to raise funds for offshore drilling ventures in the Gulf of Mexico. By this time, David Trice was the proverbial one-armed paper-hanger: "Accounting reported to me; oil and gas marketing reported to me; and I had to wear my Investor Relations hat when we were raising money." That was exactly the broad range of experience Joe Foster wanted in Newfield's first CFO.

Joe Foster Calls

Joe Foster did pick up the phone, and David Trice recalls his thoughts process, "At the time, I was with the Huffington organization, and it was reasonably clear to me that Michael Huffington would seize the corner office from his dad, Roy. Michael would likely head the company off in a different direction—or the company's assets would be auctioned off to the highest bidder."[94] Although he was a senior executive at Huffco and was one of six who were supposed to lead the company into the future, Trice (an oilfield executive sapling of a mere thirty-nine years) could not pass up the new opportunity. Foster and he agreed to meet on a Sunday afternoon at Newfield's new downtown Houston office in the 1100 Milam Building—coincidentally, the same building that housed Huffco's executive offices.

Trice notes that his effort to keep the interview confidential was destined to fail.

"I cruised into my regular parking space at the Milam Building and rode the escalator to the second floor where the elevator banks were concentrated. [Even though] it was the weekend, I came dressed in a coat and tie because I wanted to make a positive impression with Joe Foster. When the elevator opened, who was inside but Michael Huffington! Michael sees me downtown on a Sunday in a suit! I was nabbed—plus, I'm not a very good liar."[95] When questioned point-blank, Trice was forthright: "I've got the opportunity to meet a guy named Joe Foster. I need to meet [him] and hear him out. I have always admired him from afar and wanted to have the opportunity to meet him."[96]

Now Michael Huffington knew that Trice was actively looking. David scurried into the elevator and headed to Newfield's office on the twenty-second floor. Trice thinks back to that fateful Sunday. "When I met Joe, we just hit it off—I liked the way he thought about things, the no-nonsense way he described himself and his plans for Newfield. There were a lot of similarities, the way we approached business in general."[97] The position at a new startup was intriguing and offered Trice the opportunity to build something from the ground up, as opposed to his uncertain future with the Huffington family interests.

After their meeting, Foster sent Trice his "New Business Proposal Oil and Gas Start-up Company," dated November 23, 1988. Trice saved a copy of that business plan, complete with his hand-written marks, underlines, and question marks.

Trice later found out that Joe Foster had canvassed a broad group of oil executives in his CFO job search—including David's former boss, Clyde Metz. "Apparently, my name had come up repeatedly; Joe wanted someone who had been an independent and was used to wearing a lot of hats, and actually had some experience raising money. It was extremely clear that new capital was the most important single challenge Newfield had on the immediate horizon."[98] Trice was an advocate of bringing in partners for drilling programs (as he had done at Huffco); this would help defray overhead and provide broader diversification to the upstream budget.

Before David Trice had even met with Joe or read the business plan, a headhunter had sent him Joe's skeletal outline of his new company's business objectives. Trice recollects, "Joe's core plan targeted a backing of $100 million of investment. Joe and I agreed that the oil and gas E&P business was sound and—if you attracted a team of really good people, coupled with probability and statistics—it would be successful. But it was essential to have enough flips of the coin to make it work."[99]

Knowing how difficult it is to locate new investors and complete funding, David Trice was circumspect. A large nest egg of initial capital is necessary; the drain of G&A overhead can cannibalize startup funds almost overnight. Trice confronted Joe: "I really like the [Newfield]

When Joe Foster announced that he would turn over the title of Chairman of the Board to Newfield President and CEO David Trice in 2004, he left a legacy of perseverance. Newfield executives continue to follow the words of Rudyard Kipling, always remembering to "…meet with Triumph and Despair. And treat those two impostors just the same."

business plan. However, I'm challenged by the thought of raising $100 million. How come you only raised $9 million at the get-go?"

Joe had the perfect rebuttal: "Well, I really wanted to get a good CFO in here to figure out how to do it right before we went out and raised it."

I Have Never, Ever Questioned That Decision

A week or so after David had had a chance to consider the Newfield opportunity, Joe Foster called him and offered him the CFO post. Trice went through the turmoil that comes with contemplating a major career change. To clear his head he went on a ski trip, and he decided that working with Joe Foster was the right move. He took the Newfield job on his birthday in April 1989 and has never questioned that decision.[100]

Newfield Exploration had been up and running a mere three months when Trice joined. Terry Rathert was yet to come on board full-time because he was still committed to advisory consulting with Tenneco. The entire group of Newfield personnel in Houston (only Joe, Betty Smith, and David Trice) wasn't enough for a hand of bridge, since most employees were in Lafayette at the time.

In 1990, the original Newfield investors bought common stock at the split-adjusted equivalent of $1.25 per share. Had they kept it (they haven't—along the way they captured gains and diversified funds) their shares would be worth nearly sixty times as much today. Trice reflects with some degree of satisfaction, "Sixty times $37 million is certainly not a shabby return. That $37 million would now be worth more than $2.1 billion."

Trice left Newfield at the end of 1991 when Terry Huffington seduced Trice back with an incredible opportunity—to return to Huffco as its CEO and run the global private oil and gas firm. In May 1997, Trice went back to Newfield as its Vice President of Finance and International—Huffco had been sold. But during the years David was away from Newfield he had stayed in close touch with Joe, Terry Rathert, and the rest of the Newfield team. "I'd come back for the Founders' Dinner every year and once was tapped to give a speech."

When David Trice left Newfield for the top job at Huffington, it was a bittersweet moment. "I had huge respect for Joe Foster at the time but the opportunity to assume the leadership mantle was compelling—to make the key strategic decisions and run the business day to day." Huffington offered a chance for Trice to experiment and hone his oil and gas exploration and leadership skills. "At the time the core executives of Huffington believed that we held one of the most attractive exploration concessions in the world—millions of prospective acres in Indonesia and East Java, onshore and offshore. Most important about my time as CEO of Huffco was the fact that I learned a lot about myself…what it's like to be a CEO and what it's like to manage an international petroleum operation and to negotiate with leaders of foreign countries on production-sharing relationships. The Huffco detour was definitely valuable for me as an executive and, therefore, good for Newfield as well."

It's Been an Interesting Evolution

When Trice returned to Newfield in 1997, he was charged with helping build Newfield's international business portfolio and assisting on the financial side. Trice's duties evolved into working with Joe Foster on key executive initiatives and fleshing out Newfield's strategy for overseas expansion.

The Newfield board of directors took notice of David's contributions and, in May of 1999, he was named chief operating officer. For years, Joe had told Wall Street that he was going to retire when he was 65—in February of 2000. And Joe was true to his word.[101]

About the time David Trice rejoined Newfield, Joe Foster and the board of directors had begun to struggle with the question, "Now what do we do next?" Joe was a huge believer in focus, focus, focus. Newfield was successful from the get-go because they didn't have a shotgun approach. They used a very focused approach to the shallow water Gulf of Mexico. Nonetheless, it became increasingly clear that they were getting bigger and the Gulf of Mexico opportunities were not. If Newfield was going to continue to experience strong growth, they needed to do different things.[102]

Earlier, in 1996 while David Trice was on his second sabbatical at Huffco, the board had made an important decision. They considered venturing into deepwater, but decided that the company was too small. The next natural step was to move onshore.[103]

Newfield rounded up a group of talented upstream hands—all veterans of the Gulf of Mexico—and asked them to draw up a business plan for onshore operations in south Louisiana, an area favored because it offered the same geology that Newfield knew so well from the Gulf. The onshore Louisiana initiative got off to a slow start; Newfield quickly learned that doing business onshore was very different than offshore. For one, it requires substantially more manpower, particularly on the land and administration side, and all of the deals take longer. Another important but painful lesson was that it is hard to launch a true grassroots effort. They learned that, in the offshore arena, acquisitions were a great way to move into a new area because expertise can be brought to bear with the experienced people who come with a deal. Equally important with acquisitions is the structure—the upstream producing assets and leaseholdings—that come with the deal. With a foot in the door, growth can begin in an area. It is more challenging to plunge in, totally greenfield than it is using a combination of brownfield and greenfield.

Newfield's onshore effort started in 1996 and by the end of 1998, the company was only producing 2 MMcf of gas per day onshore. Foster recognized the company was entering a new level of maturity. Newfield would be ten years old in 1999 and it was high time they started thinking about the long-term. Right before Foster stepped down as CEO, he instituted an annual all-day strategy session with the board of directors, in concert with the regular November board meeting. They examined the state of the petroleum industry and the state of Newfield, and attempted to determine the best path to take Newfield forward. Above all, they focused on ensuring that Newfield's leadership and directors were on the same page.[104]

"A number of people have asked me why I would retire from the board of the company I founded— one where I was always made to feel welcome, even after I reached the customary retirement age of 70. As a director, however, I felt it was time to 'move on.' The management had pretty well figured out what my position would be on every issue. The board needed to look exclusively to David Trice and his team for leadership. We needed some fresh faces in the boardroom, with new perspectives and new alertness. And, frankly, I want to be able to make some investments in the oil and gas business without being conflicted as a director of a publicly held company in that industry.

"It has nothing to do with the love and affection I have for Newfield and its people. I will continue to host or attend its monthly birthday luncheons for as long as they invite me." **JOE FOSTER**

The New Team Takes Over

By 1999 Foster was winding down his activities as CEO, and left it to the rest of the management group to craft that initial strategy presentation for the board. The executive team determined that a key goal for 2000 was to execute a significant onshore acquisition—something to really spur onshore drillbit activity. Elliott Pew had come on board and was eager to get Newfield involved in South Texas. Pew had spent most of his career there

> "Headington was important because it gave us a presence in South Texas – gave us a footprint where before we only had little bitty scratches." **DAVID TRICE**

and done well as an explorationist. The company had started a little grassroots exploration operation in South Texas; their target was to identify and complete an accretive and meaningful onshore acquisition. And in January 2000, Newfield completed an acquisition of properties from Headington. So as Joe Foster noted, Headington is considered either the first acquisition of the new regime or the last acquisition of the old regime. In Foster's last month at Newfield, Trice and Company completed the Firm's largest-ever acquisition: Headington was a $140 million transaction.

From that point on, management began to focus on the fact that Newfield was not only growing substantially; it was also becoming much more mature. Newfield still had great opportunities in the Gulf, but they recognized that they didn't have enough core producing assets to propel production annual growth of 10 percent to 15 percent. The logarithmic decline rate had yet to catch up with them, but they recognized they needed to diversify into more places. Foster became very supportive of Newfield's global diversification effort in his new role as non-executive chairman. Trice, Rathert, Schaible, Schneider, and Pew ran the company day to day, but Joe Foster was always just a phone call away. In essence, Foster functioned as a one-man executive committee.

Naturally fit at 5'11", with an angular face, dark brown eyes, and well-trimmed, prematurely gray hair, David Trice impressed investors and his Newfield colleagues as having the utmost confidence but no airs or pretensions: the consummate leader and energy executive. While Trice bears a striking resemblance to funnyman actor Steve Martin, he is all business, all the time. Make no mistake: Trice had huge shoes to fill when Joe Foster stepped down as Newfield's president and CEO in January 2000.

The record attests that Trice has filled those Timberlands. Foster turned over the chairman's title to David in September 2004. In May 2005, he effectively "orphaned his baby" to David's care when Foster found stage left and soft-shoed his way out of his last Newfield Board meeting.

TERRY RATHERT – THREAD OF CONTINUITY

Terry Rathert has been present at virtually every board meeting and been a part of every key Newfield decision since joining the company as manager of economics analysis in Houston in April, 1989. He, as of this writing, is one of the only three original founders remaining at Newfield. The others are Bill Schneider and Mike Sewell, a senior petroleum engineer.

As manager of planning, assistant corporate secretary, corporate secretary, Chief Financial Officer, and Executive Vice President, Terry has risen from having a cat's eye seat in the back of the board room to having a catbird seat during his twenty-one years at Newfield.

From St. Louis to College Station

Terry Wayne Rathert grew up in Saint Louis and steered his sights southwest to Joe Foster's alma mater, Texas A&M. Rathert recalls, "As a kid growing up, I loved geology. In high school I would venture to Illinois where there were open pit quarry mines along the river. I would spend all afternoon digging through huge open pits looking for trilobites and other fossils. When I was a kid, and the family would travel, there were no T-shirts or refrigerator magnets; my souvenirs were rocks—hundreds and hundreds and hundreds of different kinds of rocks. I regularly squandered my weekly allowance on furthering my extensive rock collection."[105]

Rathert's dad, Robert (Bob) didn't have the opportunity to earn a college degree; he began work at age thirteen. When Terry's grandmother died prematurely, Grandpa Rathert put his son Bob to work and charged him weekly rent just to live at home. Dad Rathert later worked at the Missouri Pacific Railroad, starting in the mail room and climbing the corporate ladder to become a vice president. Despite his success, he always lectured Terry, "You need to go to college. You need to get an education." One of the senior executives at the railroad was Harold Hoffmeister, a 1932 Texas A&M chemical engineering grad. Harold had one son, but the lad disappointed his old man and did not matriculate to A&M. Hoffmeister was passionate about A&M and, meanwhile, Dad Rathert was steering young Terry toward engineering school with a focus on chemical engineering. Luckily, Terry had an aptitude for math and science.

Terry was a fine high school student and with his SAT exam scores, he knocked the academic cover off the ball. Terry considered attending the University of Missouri-Rolla, Texas A&M or Georgia Tech. Then Hoffmeister intervened: "You know, son, you ought to at least think about Texas A&M University. It's a great engineering school."

"My cousin, Steve Trauth, and I were like twins and played tennis in high school as a doubles team."[106] While approximately the same age, the boys were on the opposite sides of the date line, so his cousin went to West Point one year ahead of Terry. When Steve came home at Christmas, he raved about being a plebe at West Point. As a kindred soul, Terry was naturally attracted to a military regimen; West Point sounded great to him. After investigating Georgia Tech he determined that he would eliminate it; since he wasn't the son of a tycoon, it was way too expensive for the Rathert budget. When it came down to the University of Missouri-Rolla and Texas A&M Terry concluded that the mere hundred miles to Rolla was too close.[107]

So in the end, Texas A&M University made the grade with Rathert, particularly after he was introduced to the Corps of Cadets—it was right down his line in terms of structure and military regimen. Terry recalls his first week at A&M, when he didn't just learn to fish but became a fish.

"You are a fish as a freshman and graduate to becoming a 'pisshead' if you survive to sophomore status. Then, you improve as a junior to the rank of 'sergebutt.' Finally, you molt into top status as a senior, a 'zip' with special privileges and rank."

Rathert remembers, "I went over to the chemistry building to complete my enrollment process. They had big lecture halls, with theater seating. They put a few hundred kids in there for Chemistry 101. I'm sitting there, filling out the paperwork. The fellow next to me is Eldon Reed. He asked me, 'What are you going to major in?' I said, 'Chemical Engineering. What are you going to major in, Eldon?' He says, 'Petroleum Engineering.' I asked, 'What's that?' He says, 'Oh, it's kind of like Chemical Engineering, but it's got more Geology.' So I get the catalog and there's the geology courses. I erase 'chemical' and I put a little black mark in 'petroleum engineering.'"

"Eldon Reed changed my life. I had never met him until we were sitting next to each other in a lecture hall, filling out the paperwork to get enrolled."[108]

Terry met his match, Ginger, during the first semester of his senior year. Terry was delivering football tickets to a friend of a classmate when her roommate, Ginger, answered Rathert's knock on the door. Terry stammered, "I'm looking for Debbie Boyd," and tried to strike up a conversation. He recalls his excitement when he returned to his dorm room: "You wouldn't believe what Debbie's roommate looks like; she is cute!"[109] A brilliant gal, Ginger finished high school and college in a combined six years. Although Terry was an engineer and Ginger a sociology major—vocations not generally thought to mix well—the Ratherts have enjoyed thirty plus years of married life.

Prior to graduation, Rathert interviewed with Chevron and Atlantic Richfield and received job offers to join these major integrated oils in Utah and West Texas, respectively. However, based on an earlier summer internship experience with Amerada Hess in Hobbs, New Mexico, Terry was certain that life in the western oil patch was not at the top of his list.

Terry and Tenneco

Rathert decided to interview with Tenneco in Houston where he met a fellow named Louis Stipp. "Three-Finger" Stipp was the general manager for the Gulf Coast Division. Like many an oilman who worked the rig floor during his career, Louis had lost fingers in the "spinning chain." (Today's Iron Roughneck has replaced the spinning chain and vastly improved rig safety.) Louis was another Aggie who had graduated in the '60s, a couple of years behind Joe Foster. Tenneco's West Loop office was in the Philadelphia Life Towers. The widely diversified conglomerate Tenneco had owned insurance company Philadelphia Life back in the early '70s.

After his interview, Rathert was preparing to catch his flight back to College Station when Louis Stipp intervened. "Well, we're going up for the football game this weekend. How about you joining up with the family?" So Rathert headed to College Station with Stipp, his wife

Terry fondly remembers an annual A&M tradition: the Tour of the Great Pumpkin. A brave freshman "fish" would get dressed up in a sheet, place a huge hollowed-out pumpkin on his head, and run through the Quad, followed by the other fish. Meanwhile, throughout the "run" upperclassmen would wildly swing away, trying to knock the pumpkin off. Terry asked Ginger to accompany him to the "run" in the fall of 1974. It was a full moon, a Halloween-type night. Afterwards, he escorted Ginger back to her dorm and remembers standing on the little balcony and asking her to kiss him. When she acquiesced, Terry literally howled at the moon.

and one of their kids. That familial Tenneco spirit was a big selling factor for Rathert. A young kid interviews for his first job, and Tenneco brass reaches out: "Come on, let's spend some more time together." Instead of flying back on College Station Air, Terry Rathert got door-to-door service to his dorm. And since Ginger was still at A&M, Tenneco's Houston location was another plus.

When Rathert started with Tenneco in 1975, he had two roommates, Tony Pelletier and Mike Tiner, who remain great friends to this day. The three shared an apartment in Tanglewood Square, a "rockin' place" in the '70s between San Felipe and Woodway, a couple of miles west of the 610 Loop. Rathert was the first to marry and move out, making way for another good friend, Joe Young, to fill his bachelor shoes.

An avid outdoorsman whose close-trimmed beard and wire-framed glasses gave him a scholarly appearance, Rathert toiled at Tenneco and early 1980s as Director of Economic Planning. He reported to three people: Joe Foster, then Executive Vice President of Tenneco Inc. with responsibility for Tenneco Oil E&P, Tenneco Oil R&M, and Tennessee Gas Transmission (the energy side of Tenneco, the mother ship); Steve Chesebro, head of new business development at the corporate level; and Wayne Nance, who was acting President of Tenneco Oil E&P.

When the decision was made to sell the E&P company, Tenneco encouraged Foster to form his LBO proposal for selected E&P assets for one primary reason: his would be one more bid, and another offer could only make it a better horserace. David Schaible, a 28-year-old engineer in Lafayette, joined Joe's team, working with a group of 70 or so on

Economic Planning & Analysis (EP&A) at Tenneco was Joe's group and his brainchild. Its function was to critically evaluate business results and work on other special projects. That group was designed to help understand and analyze business performance. Comprised of financial guys and petroleum engineers, Rathert was the first production engineer in Tenneco to join EP&A, moving back to Houston from Lafayette in 1980. Next he moved to Bakersfield, California, where he worked with Harold Korell, Barry Quackenbush, and Neal McBean, returning to lead EP&A in 1988.

the LBO evaluation.

Terry Rathert was on the Tenneco corporate side—the other side—working hand-in-hand with Tom Hassen, head energy investment banker at Morgan Stanley, which Tenneco had engaged to sell its E&P assets.

When Tenneco sought buyers for its energy assets in 1988, Rathert and Hassen viewed Foster and Company as just another competitor, the same as Chevron, Exxon, Shell, Atlantic Richfield, and Mesa's T. Boone Pickens, Jr. Notwithstanding Foster's rank in Tenneco, he was treated no differently; they wouldn't play favorites.[110]

Late in the year, it became evident that Tenneco Oil E&P was going to be divided up and sold to multiple companies, and that Joe Foster's LBO effort would be unable to compete with the giant oils' deep pockets. Moreover, it was clear to Rathert, Wayne Nance, and others of the energy headquarters staff that they would be out of a job when the ink dried on the transaction. Ergo, no regular income and a brutal birth into a hostile Houston job market. However, Tenneco operations personnel in the regional division offices were likely to find stability and an employment offer. For example, an employee in Lafayette might get an offer from Chevron or an Oklahoma City employee might get an offer from Mesa.[111]

After the Tenneco energy assets were parceled out, Tenneco asked Rathert to assist in a special project involving litigation among the oil and geophysical contractors concerning ownership of Tenneco's seismic data. There were also a number of pending matters that needed to be addressed. Rathert's office was on the 15th floor of the Milam Building and Newfield's offices were on the 27th. In Newfield's early days, Rathert was underutilized at Tenneco. He approached Steve Chesebro and said, "I'll be happy to do whatever Tenneco needs me to do, but when I run out of things to do, I'd like your OK to work on Newfield business."[112]

By April of 1989, Rathert told Chesebro that Tenneco wasn't getting its money's worth. He was on salary at Tenneco but working almost full-time for Newfield. He told Chesebro, "I need to cut the cord with Tenneco—I don't feel right about taking Tenneco's money and putting in eight hours a day over at Newfield. I'm around if you need me to help with something."[113]

A Great Board of Directors Makes a Difference

Meanwhile, Charles Duncan and Joe Foster had been actively recruiting a chief financial officer for the new company and David Trice had emerged as the top candidate. Officially, Trice and Terry Rathert came on board April 1, 1989. In Rathert's initial role, he served as Newfield's Manager of Economic Analysis and Planning. Later he took Trice's job as chief financial officer, a role he continues to hold today.

Terry Rathert reflects over his twenty-one years at Newfield: "I think we've been blessed with an extraordinarily talented group of directors with different backgrounds, [from] different walks of life [and] different perspectives, and generally deeply dedicated to Newfield's success. They understand the business. It goes back to the earliest days with our original directors, Charles Duncan, Mike Patrick, Tom Ricks, and Howard Newman. These directors understood the business, let management run the company, but challenged management thinking about strategy, the business climate, the environment, and company direction. How are you going to get there? They didn't delve into day-to-day operating management issues, but they always challenged our thinking. Howard Newman is a rare and brilliant individual who approaches business from a philosophical perspective. Moreover, Newman listens as much as he talks, which is a rare thing."

Rathert also has a great deal of respect for Chuck Shultz, former Tenneco hand and Newfield Director. Shultz, Foster, and other Tenneco executives created functional "chiefs" for every technical discipline. A chief's primary role was recruiting in his discipline, and then shepherding those people within the company throughout their careers. A chief was responsible for knowing what his people needed in terms of exposure, experience, and outside schooling. "I can remember recruiting with Chuck and sitting in the motel…lounge area, with stacks of resumes and applications. Flipping through mounds of papers, Chuck kept asking, 'What do you think about this guy? How did he rank?' Sorting through all the candidates after a day's worth of interviewing was the role of the chief."[114]

Terry Rathert perceives that one of Joe's strongest suits is his ability to pull professionals together and ask a ton of questions. "Foster's mantra was to not let up until one, all the tough questions were asked, and two, all the information was laid out in plain terms. The result: This group of intelligent people will reach the right conclusions when they have all the relevant information. All the differences of opinions, and the biases, will disappear into the background when everything is out of the wrappers and on the table. But the only way you do that is, you ask lots of questions, and you get all the facts. Engage intelligent people, and they'll reach the right conclusion."

DAVID SCHAIBLE – KID TO KEY MAN, QUICKLY

David Schaible Has Time for Joe Foster

In the early days of assembling Newfield's original corps, Joe Foster was competing with Standard Oil of California (Chevron), which had purchased all three of Tenneco's offshore Gulf of Mexico divisions. Tenneco's upstream professionals faced a dilemma: "I either take an offer from Chevron or I don't have a job."[115] Joe Foster had a small window in which to offer another alternative: "I have this startup Gulf of Mexico business plan. Do you want to come work with me?"

> Betty Smith confirms one of Joe Foster's major attributes that shows up consistently. "He can recognize talent. The record is incredible; look at the team that he put together at Newfield. At the time, Joe and I were considerably older than all those people who joined us." Betty distinctly recalls a conversation about a new recruit in Lafayette who had not yet been to the new Newfield office in Houston. "I can remember Joe telling me, 'You're going to love Dave Schaible, Betty.' And he continued, 'He's really got it together. He's a smart young man.' He was a kid. When I did meet Schaible, I teased Joe, 'Am I going to have to raise this kid, too?'"

After the auction of Tenneco Oil, Foster called David Frederick Schaible, "Hey, I'd like to talk to you if you have time." At the time, Foster ranked ten levels above Schaible in the corporate hierarchy. Schaible recalls his reaction: "And what was I going to do? Tell Joe Foster, 'No, I don't have time'? So I met Joe in Lafayette at the Hilton Hotel."[116] Foster laid out his plans for Newfield and explained, "If we can get the right group of people together, with the right focus on creating value, we can beat the brains out of companies like Tenneco."

Joe's thesis resonated with Schaible, who thought, "The right group of talented people, just focused on creating value and stripped of the bureaucracy, *could* do great things in exploration and production." David Schaible was square with Foster and told him he was considering going back to school for an MBA. After all, the turmoil surrounding the auction of Tenneco body parts had caused him to distrust big oil and corporate America. Joe looked Schaible in the eye and said, "Dave, if you come to work for me at Newfield, I guarantee you that I will make sure that you get a better hands-on business education than you'll ever get at one of those B-schools." Schaible, twenty-eight, straightened up in his chair, looked squarely back at Foster, and replied, "Joe, if I come to work for you, I am going to hold you to that."[117]

There were two questions that young Schaible asked Joe about his new venture. First was the composition of the new team: "Joe, can you tell me who else you are talking to?" Schaible's second question was where he would fit in the new organization.

Schaible was the youngest professional Joe Foster had asked to join his new company; the other twenty or so all had titles like Supervisor, Manager, and Vice President. So Schaible responded, "Well, Joe, that's a pretty good group of people you've put together, and they all have a great track record of creating value. But when I look at all these titles, the way I see it is, there are [twenty] managers, and then there's me." Schaible shook his head: "I can't do all the work."[118]

Joe Foster smiled and gave David Schaible an outline of the culture that he wanted at Newfield. "Dave, I've talked to all these people about a flat organization where there are no titles. We are all going back to finding oil and gas and creating value."

> "I can vividly remember Dave Schaible stating emphatically that the essence of the oil and natural gas business is about identifying and capturing good dirt. One thing is clear to me: The talented, hard-working people that make up the Newfield family definitely have a real nose for good dirt."
>
> **MICHAEL D. VAN HORN, V.P. – EXPLORATION NEW VENTURES AT NEWFIELD**

I Come to Work Because I Enjoy the People

It took little persuasion to coax David Schaible to share his enthusiasm for Newfield during a 2005 interview.[177] "A lot of companies talk about their culture, but truly at Newfield it is our culture—Joe Foster's culture—that really does differentiate the firm. Before Newfield I was at Tenneco—an inexperienced young guy who thought Tenneco was a really good company. When I learned that Tenneco Oil would be sold, it was devastating because I had envisioned a career with that company that would last forever. I really enjoyed working there."

Schaible noted, "One of the great things about Joe Foster is that he was humble enough at the time to recognize that, at some point in our life we all say, 'Boy, if I knew what I know now, and could just go back and do it all over again...'" Joe viewed Newfield as just such an opportunity—a chance to start afresh with a *tabula rasa*. Schaible recounts Joe Foster's words verbatim when he was hired: "Although I will take some credit for some of the things that made Tenneco successful, I will also take the blame for some of the things that held Tenneco back as an organization. And so my goal at Newfield is to take the things that worked well at Tenneco and instill them at Newfield, and be vigilant about the things I know we did that held Tenneco back. And always be vigilant to keep those out."[178]

In every interview with a prospective new hire, Schaible reiterated that it was the culture of Newfield that set the firm apart: "The flat organization. Employee ownership. The camaraderie. Hiring world-class technical people and giving them the resources they need and then turning them loose. Every day that I come to work, I come to work because I enjoy the people who work beside me. And that's why I came to work at Newfield the first day the company was formed in January 1989. And when I got up this morning and decided to come to work at Newfield, the reason I came to work was because I enjoy the people.[179]

"Today we remain vigilant about things that will dilute our culture and start seeping into the organization. And, as we have grown, it has become more of a challenge.

"Because once you start doing those [bureaucratic] things, you become like them—guys that we strive not to be like...Newfield's leadership team could probably sit around on the twentieth floor and justify a company plane because of the amount of time spent on the road and the inconvenience. We could probably convince ourselves, 'Hey, we ought to do that.' But on the other hand we ask, 'Is that the tone that we want to set from the top?' If we are going to instill this culture, and if we are going to expect our people to maintain this culture, we have to set the example from the top."[180]

Newfield Is Not About Me

Joe Foster would be the first person to say, "Newfield is not about me".[181] Dave Schaible recalls, "Newfield then and today is about a lot of people who all shared in the vision of what they could accomplish. The way the company has incentivized people is: you have a prospect, and I have a prospect, we all get to see them…you know, it's not just the managers who make the decisions on the prospects. We have our peer reviews where the staff comes in and whoever is the generating team, they will present their prospect. Well, the great thing about Newfield is, if I have a prospect and you have a prospect, and if I think your prospect is better than mine, I am going to make a recommendation: Drill yours first. Because we as an organization, we as a Company, and we as individuals will prosper more by drilling the best prospects first."

"Now my prospect is good, and I still want to get it drilled, and as long as there is enough money to go around, we'll get to it. The culture is always: Let's drill the best prospects first. And that gets back to the key point: we all work together. We all share in the highs. And we share in the lows. There is that kind of underlying peer pressure that helps us pick each other up. Usually I tell people that the great thing about it is that it is not a negative thing. It's not debilitating competition. If you drill a dry hole, I suffer with you."

> "I drilled that dry hole too. In the early days of Newfield, back before we had PCs, cell phones, and satellite communications, when we drilled those first several wells beyond the three dry holes, the log would be coming in over the fax machine, and there would be 15 people gathered around that fax machine; and we all shared in the discovery. Yet we all shared in the dry holes just as equally." **DAVID SCHAIBLE**

"As Newfield has grown, one of the questions among the management was, 'Well, how long can we keep doing what we are doing? How long can we keep managing the way we are managing?' And as we began to diversify the company, and the employees grew from twenty to fifty, to 100, and now to north of 600, we look back and say, 'Well, how do we maintain that culture?' Our answer has been to create new teams of twenty to twenty-five people—where each individual has meaningful accountability to one another."

"Newfield used to have its Monday morning staff meetings when the entire company would sit around a conference table. Well, with more than 1,000 people, we can't do that anymore. While we don't have company-wide meetings, each team has its own Monday morning staff meeting."[182]

Joe Foster Loved Dave

"Bob Waldrup is the guy who suggested I talked to David Schaible. That was a solid endorsement, though I was not sure, at age twenty-eight, if he had enough experience to do what we needed in the new company where there would be only minimal supervision. He convinced me otherwise in that interview in Room 711 of the Lafayette Hilton. He was eager, ambitious, and became a joy to work with. It was clear to me and others in management, by the second year of Newfield that Dave should be CEO someday. He could not only do good engineering, he could analyze the work of others, and see both opportunities and risks that others did not see. Though quite young, he could be a bulldog in defending his views and could be very frank in critiquing the presentation of others. Importantly, he became the key guy in Newfield's acquisition effort. Our whole management team helped David grow and develop. He never behaved as a fair-haired boy, and, before long, very few decisions got made in the company without getting Dave's input. He then became a vice president and member of our Decision Group. He never lost the ability to communicate well and objectively with people at all levels of our organization, including the board.

I can't imagine anyone handling the fate he was dealt with better. He continued to flash that great smile of his, and was positive to the very end.

I was so proud that Newfield's board acted to name him President and Chief Operating Officer, even though it knew Dave's death was imminent. It was an expression of respect and love for Dave that we all felt.

To have an energetic and intelligent young guy in Newfield from day one who was a "believer" in what we were trying to accomplish had immeasurable impact on Newfield's growth and success.

I loved David Schaible."

> David Schaible was young when he joined Newfield; 15 years later, he still looked like he'd just returned from tossing a Frisbee on the campus quadrangle. Until his untimely death from cancer in 2007, Schaible—with his broad tanned face and infectious smile—served on the Newfield board and held the title of President and COO. **ART SMITH**

Hunting and Dave Schaible's Legacy

Terry Rathert laments the loss of Dave Schaible, one of the toughest challenges ever faced by Newfield's board and executives. Rathert's comments are echoed among the top ranks: "Schaible left a legacy; we all hope that we have such an enduring presence."[119]

Rathert elaborates, "Dave Schaible didn't hesitate to question the status quo. He had a really sharp mind and was able to identify what mattered, what didn't, to identify opportunities. He didn't hesitate to step up, and his clear thinking and geoscience skills were held in esteem by the technical folks. Dave could turn it on and turn it off. When he knew that he was really ill, he continued to work but he stole as much time as possible to be with his family."[120]

More than anything, Dave Schaible loved to hunt. He had gone to Africa with his best friend, Maurice Bledsoe, and scheduled a second Africa hunt for the Summer of 2007, after the cancer diagnosis. Dave went anyway, full speed ahead, notwithstanding the fact that his physical condition was failing. He spent roughly three weeks hunting, walking miles every day. He was determined, and he had a great time. It gave him something to focus on. But it seems that last hunt in Africa drained the final amount of energy he had been able to muster.

When Dave was promoted to Newfield's president, everyone knew of his grave condition but hoped and prayed that he could beat the cancer. Meanwhile, Schaible experimented with various treatments, some of which seemed to help. But just when things seemed promising, he took several steps backward. He realized there was not going to be a solution, a cure. Rathert comments, "There was never a question in anyone's mind that he was destined to be our next leader, and we just needed him to pull through. But the Lord had other plans for him. He left a legacy, in the way he approached things. He was really a huge part of Newfield.[121]

"David Schaible was a driving force, not only [in] our culture and our early success, but [in] just how we run the business and how we approach the business. Those same characteristics exist today. There's not a week that goes by that Schaible's name doesn't come up in a meeting, or he doesn't come up in conversation, because we know he is still present in the way we run the company today."
STEVE CAMPBELL

CHAPTER VI
THE IPO

NEWFIELD'S INITIAL PUBLIC OFFERING – JOE GOES PUBLIC AT THE AGE OF 59

By mid-1993, Newfield's total assets had grown to roughly $105 million and the company had 42 full-time employees. It held proved reserves of 113 billion cubic feet equivalent (Bcfe) from 27 net productive wells in the Gulf of Mexico. Reflecting Joe's fiscal conservatism, Newfield had no long-term debt and a positive working capital balance of $9.6 million.

At a Newfield board meeting in early 1993, there was a heated discussion about the merits and timing of taking the company public. With only 100 Bcfe of proved reserves, Joe felt that Newfield just didn't have the critical mass they needed. Howard Newman, the Director from Warburg, passed on this gem of advice: "Joe, you take the cookies when the tray is passed—not just when you're hungry."[133] Newman's position prevailed, and the company hired consultant Jim Alexander to investigate the IPO market and whether Newfield could be successful. John S. Herold, Inc. was retained to perform a valuation of Newfield and to provide its opinion on the estimated public market value the company might obtain.

Newfield decided they would have a shot at going public and held a beauty contest among the investment banks. Goldman Sachs and PaineWebber won the lead positions

Betty Smith worked among the top dogs of Tenneco for many years. She often said to her colleagues and friends that Joe Foster was the only officer on that 30th floor who could take care himself. "For most of them, a limo picked them up at the front door, took them out to the airport to get on the company plane, and then the limo drivers patiently waited to escort them home at night." Joe was different and eschewed expensive first-class tickets. Betty remembers, "Joe was on a commercial airline business trip once and was sitting back in tourist with the regular people. At the same time, a lower-ranking Tenneco Oil executive was enjoying the wide seats and comforts of first class. It was very embarrassing to him when he saw that Joe Foster was sitting in the back of the plane. As always, [Joe was] as careful with Tenneco money…as he was with his own. Joe has not changed to this day."

as deal managers. After the traditional road shows had been held for the investment advisors in Boston, New York, Chicago, and on the West Coast, Joe remarked, "There sure is a lot more road than there is show in a road show."[134]

That first week, the Newfield team took cabs. The second week, Bobby Tudor, managing director of Goldman Sachs [*Author's Note:* Tudor is the lead principal in the research and investment bank Tudor Pickering Holt & Co. where Joe Foster now directs a private equity investment fund.], said, "Look, Joe, we're going to get limos and Goldman Sachs will pay for them. Don't worry about it. It's not coming out of Newfield's pocket." Tudor's rationale was that arranging the logistics for all of them was just hell on the secretaries.[135]

> "Two things about Joe that have always impressed me: one is his listening—his ability to be an acute listener. Two, his keen observation skills."
>
> **DAVID TRICE**

RINGING THE BELL AT THE NEW YORK STOCK EXCHANGE

After Newfield's IPO, Foster—the inveterate penny pincher—splurged on "T and E" expenses. Newfield did not require that Messrs. Waldrup, Schneider, Rathert, and Schaible drive those 1,800 miles from Houston to New York City in a "Rent-a-Wreck." Newfield's key executives were given the latitude to fly coach to LaGuardia and share a cab into Manhattan. The date was November 11, 1993—Newfield would be featured on CNN "ringing the bell" at the ten o'clock opening of the New York Stock Exchange. Newfield Exploration Company (symbol: NFX) began trading that day at $17.50 per share (on a split-adjusted basis equivalent to $4.38 per share today). When the day ended, the NFX shares closed up ten cents.

Those beaming oil and gas professionals in the photo knew that the proceeds from the IPO should be guarded and protected; Newfield could scant afford to go on a bender and dissipate the $65 million they had worked so hard to bring together over the five previous bootstrapped years.

> You and I should have "backed up the truck" and bought as many shares as our 401(k) could fund! If you missed the Newfield Exploration IPO, there was no reason to despair. In a weak stock market with volatile and downtrending oil and gas prices, the NFX shares got cheaper and traded as low as $15.75 per share before ending the year at $18.70 (1993 shares).

Newfield's IPO was met with strong interest, and the company placed the equivalent of 11.6 million common shares (adjusted for the two separate two-for-one stock splits effected in 1996 and again in 2005), raising $51 million. At the completion of the offering on November 11, 1993, Joe B. Foster owned or had options on 3,109,000 shares of Newfield, representing roughly 5 percent of the post-offering ownership, with a 1996 stock market value of $14.8 million.

Foster felt Howard Newman deserved the credit. More than anybody else, Newman was the one who had pushed him through the gates to do the IPO. Newman didn't hesitate when he said, "Going public is not a matter of your own critical mass. Going public is a matter of the market. The energy market's good now—it may be five years before it's good again."[136]

> Joe Foster wrote to his new investors, "There are two sides to the corporate finance coin; one says GTM—Get The Money; the other says SIW—Spend It Wisely. My experience tells me the opportunity to invest the money wisely will come—perhaps all at once, perhaps over time. Please permit us the discipline to spend it wisely."

New York Stock Exchange, November 11, 1993

Newfield Exploration Share Price versus Appraised Net Worth (ANW)

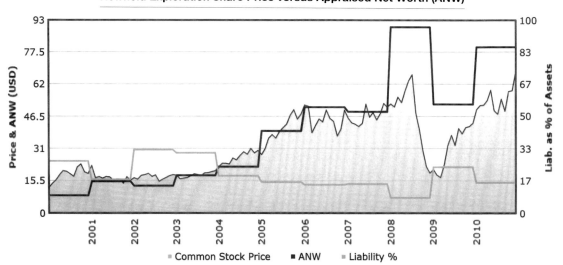

Source: IHS Herold

CHAPTER VII
KEEPERS OF THE CULTURE

Newfield continued its growth following its IPO (See Herold Chart at left from 2001 to present) and its employee headcount continued to increase, from forty-two at the time of the IPO to 100 at year-end 1999 after Joe Foster stepped down as CEO, to roughly 1,000 at the beginning of 2010.

With this growth in headcount and the retirement of some of the founders, a number of new management employees were brought in… not surprisingly, many former Tenneco Oil E&P employees.

It is time that literally hundreds of current and past employees of Newfield count themselves as keepers of the culture and the spirit at Newfield.

In this chapter, we record the thoughts of five officer-level employees about the evolution of Newfield.

ELLIOTT PEW – THE NEW GUY ON THE LEADERSHIP TEAM

Elliott Pew has a certain joviality about him. Perhaps that slight gap-tooth when Pew smiles brings to mind the late-night talk-show host, David Letterman. Then again, Pew's good nature may be due to his perfect timing in 1998, when he left Louis Dreyfus Energy and joined Newfield Exploration. Pew was, relatively speaking, "the new kid on the block" in the Newfield executive suite, among Messrs. Trice, Waldrup, Rathert, Schaible, and Schneider.

Pew received his BA in Geology in 1977 from Franklin & Marshall College in Pennsylvania, and he first worked in the industry as a mud-logger in West Texas. When he realized how much fun it had been to be a student he matriculated at "The University" in Austin, where he completed a Masters in Geosciences in 1982. He was fortunate to concentrate on the emerging interest in deepwater Gulf of Mexico geology and geophysics.[151]

Pew's first Tenneco Oil experience started in San Antonio, where he labored to understand West Texas geology. In the heady days of the oil boom in the early 1980s, did a geologist like Elliott Pew ever cross paths with Joe Foster at Tenneco? Yes—but at a great distance. Foster was beyond the reach of the average Tenneco "rank-and-file" hand. Pew saw Joe at Tenneco's budget meetings, and remembers the thrill of shaking Joe's hand at these events.

Pew left the embrace of Mother Tenneco in 1984. A University of Texas professor who had taught him Gulf Coast tectonics owned an Austin-based independent oil company, and he set Pew up in business to generate and drill oil and gas prospects.[152] In the late '80s, Pew switched from working West Texas, to working the Gulf Coast. In 1986, oil prices crashed and the upstream industry was in shambles. There were some scary times, because Pew knew he had to generate and sell drilling deals to pay the bills each month. Somehow, he managed to survive.[153]

Pew joined Fina in 1989 and was content until 1991, when, after a strong run in exploration and production, Fina changed course to pursue more downstream investment. "We went from being very active drillers to paper shufflers when the money dried up. A number of us left for want of activity." Pew left Fina in 1992 to join independent American Exploration, working internationally as a senior geophysicist. Run by Mark Andrews, American Exploration had stumbled through the '80s and had survived more due to its acquisitions than the gushers its name implied. Pew was promoted to Vice President of Exploration in 1993 and assigned a South Texas startup effort. He rose to Senior Vice President four years later, leaving shortly after the American Exploration board agreed to be acquired in a friendly merger with Louis Dreyfus Natural Gas in October 1997.

Another Tenneco Connection Pays Off

After the American Exploration-Louis Dreyfus merger was announced, Joe Foster called Pew and asked how it was going. At that point it was going very well; Pew told Foster they wanted him to stay on and run the Houston office for Louis Dreyfus. Foster planted a seed with the comment, "You know, sometimes things change—not long after the buyout money changes hands." Pew responded, "I understand your point, Joe, but at this juncture I'm going to stay put. I've put this thing together and I feel an obligation to stick with it." Foster must have been impressed with Pew's expression of loyalty. Nonetheless, he asked Pew, "Do you mind if I call you back in a month or two?" Keeping his options intact, Pew replied, "No, not at all."[154]

True to his word, Foster called Pew later on and opened with the standard icebreaker, "How's it going?" Pew replied honestly, "Well, it's not going so hot now, Joe." So the two executives, senior and junior, started talking, aiming for a meeting of the minds. Pew liked Joe on a personal level, but he had just been through the scars of a buyout. One of his questions concerned Joe's vision for Newfield, five or ten years out: "Are you going to grow to a certain point and sell?" Pew wanted to avoid another American Exploration experience.[155]

Foster's response impressed Pew tremendously: "We want to build something of lasting value that will go on indefinitely." He stressed the big picture: Newfield would create jobs for the community and economic benefit, and not be an ephemeral organization thrown together for a quick sale. Elliott Pew was ready to embrace that vision.

Sometimes You Just Gotta Say, "What The Heck!"

Newfield made Pew a strong offer and he came on board in January 1998. The company had a very small, fledgling onshore effort in south Louisiana that had been launched earlier; it had only modest onshore production. Immediately, Pew found himself involved; good luck prevailed and the Broussard prospect turned out to be a very nice onshore discovery. In his early days at Newfield, Pew took a lot of interest in the company's offshore exploration since that's where most of his experience had been. But he still devoted energy on a strategy for building a significant onshore presence for Newfield. Pew concluded that the company was not in the right areas of the onshore Gulf Coast.[156]

Pew knew that the real action onshore was in the tight gas plays in South Texas, and made a pitch for Newfield to become a player there. Such a move was highly controversial at the time because Newfield had been very focused offshore. Moreover, most Newfield personnel didn't know how the Texas geological trends worked, so they were skeptical.[157] Newfield management and board were also well aware that Wall Street investors had their doubts about the company's transitional move to the onshore.

Fortunately, Pew enjoyed the backing of Joe Foster and David Trice, and they gave him the latitude to ramp up the onshore initiative. He took two Louisiana hands and moved them into the central coast Wilcox, which was going great guns. He ended up hiring some people from American Exploration, Dreyfus, and Tenneco who Newfield had worked with previously. They had a vast amount of experience in the trend, and became the nucleus of Newfield's onshore team.[158]

A venture with Shell in 1999 became the defining moment in building Newfield's onshore exploration and production business. Newfield had negotiated a joint venture transaction with Shell and they had the deal terms down to the brass tacks. Shell required Newfield to make a commitment to drill a minimum of three wildcats—expensive wildcats, at $4-5 million per well. There was quite a showdown. Newfield had to present the Shell deal to the entire leadership group and get concurrence. To many senior Newfield executives, expensive, deep wells onshore were a foreign concept they deemed very risky. Pew felt it was nip and tuck whether the joint venture would be approved. There were heated discussions, arguments, and debates.

Pew likes to believe that Foster was clairvoyant, but more likely it was Joe Foster's vast experience that led him to caution Pew about change after a transaction is completed. "Within days of my conversation with Foster, things around the Dreyfus Houston office started falling apart," said Pew. "Broad sweeping changes were being implemented which, if advertised, wouldn't have been so upsetting. I was being told, 'Don't worry, you're going to run this thing; everything's going to be the same,' and so on. But I didn't feel like that's where it was headed." Pew had no trouble working with the senior executives at Dreyfus—Simon Rich and Mark Monroe—and he had no trouble with regular treks to the Dreyfus headquarters in Oklahoma City. However, he didn't know who would be calling the shots in the Houston office—but he was pretty sure it wouldn't be him.

Joe Foster listened and listened. Finally he stood up and cast his decisive vote: "Sometimes you just gotta say, 'What the heck!'"[159]

That deal led to the Provident City drilling program, which became the largest field in Newfield history at the time. Though no longer the largest, it's still high up in the asset rankings. Pew says he will never forget that it was Joe's influence that made it happen.[160]

> "Early on, I'd been here about three or four months and Joe came in one night and asked me what I thought about Newfield, how things were going. And I said, 'Well, it's real quiet here. People are working a lot and people don't seem all that friendly.' He said, 'Really? What do you mean by that?' And I said, 'Well, right from the beginning, it seemed like everybody's been trying to figure out if I'm gonna be accretive or dilutive to the bonus pool,' because we were the new kids on the block trying to get the onshore up and going."
>
> **ERIC FREEMAN, GEOPHYSICIST, NEWFIELD EXPLORATION**

Pew Earns His Stripes

Joe Foster's broad experience served Newfield well as the company moved to establish new core oil and gas producing areas. Joe brought his experience from Tenneco's global upstream and transmission business—not just from the Gulf of Mexico. He recognized that business is done differently from one area to another; what a prospect looks like here is not what a prospect looks like there. Joe worked to see that the Gulf of Mexico teams could appreciate the different *modus operandi* required to be successful in South Texas.[161]

Elliott Pew did have four years of experience working for Tenneco Oil, but he was not a purebred Tenneco man like Foster, Waldrup, Rathert or Schaible. When he joined NFX in 1998, he was accepted from the get-go, but there were definitely some rocky times: "There was a lot of debate, honest debate. It was never rancorous but I definitely had to earn my stripes." Pew's decision to lead the charge to build an onshore business made him the agent of change. The new team Pew had hired knew onshore exploration and production, but they weren't Newfield GOM offshore people. Pew felt there were cultural differences and tensions between the groups. But once the onshore team started drilling good wells, those differences evaporated.[162]

> In 2005, Elliott Pew noted that the company earmarked in excess of $40 million on seismic surveys—a very large budget for a company Newfield's size. Pew cited a truism in oilfield exploration: "A seismic dollar typically is the hardest damn dollar to find in the oilpatch."

Elliott Pew's Top Ten List Of Newfield Exploration's Basic Tenets (Circa 2005-06):

1. We're an empowered, bottom-up driven organization. The role of NFX management is to define the "what." The role of NFX teams is to give us the "how." Throughout the organization we all concentrate on establishing goals we all believe can be achieved. We want people who have fun doing their jobs. We give our people—empowered professionals operating in a very flat organization—a lot of individual responsibility, and expect them to judge and police their own actions.

2. We despise structure and cookie-cutter answers; we recognize there are many ways to skin a cat. We give Newfield teams the latitude to attack a problem in whatever way they need to get the desired result.

3. From a cultural standpoint, teamwork is extremely important to us—people working together. But at the same time, it's essential that we're not afraid to question one another; it's professional, it's not personal.

4. Mutual professional respect is an important part of our culture. It may appear a contradiction, but Joe would *encourage* debate, sometimes heated debate. Foster always stressed professionalism, not personal gain or loss. Newfield people are never afraid of or concerned about taking a contrary view. Newfield seeks "collective wisdom." We work very hard to make sure that we have *all* views. It doesn't mean that we *agree* with all views, but we want 'em all out there and then we decide. We want the right answer.

5. Part of the innate Newfield culture is to be very active; we're all about drilling and acquiring oil and gas properties. We like to work hard—be achievement oriented.

6. Newfield is not afraid at any time to take risks—measured risks. But we like to hedge our bets. We like the balance of risk and potential—for there to be a counterbalance.

7. Newfield concentrates on a very strong peer-review process called the "technical review." We want the *staff* of the company to do the technical due diligence and to recommend which prospects we drill and which prospects we don't drill.

8. Since the beginning Newfield has prided itself on significant employee ownership. It's a really important thing that links up the peer-review process. We tell people, vote your shares on each prospect and project. Choose investments that you believe will increase your individual wealth through the shares that you own. Put yourself on the same side as the investor. It works quite well.

9. The company puts a strong emphasis on talented people. We spend an awful lot of time looking for the best people. One of the criteria for screening new hands in geology and geophysics is that if you don't have a proven track record of consistently finding oil and gas, it doesn't matter how much you know about this, or how much you know about that. You must show that you can do it.

10. Finally, at heart Newfield is conservative and cost-conscious. I sit behind a fully depreciated desk that once belonged to another geologist at Houston Oil and Minerals some thirty years ago. It serves me well.

We Have A Lot Of Ways To Win The Game

Joe Foster always stressed the value of looking back and accessing the situation. Pew over-saw an ex postreview of drilling results. He sought to identify variances between what they predicted and what they actually found. What were the factors contributing to the variances? How they could be resolved in the future? These studies were part of the challenge of building intellectual capital within the company.[163] Foster and Pew agreed on the importance of squeezing bias out of estimates, noting that it's easy to be optimistic on every prospect. But each Newfield team has to walk the plank; to be optimistic is bad, but not as bad as choking off creativity and reasoned risk. To fear taking risks is also bad. Newfield is always looking for that middle ground.[164]

Elliott Pew compares Newfield's oil and gas exploration and production business to football: "We have many ways to excel. We do acquisitions and exploration extremely well. We don't have any one aspect of the company that we absolutely have to rely on. We run, we pass, and we kick. As a company like Newfield gets bigger, it becomes more and more important to have multiple talents and spare capacity. We have to more than replace the hundreds of billions of cubic feet of natural gas we will produce. We've got to do a lot of things well."

Elliott Pew resigned from Newfield in 2007 to pursue private interests and enjoy an early retirement. However, in short order, Pew was back in the E&P business with a startup, Common Resources, L.L.C. Working beside CEO Roger Jarvis and CFO Robert Snell (deceased January 2010). Pew assumed the role of president and COO. Jarvis and Snell enjoyed great track records creating value in offshore Gulf of Mexico exploration with their predecessor company, Spinnaker Exploration Company. Norwegian oil Norsk Hydro (now Statoil) acquired Spinnaker Exploration in late 2005 for the princely sum of $2.6 billion. Common Resources was launched with strong equity backing of $500 million: $375 million from large Houston-based EnCap Investments, L.P., and $125 million from Manhattan-based Pine Brook Road Partners, LLC. EnCap Investments is one of the largest and most successful energy private equity firms, run by principals David Miller, Gary Petersen, Marty Phillips, and Bob Zorich. Pine Brook Road Partners features several old hands in energy private equity firms, notably Michael McMahon (a former Salomon Brothers investment banker and investment guru with the Harvard University endowments) and Howard Newman (the key investor in the launch of Newfield at Warburg Pincus).

GEORGE DUNN – A MINER FROM THE TENNECO MAFIA

George Timothy Dunn is a Mines guy—that is, he received his BA in petroleum engineering in 1979 from the prestigious Colorado School of Mines in lovely Golden, Colorado. Golden is known for two important landmarks: the School of Mines and a very large Coors Brewery.

Like many others in Newfield's "Tenneco mafia," Dunn's first position upon graduation was with Tenneco in Lafayette. However, Dunn did not immediately join Newfield after Tenneco's oil and gas assets were parceled out in 1988. Although Dunn wasn't one of Newfield's celebrated founders, when Foster relocated the main staff to Houston and a couple of hands left the organization, Dunn was recruited vigorously to rejoin the fold. "This is how I like to tell the story….When David Trice left to start Huffco International, all of the key [Newfield] executives basically ratcheted up a notch: Terry Rathert to CFO, and David Schaible went to Terry Rathert's spot. So I was hired, I always like to say, to replace David Trice, although it was actually to replace David Schaible." Waldrup, Rathert, Schaible, Trice, and Foster all knew Dunn, and he won the position, given his advantage of being "the devil you know."

In the thirty-six month interim between Tenneco and Newfield, Dunn went back to the high altitude he knew and loved from college—landing in the Rockies with Meridian Oil, the energy subsidiary of Burlington Resources (now Conoco Phillips). Hearing that his Tenneco position was being subsumed into giant integrated Conoco, Dunn exclaimed, "Well, you know, that's going to be too big," leading him to search for a smaller company, something that related more to Tenneco. At Meridian, his Tenneco connections worked well; Meridian sent Dunn to the heart of the San Juan gas basin in Farmington, New Mexico. The number-two guy in that office was Steve Nance, son of Wayne Nance, who was president of Tenneco Oil when its upstream business was sold. Steve Nance did a background check on George Dunn the old-fashioned way: he called his dad. Dunn was offered a significant position exploiting one of Meridian's core natural gas producing assets.

George Dunn remembers first meeting Joe B. Foster during a "Tenneco new-hire day." All the district office leaders would gather at Houston headquarters and President Joe Foster would speak to the group. Dunn believes that Joe must have received some kind of briefing book with information and photos on the new hires. To this day, he is amazed that Foster knew his name at that first meeting. Dunn notes, "That was a lasting first impression of Joe. How the heck does he know my name? And of course that continued through the years. Every time I ever saw him, prior to actually going to work for Newfield, he always knew my name. And how he did that, I don't know—somebody taught him how to learn and recall names. It's one of Joe Foster's great talents and it has lasting value."[141]

"Last summer I learned a lesson from a young man wise beyond his years, Ben Olson, our fly-fishing guide on a trip. Six of us, three boats, two fishermen [per] boat, Olson as our guide. While we were fishing in this beautiful canyon in the Gunnison River Gorge, we were staring down, looking for fish, fly-casting to the fish; it was great. About every fifteen minutes on the first day, Ben would say, "Look up." Well, okay. Back to fishing. Right? Go through the whole first day that way. The second day, about halfway through the morning, Ben says, "Look up," again for the fifteenth time. And I looked up and it hit me. I mean, what am I doing? I'm just looking down and I'm in this fabulous beautiful place. There was an analogy to life. Always take the time to look up, always. No matter how involved you are in whatever situation. If you're stuck on a problem, look up. If you're in a meeting, somebody's talking and you're not really sure you like what they're saying, look up because they have a perspective that maybe you need to listen to. Look up. Take a break. Don't be protective of your ideas. And looking up works at home and with your children just as well as it does at work. It's all about balance. Do your best to enjoy every moment of every day and look up." **GEORGE DUNN**

Winners And Losers

Dunn also recalls that it was July 1979 when President Joe spoke to the new Tenneco hands and handed out a small book titled *Winners and Losers* by Sydney J. Harris. One page says, "A Winner," and the facing page describes a winner; the next page says, "A Loser," and the facing page describes a loser. Joe Foster recommended the small volume to his Tenneco brethren and exclaimed, "You can read it in about fifteen minutes." The same book was distributed again in July 1996 at Newfield, with a similar note from Foster: "It's worth your attention, and you can read it in fifteen minutes."

Winners and Losers is not only a good quick read, but deep down it reminds you of Joe Foster. Dunn quoted one of his favorite passages at Foster's retirement dinner celebration: "A winner, in the end, gives more than he takes. A loser dies clinging to the illusion that winning means taking more than you give." Joe definitely has always given more than he takes. Dunn continues, "When I re-read that little book…the whole thing flashes back to Joe and his simple leadership messages."

Apparently, the spirit of *Winners and Losers* permeates the Newfield Exploration culture. George Dunn states emphatically, "I can't recall that I've ever had a bad boss or a bad person to work with at Newfield. I've learned from them all. But Joe would be the maximum learning experience…by far."

Project Jumpstart

Dunn recalls working on Project Jumpstart in 1992, the potential mega acquisition of properties from Chevron. It was the first time he got to work closely with Joe Foster and the Newfield leadership team. The team, working on "due diligence" in Midland, Texas, was comprised of Joe, Bob Waldrup, Terry Rathert, Dave Schaible, and Dunn. Because Dunn had been in Farmington, New Mexico and Meridian had an office in Midland (which he had visited two or three times, maximum), Dave Schaible decided that Dunn must know all the top restaurants there.

Ordering Wine In Midland

George Dunn became the Zagat guide of Midland. For the first night's dinner—and Dunn's first elbow-to-elbow gathering with Joe Foster—a small Italian restaurant was selected. Dunn recalls that he only knew of three restaurants, and luckily the Newfield team only required two lunches and one dinner. Dunn plays back the evening: "Our waitress asks Joe first, what would you like to drink? And he says, iced tea. And then she goes to Bob Waldrup, and he says, iced tea. And then Terry Rathert follows suit, iced tea." When the waitress asked Dunn, he blurted out, "What kind of house wine do you have?" Knowing of a reasonably priced Chianti, Dunn broke ranks: "Well, I'll try a glass of wine." And then Schaible chimed in, "I'll do a glass of wine." And Bob Waldrup: "I think I'll change my order to a glass of wine." And Terry Rathert: "I think I'll take a glass of wine, too."

Now Joe didn't flinch or change his drink order; he stuck with his iced tea. Dunn recounts: "Joe Foster is more like your grandfather versus your dad. It's different with a grandfather.

In 1991, by accident or just plain old snafus in the computer system, the Newfield accounting department was unable to meet its scheduled February 12th date for bonus and compensation distributions. When it was clear that the checks wouldn't be distributed until February 14th, Joe and his executive assistant Betty Smith came up with the idea of not only passing them out on Valentine's Day, but of putting them in a red envelope. And so to this day, Newfield bonuses are disbursed with fanfare on February 14th in a red envelope. George Dunn recalls the tradition. Foster would shake your hand, give you your envelope, and encourage you further with, 'And make sure you take something out of that envelope and do something nice for your spouse.' Classic Joe."

"We'd go in, and we'd do these acquisition reviews—we called them decision reviews—with Joe. And we'd go through the whole analysis and research and work to determine our bid and bid strategy. And on this specific acquisition, Amoco, Dunn recommended a bid in the range of $45 [million] to $50 million. And Joe really surprised me when he topped my assessment with a very strong $66 million." Dunn was flabbergasted and extremely nervous regarding the project economics. (Note: The bid was successful and the properties exceeded expectations.)

"Foster created a Leadership Group, and we still call it that today. The Leadership Group consists of four to eight people, depending on the dimensions of the project or problem. David Trice carried on the mantra of keeping a lot of people informed and knowledgeable about why and how decisions are made; such buy-ins assure that many people can pick up the ball and run with it when called upon. Newfield has a strong bench." **GEORGE DUNN**

GARY PACKER – FROM OPERATORS, INC. TO CHIEF OPERATING OFFICER

Hailing from Pittsburgh, Gary Donald Packer became a Nittany Lion and received his petroleum engineering degree from Penn State in 1984. In the early 1980s, Packer easily secured lucrative and challenging summer internships with Pittsburgh-headquartered Gulf Oil Corporation. However, by the time he graduated, times were tough in the oil patch and Gulf Oil was under siege by T. Boone Pickens' Mesa Petroleum. (Note: Gulf eventually succumbed to a takeover by San Francisco-based Standard Oil of California, now Chevron.)

Facing a bleak job outlook, with more petroleum engineers being laid off than hired, Packer grabbed a bargain fare on the now-defunct People's Express and flew to Houston. Packer recalls, "My buddy and I plunked ourselves into a cheap hotel that was more like a walk-in closet. We then threw open the Houston Yellow Pages to the listings for oil and gas companies and started dialing."[143]

Packer immediately received job offers from both Big Red and Big Blue, the giant oil-field service companies: Halliburton and Schlumberger. However, Packer did not veer off into oilfield services; he was most interested in the upstream—exploration and production business. He recalls, "I'd always admired Tenneco, which, when times were strong in the oil patch, was an active recruiter at Penn State. Tenneco had an operating company that managed all their production operations in the field, appropriately named Operators, Inc. I had heard about Operators, Inc. and went in to visit with R.H. Boyd, a nice older gentleman." Rocking back in his desk chair, Mr. Boyd informed Packer, "There is a new initiative at Tenneco to bring in young engineers and take advantage of the downturn in the industry. The concept is to develop bench strength from these young recruits—shipping them off-shore to get their sea legs and field experience." Then Mr. Boyd paused, and Packer's hopes were dashed. "The only problem is, at this time, Gary, I don't have a position open."

Packer recalls the emotional roller coaster that then ensued. "Just as Mr. Boyd had delivered his 'but unfortunately' message the phone rang. A senior manager from the Operators, Inc. training facility in Lafayette was on the line. After a moment, Mr. Boyd covered the mouthpiece and exclaimed: "This is your lucky day! Do you know where Lafayette is located?" Packer admitted, "Well, no. But I'm sure I can find it!" Mr. Boyd offered these simple directions: "Well, just get on I-10 and head east."[144]

Packer wasted no time and put pedal to metal. "I remember being interviewed again by the manager of the Lafayette training center, the highlight of which was the penetrating inquiry, 'Can you pass a drug test?'" Packer cleared the test and was offered the position. "I immediately drove home to Pittsburgh and packed up my modest belongings. I emigrated to Louisiana and began working offshore, the standard seven days on and seven off. I held that position with the Tenneco subsidiary for about 18 months."[145]

"The Rules of Joe: No company cars. No company airplanes. Eight holidays a year. [*Author's Note:* Newfield now has eleven.] You know, in the climate we're in, we've had to do [everything]—so we now…work four and a half days a week, put in an extra hour Monday through Thursday [and] get a half day off. Pay part of your own insurance is another legacy of Joe Foster. Medical, dental, life insurance is a cost to the company, and you can't be frivolous with shareholders' capital. We know that when NFX people pay part of their insurance premiums then they have some ownership in it. Just like ownership in the company, which continues to be a philosophy that is a keystone of the founding principles." **GEORGE DUNN**

George Dunn is a keeper of the Foster traditions at Newfield. He recalls, "I have a great memory of witnessing the Houston office children's Christmas party a few years ago when Joe was still Chairman…they dressed up Joe Foster as Santa Claus, and [there were] photos…holding kids on his lap, doing the Santa Claus thing. It was just a neat picture to see Grandpa Joe in that situation." **GEORGE DUNN**

After the Tenneco Oil sale, Gary Packer joined Amerada Hess (now Hess Corporation). He had a lifelong friendship with David Schaible; Schaible often sought to recruit Packer for the Newfield team. Packer's original response was, "No! I have a fine job at Amerada. But while I declined Schaible's offers repeatedly, I always left an opening: 'The next time Newfield has need for a senior reservoir engineer I'll be happy to consider it.'" Sure enough, Schaible called again in the mid '90s and the timing was right.

Packer recalls, "As we continue to do with all recruiting at Newfield, senior management—at that time, Joe Foster—was responsible for interviewing and approving every new employee applicant." As Packer entered Foster's office on that important date in 1995, he reminded Joe that they had crossed paths in 1988. He blurted out, "Joe, it's really destiny that I would come to work for Newfield." When Foster questioned this, Packer replied, "Well, as I look out the window, the building where I was interviewed for my first job, with Operators, Inc., is right across the street. Then located adjacent [to it] is the Hotel Sofitel, where my bride and I spent our wedding night."

Joe replied, "I didn't realize you worked at Operators, Inc.," and inquired who he had interviewed with there. When Packer told him that it had been R. H. Boyd, Joe smiled and completed the cycle: "Gary, you're right—Newfield must be in your destiny." R. H. Boyd had been an early associate of Joe's and they had been friends until Boyd passed away.

Parker reminisces, "Incredibly ironic how we had come full circle; it was Joe Foster who was one of the key management backers at Tenneco to proactively contact strong universities with the goal of finding bright young people and introducing them to Tenneco's offshore oil and gas business." Packer continues, "So indirectly, Joe Foster was responsible for my first position and . . . ultimately, Joe hired me into what I hope will be my last position."

Coldcall With Tenneco

To make the move to Tenneco, Packer cold-called one of the senior managers with the E&P company in Lafayette and got an interview on one of his days off. Through that lead, Packer was able to secure a position with the help of a VP and senior executive at Tenneco, Clyde Crouch. Packer explains, "That got me in the door and I worked as a reservoir engineer until the sale of the company in 1988."[146]

Packer recalls his first real interaction with Joe Foster: "It was during the sale process of Tenneco Oil that I first was exposed to Joe. Foster's so-called 'LBO group' was evaluating an offer for Tenneco's Gulf of Mexico Division." Packer recounts: "I was responsible for making a presentation to prospective buyers of the assets of Tenneco's western Gulf of Mexico Division. Joe Foster, notorious for filling up yellow legal pads, sat in the front right corner of the room. During my presentation and question and answer session of forty-five minutes, Joe Foster wrote copious notes without a pause. I don't know whether Joe ever looked up; [he seemed to be] hanging on every word. Foster's intensity, patience, and attention to detail that I observed in Lafayette are valuable traits I came to cherish in the later years [when] I worked with Joe at Newfield."[147]

Packer vividly recollects that during his early tenure, Newfield senior management gathered for a "PFC (push for closure) meeting" around a big conference table early every Monday morning. He explains, "Everyone would preplan for this meeting to make sure that you always had the right answer, because Joe would pepper each team with direct pertinent questions—how we were pushing for closure on various projects. It was not unusual to rehearse your script with your team since it was downright dreadful if you didn't have the right answer!" Packer continues, "Joe would look at you and then he would slide his glasses down his nose a little bit so he could see over his glasses. And that's all he needed to do. In my career, I've been around executives who ranted and raved and resorted to public temper tantrums to express their displeasure. Joe Foster never needed to do that. He'd just look over his glasses and make you melt. At Newfield, we know we have to be moving things forward all the time. Today, the Denver office PFC is held on Friday afternoon; that meeting is part of our Newfield heritage and it's something that we'll always continue to do."

Negotiating A Deal

Gary Packer recalls a key transaction with Phillips Petroleum where he worked side by side with Joe Foster. "Phillips was selling a package of Gulf of Mexico properties and I had taken a lead role in the evaluation as senior reservoir engineer—crunching numbers and assumptions." Dave Schaible was on vacation, so Joe Foster intercepted a call from Phillips and stepped in. Packer was caught off guard: "Joe comes down the hall and saunters into my office with the remark, 'Look, we need to go present our proposal and I'd like you to come with me.'"

Packer continues, "At the time many of my NFX colleagues had plenty of experience working with Joe hand-to-hand and face-to-face, but this was the first time for me. I remember sitting in Joe's car en route to Phillips' office while reviewing all the numbers—where my low valuation came in and where my maximum range fell; where I thought we could make this deal work. It was approximately $40 million. And while by today's standards it may seem relatively trivial, at the time it was a very big deal for Newfield.

"When we arrived at the Phillips senior management's office [on the] top floor…it was clear that the news had not made the rounds: few were expecting Joe Foster to be there in the flesh. Several VPs walked in and discussions began regarding valuations and the framework of our acquisition proposal. After a torrent of numbers was thrown around, Joe, got to the point: where he wanted to stop—well below my maximum. Joe turned to the Phillips VP, an executive in his early forties, and slowly slid his reading glasses down his nose with the adamant statement, 'That's as far as we're willing to go.'

"The negotiations stopped and there was no further discussion. At this point the young Phillips manager backed away from the table and said, 'Well, thank you, Mr. Foster. We'll go talk about this.' He then led his Phillips contingent out of the room."

Riding back to Newfield headquarters, Packer confided, "Joe, only you can get away with that. If Schaible or I purport to give our best number, our counterparts still think they've got another ten percent to get out of us. Joe, [your] reputation [is such] that when you say 'discussion's over,' [they realize] this is it…we're done. [*Author's Note:* In the end, Phillips accepted Newfield's offer at face value.]

"Joe has always been able to mix genuine heartfelt concern and compassion for people while developing a balance—the key work/life balance…Joe has always been able to get folks to give the old cliché within Newfield, 'whatever it takes' and, at the same time, have intense, personal concern for you personally, and your family, and that you do the right things by them, as well. That's a very unique characteristic of Joe B. Foster."[148]

Transmitting Culture

Gary Packer reminisces on Dave Schaible and the evolution of Newfield, "Dave was a wonderful leader—like Joe. I tell people that Newfield is no longer a company driven by one or two or three persons. When I joined the company, I was the forty-eighth employee and today we're now more than 1,000."

"In 1995, an individual such as Joe or Dave or Bob Waldrup could individually alter or change how the whole organization acted. At 1,000 [employees], we're beyond that as a company. Joe and Dave and Lee resonate as key leaders today—even though one's retired, one's passed away, and one's taken the reins recently—because they've essentially developed a whole army of disciples to take this enterprise to a very different level.

"Their thoughts and way of conducting business are now magnified; their influence is strong because now business units have adopted their same mindset…I came to Denver with only two original Newfield souls and now had an organization with an eighty-plus team conducting business as I was instructed ten years earlier. I spread Dave's and Joe's thoughts to another eighty people and they're doing the same thing as we continue our growth. It's a marvelous thing because Dave continues to live, from a business standpoint, in all of us…There are only a handful of people still around today who were present at Day One when Newfield's founding principles were unveiled. I wasn't there Day One and I wasn't there the day the company listed on the New York Stock Exchange. But when I share the history with new people about Newfield, I tell the history as if it's mine, because it is."

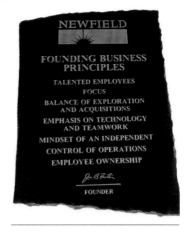

Granite stone commemorating
Founding Principles

"One of the proudest moments I have ever experienced was when I overheard an employee in Denver—hired maybe two or three years ago—tell the story of Newfield's founding. I was filled with emotion. Rightly, they took credit for our history of growth and adherence to Joe's principles. And, in a natural quid pro quo, I shamelessly take credit for the motivation and success of my new Newfield colleagues.

"Newfield's never put itself up for sale; our attitude has been that if we continue to create value, and create a premium in our valuation in the marketplace, then we are not at the top of somebody's speed dial.

Newfield Not A Sweatshop

Gary Packer describes the hiring waltz for upstream personnel in an overheated market for energy professionals. "They'll interview up and down Denver's 17th Street. They'll start at one end and they'll gradually work their way up to the other. I've heard this time and time again: that when new prospective employees walk down the halls at Newfield—in Denver as well as our other office locations—they know that something's different. They can sense it. They see the energy level. They see the passion. And they also observe that Newfield people have fun, too.

"We have been told repeatedly that the HR department of one of our large E&P peers created a PowerPoint presentation (after several of their staff joined the Newfield team) where it was suggested that the type of folks who come to work with us here at Newfield are raging workaholics. More than once, I have had a prospective employee or business associate [remark], 'Hey, they say you're a sweatshop.'

"And, I guess from the outside it may appear that this is the case and we may have earned it and wear it as a badge of honor. In actuality, I believe it is a reflection of Newfield's culture and a result of bringing together so many quality professionals, and their internal drive to succeed…these folks work themselves into a bit of a frenzy and others just assume it is a result of management expectation. Joe established a culture where we removed many of the obstacles and processes encumbering many before [they joined] Newfield, and we make no excuses for the environment that results from this.

"Joe has the ability to blend a grandfatherly image and persona and, at the same time, demand a tremendous amount of respect and get the most out of you. It's a characteristic that's hard to replicate. He's a very warm person and his reputation precedes him in all circles."[150]

LEE BOOTHBY – A DELAYED TENNECO CONNECTION

A Louisiana boy transplanted from Maine, Lee Kenneth Boothby graduated with a degree in petroleum engineering from Louisiana State University (LSU)-Baton Rouge in 1983. One year earlier, all of LSU's petroleum engineers had been hired. When Boothby graduated, the oil bust was well underway, and only three of fifty-three students in that December graduating class found jobs with traditional E&P companies.

> "You know, when Dave Schaible died, I called Tina, his wife, and said to her, 'I loved Dave Schaible.' And I don't think it's uncommon in the kind of environment you have in a working situation where you find love which exists among men at work and women at work, as well. Betty Smith comes to mind. It's just as genuine as the love you find in a family. It's built on mutual respect, on trust, admiration, a lot of needling, and camaraderie. But it is love. And one of the things that I'm proud of is it exists at Newfield; it's one of the keys to continued success." **JOE FOSTER**

After graduating, Boothby returned home to the epicenter of Cajun culture, with the best etouffée and the best zydeco music. He migrated 60 miles west to Lafayette, where he joined Tenneco's Eastern Gulf Division. After five years of increasing responsibility working offshore exploration and production, Boothby was selected to support Joe Foster's LBO group when the parent company put the business up for sale in 1988. While it was a great experience working alongside Foster and the LBO team, it was a huge letdown when Joe's efforts came up short. Boothby reflects, "Our hard work and effort didn't play out to where we finished in the money. Moreover, having the company sold out from under me left a bad taste in my mouth, so I became hellbent on going to business school.

> "I was born a military brat in Quantico, Virginia, and spent my early years in various military posts along the East Coast and a few years in Maine. As a young lad, my parents divorced and my mother's solution to the divorce was to put distance between her and my father, and we ended up in south Louisiana. So that's how I ultimately made the long trip south and made my way into the energy business." **LEE BOOTHBY**

In 1989, British Gas (now BG Group, Plc), the buyer of Tenneco's large international package of petroleum assets, offered Boothby a job, plus help with his tuition at business school. He picked up from Lafayette and headed another 220 miles farther west to Houston. Young and single, without any encumbrances, Boothby rose to the challenge of holding a full-time job while carrying a full class load. During his four years at British Gas and while earning his MBA from Rice University, Boothby stayed in contact with the folks at Newfield. He recalls constant updates from his good friend, Dave Schaible: "Dave started six months before I did at Tenneco and was one of the founders, the youngest founder, of Newfield. He stayed after me, telling me repeatedly, 'You really need to be here at Newfield.'"

> "I remember when I first heard that the new venture was to be named Newfield Exploration. Some so-called friends on the street were skeptics and joked that that wasn't the right name for the company. Call it "No-Field," they jibed, because they didn't have any production, assets or leases. Their only assets were a small dollop of cash and some very talented people, and their immediate liability was a significant weekly payroll." **LEE BOOTHBY**

Newfield Comes Calling

Fast forward a decade: Boothby is working the domestic offshore with Gulf of Mexico private Cockrell Oil, Ernie Cockrell's company. On a sultry morning in mid-July, 1999, Boothby was driving to work in downtown Houston when he took a call from Newfield's Dave Schaible. Schaible surprised Boothby with this question: "How would you like to go to Australia and run a company we just acquired down there?"

The conversation was short. Prior recruiting efforts by Schaible had not pulled Boothby across the line, but this morning was different. He responded, "Well, that sounds really interesting. I think you just might have me." Later Boothby visited Newfield's headquarters in Greenspoint, meeting with David Trice, Dave Schaible, and Bill Schneider. After a handshake and three days after his two weeks' notice period, Boothby and his wife, Janice, and three children were on a plane to Australia. He had never been "down under" before. Boothby and his family were all committed to going to Australia, sight unseen.

Boothby served Newfield in Australia for two and a half years, an experience that completely rejuvenated him and reminded him of what he really loved about the oil and gas business. Newfield's entrepreneurial can-do, make-it-happen spirit stood him in good stead. He was immediately confronted with resistance from Australian unions, enterprise bargaining agreements, and engineering snafus on FPSOs (floating production, storage and offloading vessels), not to mention the challenge of living and working in a foreign country.

Boothby reflects on how he came to accept Newfield's decidedly risky and challenging offer to head up its Australian business. "Down deep, it was the opportunity to reconnect with exceptional people — I call them the fingers and toes. I hadn't used all my dedicated fingers and toes up at that point. Several of the people that I had reserved digits for, if you will, were with Newfield; plus, who doesn't want to be with the best and the brightest? And that's why it felt a lot like coming home. There was a level of comfort and knowledge within the group that made things easy.

"What Newfield didn't take into account at the time of the evaluation was that Australia operated under a joint venture operating agreement and the budgets were only approved annually. We needed to drill several wells but were in a bit of a pickle. Enter Joe Foster, who was getting toward the end of his time at Newfield. He flew coach class to Perth, Australia.

"I took the summer intern job in 1983 with Tenneco Oil Company in Oklahoma City and was assigned a natural gas field study. I later learned that Joe Foster had earned his stripes in a similar assignment. Oklahoma City was a great experience; I spent all summer working on that field study and did a lot, learned a lot, met a lot of neat people. I completed my research project and gave a presentation on its findings, which is the traditional intern role. When the summer gig ended, and as I was driving south out of town, heading back to Louisiana, I reflected on the experience—what Tenneco had invested in a greenhorn LSU petroleum engineer who spent the summer working on analyzing a decrepit old field. I had focused on the etchings in the Pyramids— so to speak—production enhancement projects that had been orchestrated ten to forty years earlier. I thought: interesting work, but not for me. The new and exciting place in that timeframe was the Gulf of Mexico. In 1983, we had the first areawide MMS lease sale; I wanted to be out there where wildcats were being drilled and new fields were being discovered and developed. I wanted to be the guy making the mistakes, not the person to come along thirty or forty years later thinking, 'Why the hell did they do it this way?'" **LEE BOOTHBY**

Foster went up to Darwin, helicoptered offshore, and walked stem to stern on those vessels. Started early, finished late, and just impressed the hell out of all our employees. They'd never seen somebody at his level show up to do that."

"Foster started at the crack of dawn and went full tilt until late at night; he was the Energizer Bunny. In addition, we made a trip across to Adelaide, where Santos was headquartered. Santos was, and remains, a pivotal player in Australia. Joe joined me and Bill Schneider for dinner with the senior management at Santos. Luckily, one of the Santos executives had spent time here in the U.S., knew the Newfield story, and was positively predisposed to support our initiative. Ultimately, because of Joe's efforts, the joint venture approved Newfield's drilling plan off-cycle, outside of the normal protocol — something unheard of at the time."

Boothby saw first-hand the power of Joe Foster's personality and the respect that he had earned. Boothby turned Newfield's Australian acquisition into a true "Newfield Down Under." This organization was an extension of the company's success. A strategic decision was made by the Newfield board to divest its Australian operations in September 2003 to privately-held Coogee Resources Ltd. Boothby's next assignment was Tulsa, OK.

Joe Foster, Australia

"What's unique about the E&P business is it's really a very small business circle. Think about it; you graduated from some college in chemical or civil or mechanical engineering, those people go like the wind. Right? However, if you are a petroleum geologist, a petroleum landman, or a petroleum engineer, it is a very small clique – a brotherhood of sorts. Oil and gas companies come and go, but Tenneco seems to have left a unique footprint, as a disproportionate number of Tenneco executives have found their way to significant positions in public companies. I see these friends from twenty-five years ago, and they're everywhere. For example, Harold Korell recently announced his plans to retire from Southwestern Energy in January 2010—another Tenneco hand who made good and built a very successful E&P Company. I can't pinpoint what it was at Tenneco that produced exceptional leaders. When I reflect on my business career in the petroleum business, I appreciate the opportunity to have worked shoulder-to-shoulder with the Fosters, Schultzes, Nances, Trices, Schaibles, Korells, Chesebros, et al. In short, I am honored and thank the Lord. What a blessing!" **TERRY RATHERT**

Boothby Gets Lassoed

"The Lariat deal was a different story. The question at that point in time was, 'What the hell does a shallow water Gulf of Mexico company know about the Mid-Continent?' And Wall Street didn't like it at all.

"Lariat was a jump-start rather than a startup, and it brought with it all of the challenges of a jump-start type opportunity, acquiring an organization and assets and a different operating firm. So the first year wasn't a lot of fun. It wasn't a lot of fun because Newfield has always run very lean. We exited the first decade with less than a 100 total employees — ninety-six, to be exact. Then in 2001, the Lariat acquisition alone added 110. We made the classic mistake that every successful company only makes once. We tried to just send money with no material changes to management and staff, and that rarely ever works."

Six months after the Lariat acquisition, David Trice mentioned to Boothby, "I'd like you to think about Tulsa." Boothby recalls, "The last thing in the world I wanted to talk about in mid-2001 was Tulsa. I hadn't thought about Oklahoma since I'd driven south out of Oklahoma City in August 1983, when I had the attitude of a young twenty-one-year-old that 'this isn't the end of the world, but you can damn sure see it from here.'" However, Boothby was savvy enough to never say "never." David Trice, just like Dave Schaible before him, was incredibly persistent.

Boothby continues, "Here's David Trice—let's call him the coach. He says, 'I'd like you to think about Tulsa.' Let's put it in baseball terms: 'I'd like you to think about playing shortstop.' 'But Coach, I'm enjoying playing third base.'

"Third base is a good place. And I ultimately got kind of conflicted, like a lot of us have. Now, wait a minute. I made a commitment. I'm part of the team. And if coach needs you to play shortstop, you play shortstop. And after a few months of chatting back and forth, I made the commitment to come back to the States and move directly to Tulsa. Shortly after I arrived, I regretted that I had not accepted David's coaching message six months earlier, because the hole we had to dig out of was only that much deeper."

"Let's take what's good about Tenneco and let's shed what's bad about it and create Newfield, in this vein of what we know are the best of experiences that we've had. Stress constantly an attitude of achievement, the best and the brightest. Run hard, run fast, jump high. Assemble a group of folks who have these great traits and then create an environment of success that attracts more of those types of people into the firm. When Tenneco sold, it was a traumatic event for most folks. But in the years after that, it had a neat effect in that it scattered all of these talented people all across the industry. So suddenly—if you thought long enough—you knew people just about everywhere. Looking back, it is amazing how many Tenneco folks landed on their feet and went on to do very, very well; and more importantly, the sale led Joe Foster to found NFX." **DAVID SCHAIBLE**

"I remember the first Tenneco assignment I had. I was green as an unripe banana—twenty-two years old. I landed by helicopter on an offshore platform…in the federal waters of the Gulf. I was working as a project engineer at the time and there was a big crew on hand. We were going to be working together for the next two weeks. We had a little pre-job meeting and had the entire team standing around with blueprints and diagrams—everything laid out. I remember looking out across that room of forty experienced oil hands and thinking, 'Holy hell, a lot of these guys in here are old enough to be my dad. Some of them are probably old enough to be my granddad.' But I thought to myself, the golden rule goes a long way. Treat others like you want to be treated yourself. Probably the smartest thing I did on that first trip was, I laid out the plan and I asked the guys if they had any questions or suggestions on how we could do things better. After a strained minute of silence, the first response was from a senior guy on the platform who asked, 'Are you serious?' I said, 'Yes, I am.' And he says, 'Well. All right… we ought to do this instead of that; that instead of this. And, this is out of sequence and doesn't make any sense.' I said, 'That sounds pretty good. Let's do it that way,' and didn't think anything of it. Those guys came up after the job and said that's the first time they'd ever been asked that question. The lesson I never forget: 'There's a lot of good that comes from being in the fray.'" **LEE BOOTHBY**

"We want Newfield people [who], when the game's going on, want to be on the field playing the game, not on the bench playing the pretty-boy quarterback routine. And not in the stands watching the game. We don't need those folks. The bench is where you go when you're injured. Again it's all tied together, part and parcel, [with] the founding principles. Joe led off with talented employees. I call them the fingers and toes …what gets you up in the morning and keeps you excited about what you're doing. We used to call it TGIM: Thank God it's Monday…Get people out of the mentality that they're working for the weekends; [we want them to] come in fired up on Monday and raring to go." **LEE BOOTHBY**

Trice Hands The Reins To Boothby

David Trice and the Newfield board were on record that Dave Schaible would assume the CEO role when Trice exited stage left. A different succession plan had to emerge following Schaible's cancer diagnosis. The board had confidence in Lee Boothby's leadership abilities, but he wasn't as well known as Schaible because Dave had been on the board for a number of years. Rathert comments, "Lee had successfully run our business in Australia and is credited with Newfield's presence in the Woodford Shale in the Arkoma. But Lee was never 'stationed' in Houston and it took a little time for the board to get more familiar with him."[122] Lee Boothby worked for Newfield for nine years, but had never been a fixture at headquarters until 2008; he earned his stripes with repeated success in difficult assignments — first in Australia and later as Mid-Continent President.

When Boothby came to work for Newfield in 1999, he was awarded the illustrious assignment to go "Down Under" and run a notoriously dysfunctional E&P operation. "Here: You don't know squat about Australia, but you do know the oil and gas business. Here you go: Let me hand you an international airline ticket. By the way, it's coach." In line with the Newfield culture, Boothby responded cheerfully, "That'll work. It'll be good. I'm ready, willing, and able."

Rathert recalls, "So Boothby jumped on a plane his first day on the job and spent the next two en route to Perth." He says the group Boothby inherited from Gulf Canada was quite a duke's mixture of talents: "mostly Canadians, Australians, and Brits — a whole stable of wild horses with a very different work ethic and culture than we at Newfield were used to. Different thoughts about what you do and how you do it, and different approaches to structure and organization. All these things on paper, like organization charts and title, may seem important at many oil companies, but at Newfield, that's not how it is done. Our emphasis has always centered on your individual contribution to corporate success, not the pursuit of a grander title. Dealing with hundreds of executives in the oilpatch during my career, I learned first-hand that just because you have an executive title doesn't mean you are competent. So, it was quite a rude awakening for the Gulf Canada Australian contingent to be introduced to the Newfield Exploration Company through Lee Boothby. Lee is straightforward but diplomatic and reads people well. Newfield's bottom line has always been about making strides to corporate success, not just flitting around with titles and showmanship. It's about making money. And some of our new Australian brethren didn't understand. At Newfield you've got to deliver 'on time on spec' and be consistent."[123]

Lee Boothby has a prominent frame in his office: in it is the first business-class ticket Newfield ever purchased. He cut a deal in Australia where Newfield could buy business-class tickets booked from Perth to Houston, for the same price as economy class out of the States. The first officially sanctioned business-class ticket was personally approved by David Trice. The first six trips that Boothby took to Australia were economy-class. "You can't appreciate how miserable it is to sit in the back of a fully loaded 747 and 'look forward to' the next 26 hours—a day plus two hours from leaving the airport here to exiting the airport in Perth and vice versa." **LEE BOOTHBY**

STEVE CAMPBELL – HORSE TRADES ANADARKO FOR NEWFIELD

The 100ᵗʰ Newfield Employee

A born natural for Newfield Exploration, Stephen Carter Campbell graduated in 1990 from Texas A&M with a communications degree and soon joined one of Newfield's largest and toughest competitors, Anadarko Petroleum Corporation (APC). Those were the years when Bob Allison was Anadarko's cerebral CEO. Allison had a loyal investor base and commanded respect for his vision that natural gas was a premium energy fuel, albeit one with a Rodney Dangerfield complex. Campbell left Anadarko for Newfield in 1999, about a year before Anadarko made a defining acquisition of Union Pacific Resources (UPR). In those heady days, Wall Street could not praise the APC/UPR merger enough. Flush with that success, the Anadarko board made an error of bravado and corporate ego, approving the construction of a corporate Taj Mahal some twenty-five miles north of downtown Houston in The Woodlands. Still not fully occupied, the thirty-story Anadarko tower looms above the Interstate-45 Houston/Dallas corridor today.

When Campbell left Anadarko for Newfield, the two competing companies were only several blocks apart in the Greenspoint area of north Houston. Campbell recalls that he was Newfield's hundredth employee—recently, the firm has tested the ranks of 1,000.

Campbell was recruited to build an investor relations program at Newfield—one that recognized the significance of the company's growth and its access to Wall Street capital. When Campbell joined up, most of those duties were shared between Jim Ulm, the treasurer, and Terry Rathert, the CFO. At the time Campbell arrived in late September of 1999, Newfield did not have a human resources department or an IT department. Campbell notes that much has changed in the past decade at Newfield, the natural progression of a company building an infrastructure to accomplish what it could not have with only 100 people on the payroll.

Work Papers On Lap And Reading Light On

After two days with Newfield, Campbell accompanied Joe Foster to the John S. Herold, Inc. Pacesetters Energy Conference in Greenwich, Connecticut and was quickly introduced to Foster's intense work ethic. "Joe liked to fly after business hours because it allowed you to get in a full day of work in the office."[138]

Newfield always flew coach and there were no exceptions, even if you were Steve Campbell, who at six feet-four inches could easily pass for a football tight-end. "Remember that I had come from Anadarko where I had become accustomed to flying on a corporate jet. And even when flying commercial at Anadarko, I didn't realize there were seats that actually went beyond Row Four on the airplane. So we boarded that aircraft, and I was in Row Fifteen, and Joe was in Row Twenty. It was eight o'clock at night, and I promptly went to sleep and slept most of the way up to LaGuardia. When we landed at LaGuardia, it was almost midnight. As we prepared for the long drive out to Greenwich (Yellow Cabs, no limos) Joe walked up to me in the terminal and put his arm around me. 'You know what I like about flying coach? It's so damn uncomfortable, you can get a lot of work done!'"[139]

After that, whenever he flew with Foster, Campbell made sure that, before he dozed off, he had some work in front of him and the overhead reading light was turned on.

Steve Campbell recollects, "Even in his final years at Newfield, Joe flew coach to Australia just to show the rest of us that it could be done. And that was the culture. No [company] airplanes. No perks. We hire the best and the brightest, and we'll pay you well enough to join your own country club and buy your own first-class tickets; but on company dollars, shareholder dollars, we're gonna run it the right way—with owner-mindedness."[140]

"In the early days of Newfield, and even after life as a public company, we flew commercial. Back of the bus. We have never had a charter plane. We traveled in [Yellow Cabs] and purposely avoided fancy stretch limos. But every once in a while, an investment banker would insist on coordinating travels with a limo. Reluctantly, Joe would slide into in one of those big stretch Cadillacs or Town Cars. What was Joe's typical comment after he struggled to extract his lanky frame from an oversized vehicle on the streets of Manhattan or Boston? 'These limos are a lot like trouble. They are a lot easier to get into than get out of.'" **DAVID TRICE**

CHAPTER VIII
FROM NEWFIELD TO BAKER HUGHES

THE BAKER HUGHES SABBATICAL – "IF MY BLADDER WAS LARGER, VIC BEGHINI WOULD HAVE HAD THE JOB."

Foster was recruited in 1992 to join the board of oilfield service giant Baker Hughes Incorporated (BHI), where he served for a decade.

For most of his board tenure there, Joe worked closely with BHI's CEO Jim Woods, a somewhat understated but strong willed executive. In the late 1990s, the Baker Hughes board was faced with one of the toughest jobs outside directors ever have: selecting a successor to a retiring chairman and CEO.

It had been known for some time that Jim Woods was going to retire and that he would recommend his successor, although the appointment would require board approval. There were several lengthy board meetings, and everyone agreed that Max Lukens would be the new CEO.[165] Lukens had risen quickly in the Baker Hughes ranks and, despite his tender age at the time (forty-nine) and lack of seasoning in tough oilfield service markets, he was Woods' apparent fair-haired boy.

When Woods retired, he immediately left the board, thus ending his influence on its decisions.[166] In a highly charged atmosphere, newly appointed CEO Max Lukens presented the BHI board with a major acquisition initiative. The BHI board approved the cash acquisition of Western Atlas from Texas Instruments, but Joe missed that important meeting.

Although the board supported Lukens in the Western Atlas transaction, there were unanswered questions immediately afterward that raised the stress level in the corner office. Tensions within the board escalated measurably and communication with the new executive worsened. In short order, it was clear that the post-merger integration of the Western Geophysical portion of Western Atlas into Baker Hughes was not going according to plan.[167] Then some even more troublesome issues came to light that were worthy of early disclosure to the BHI board.

Some accounting irregularities had taken place in the old Baker Oil Tools. The situation was then exacerbated by inquiries from the press questioning the company's transfer of certain funds overseas. The BHI board felt the daily repercussions of a hammered stock price as confidence in their new CEO waned.[168]

It was a moment reminiscent of "Casablanca," when Humphrey Bogart and Lauren Bacall share a cigarette and look over the fog-shrouded runway before parting. At the next

Baker Hughes board meeting, many carafes of black coffee were downed following the critical moment when an "executive session" was declared and Max Lukens was asked to leave the room. It was clear that a change at the CEO level was necessary. Even though Lukens was not guilty of any illegal activity, he had lost credibility with the board and with Wall Street.

There was no potential successor that the board felt comfortable in naming without first going through an external search. The immediate solution was to appoint an interim CEO while conducting a search, both internally and externally. At the time, it was common knowledge that Joe Foster would soon retire from Newfield. And Vic Beghini, a longstanding Baker Hughes director, was about to retire as CEO from Marathon Oil, the multi-billion dollar integrated oil and gas company.

Joe recounts, "The board was under great stress with the Baker Hughes shares in free-fall, and I was way overdue for a hydraulic break." Joe took a leisurely visit to the men's room. When he returned he learned that Max Lukens' resignation would be sought and that he had been voted in as the new interim chairman and CEO of Baker Hughes. "I regret that my bladder gave me up; otherwise I would have argued strongly that Marathon's Vic Beghini [take] over the interim CEO reins at Baker Hughes."[169]

"After more than forty-one years in the oil and gas business I understood very well the way the oil service business worked—check that comment: I didn't understand the oil service sector as well as I thought, once I climbed into the Baker Hughes CEO seat. However, I knew how to work with employees and with investors and analysts. I was convinced that Baker Hughes needed to improve its communications with Wall Street and felt that if BHI would work openly with analysts and investors and tell it like it is, we were going to be okay, despite the problems of the recent past." **JOE FOSTER**

In his new role of "Interim Big Dog," Foster's first decisive action was to meet with as many members of management and groups of employees as possible to tell them that the board and senior officers management would not delay or defer any significant decision during the new CEO selection process. And as the new CEO, Joe immediately received an outstanding vote of confidence: the Baker Hughes shares rallied strongly on the announcement.

Back at Newfield a few eyebrows were raised: "Joe's retiring one day from here and before he can take a nap he's taking on a huge new job at Baker Hughes!"

The new challenge sped up Foster's retirement from Newfield. In fact, Foster retired two weeks early so he could become interim CEO at Baker Hughes. Joe strolled into Trice's office one day and blurted out the news, "You were going to get this job two weeks from now, but you've got it today!"

"We Are Going To Do Those Things That Need To Be Done Now."

"One of the things that I have found over and over again is that you must manage intelligent people in an adult-like, responsible environment. That is, if a management group can share problems, divulge aspirations, and ultimately trust one another, the company can accomplish great things. Conversely, when there is a lack of trust, no amount of lip service is successful, and it is chaos. If you don't know who is with you and who is against you or what they are really thinking, you just wind up with more politics than you do decisions."

JOE FOSTER

One of Joe's early victories at Baker Hughes was to land a new CEO for the company's flywheel division, Baker Atlas. The Baker Atlas position had been vacant for three or four months prior to Max Lukens' departure, and it was clear that the key division's performance had suffered.[170]

Another trouble spot at Baker Hughes was the newly acquired seismic initiative in Western Geophysical. Under Joe's leadership, they managed to negotiate a win-win venture with Schlumberger, the market leader of the oil service business. BHI and SLOB, the affectionate nickname for NYSE-listed Schlumberger (SLB) created a new joint-venture company, Western GECO, in which BHI retained a thirty percent stake. More important, Schlumberger forked over a much-needed $500 million to Baker Hughes and BHI retained major exposure to the upside.[171]

Trust was renewed at Baker Hughes. Andy Szcellia served as COO, and Steve Finley as CFO. When Joe showed up for work at Baker Hughes in January 2000, the depressed BHI stock price—bouncing off a multi-year low value—closed at $17 per share. By August 12, 2000, when Mike Wiley (former chairman and CEO of Atlantic Richfield) took the reins from Joe, the stock was priced at just over $40 per share. Joe says, "At the time, it seemed to be an unconventional decision to hire a guy with an exploration and production background to run an oil service company. What the hell? Mike was a seasoned chief executive. Baker Hughes has been running fine under an E&P guy."

When Joe retired officially from Newfield on January 31, 2000, he moved out of the company's headquarters in the Greenspoint area near Houston's Bush Intercontinental Airport and set up his own office in west Houston's Memorial area. "It was important to me to get out of the building and not to cast a shadow that could undermine David's effectiveness as the new CEO. My interim appointment to run Baker Hughes that year turned into a real blessing; for that seven or eight months, I was just up to my ass in alligators and didn't have an ounce of energy to second-guess any decisions going on back at Newfield." **JOE FOSTER**

"Maybe it was very good fortune that Joe had a full-time challenge when he picked up the interim CEO job at Baker Hughes. Joe's style is to stay out of your hair and to be there as a mentor, to be a sounding board, to be that one-man executive committee, but not be the guy who is back there second-guessing your decisions."
DAVID TRICE

CHAPTER IX
TRANSITION OF NEWFIELD

IT'S BEEN AN INTERESTING EVOLUTION

The management segue following Foster's departure wasn't entirely seamless, but it did work reasonably well. It was a challenge for David Trice to go in as Newfield's new CEO and deal with the board of directors; Newfield had been blessed with a very independent, very strong board, but it was very much Joe Foster's board. Trice kept Joe Foster informed of every key management initiative. Joe would always be available to come in and view prospective acquisitions; if Joe was in agreement, it was an easy sell to the board.[184]

Well before Joe Foster formally stepped down as Newfield's CEO, he invested considerable time and energy learning about succession and transition planning. Trice recalls, "He spent a lot of time to get it right. Most founders and CEOs have a hard time planning for their departure. That's something that Joe Foster spent a lot of time thinking and reading about: How to best turn over responsibilities before he left and how to smoothly transition to disengagement. It was not an easy path because Joe Foster is quite a presence to have around."[185]

Every day Trice remained at the helm of Newfield, he was grateful for the extra effort Foster put into designing Newfield's succession plan and for orchestrating a smooth transition (Trice moved to non-executive chairman in May 2009; then left the board in 2010, handing the reins to CEO Lee Boothby. Effective February 2010, Trice—following Foster's lead—passed the chairman's title to Booth.). Human resources development gets a lot of attention today at Newfield. The Compensation and Management Development Committee devotes one full summer meeting to "people planning." It's not just about CEO or CFO succession. They look at their bench strength throughout the organization. They ask, "How are we going to fill the ranks? From where will our new leaders emerge? And how do we continue to build Newfield?" Trice certainly learned all those things from Joe Foster.

When Newfield started it would have been easy to open a Mid-Continent or Rockies office, to have some oil and gas production here and there. However, Joe Foster recognized that he could only hire so many people, which meant overhead, and Newfield could only raise so much money. So they had to concentrate on one key core producing area, where they could build a base and consistently regenerate value-accretive investment options. Joe was wedded to the notion of geographic focus, and without his dogged dedication to focused operations during Newfield's first years, they wouldn't have been successful.[186]

Newfield changed directions dramatically in the first few years after Joe stepped down. Joe always supported David Trice's leadership, even though the company took on some significant risks. Wall Street didn't like it at first, particularly when Newfield made the Lariat acquisition and moved into the Mid-Continent.

Newfield's growth had been in concentric circles around the Gulf of Mexico, expanding in the GOM and throughout the onshore Gulf coast. They didn't wander very far from home. When Newfield did the Lariat deal in January 2001—their first large corporate acquisition—they bought a management team they thought

> "It's very difficult to buy management teams, especially after you've just made them rich in a transaction." **DAVID TRICE**

had similar business principles and practices. They quickly learned that the two cultures didn't mesh. In Lariat, Newfield launched a significant and valuable entry into the Mid-Continent region, but they fell short in transferring Newfield's basic business principles and strategies.

David Trice learned that when Newfield acquires a company or buys a significant asset, it is essential to put a Newfield hand in charge from Day One—even when there are great people in the acquired organization. Trice argues strongly, "Culture and business principles—even those as unique as Newfield's—can't begin to be imported until established Newfield people are leading the organization. We learned quickly that we needed to put multiple people in the organization, and it takes some time to nurture valuable cross-pollination among organizations—to allow the Newfield culture to infuse."[187]

CRITICAL STRATEGY SESSIONS

In January 2001, Newfield's stock took a tumble and then traded sideways for a couple of years. It took some time and better industry fundamentals to convince the Street that Newfield was doing the right thing under Trice. Joe and the board of directors—through the strategy sessions that Joe first initiated in 1999—were critical. It was essential that the company take its bearings and determine that it was on the right long-term course, even if Wall Street was not going to appreciate that overnight. From the outset Foster, Trice, and fellow Newfield executives listened to Wall Street but were not afraid to shun fads and bogus advice. They were determined to run Newfield for its shareholders for long-term value, not short-term fluff.[188]

IT LOOKS A WHOLE LOT LIKE NEWFIELD

"It took a while for the benefits to materialize with our first corporate acquisition in Tulsa, but it worked. Hell, we were eventually able to make it work in Australia—and you talk about a place that is really different!" said David Trice.

"Newfield moved into Australia and found itself with a disparate and dysfunctional organization. Three years later, when we divested Australia, it was rewarding to observe how the Newfield work ethic had flourished—how people reacted favorably to our incentive programs, our philosophy, and way of doing business. It was extraordinary."

Success only comes in these acquisitions when Newfield transplants people who have daily lived and breathed its culture. Newfield's significant ($650 million) EEX Corporation acquisition in 2002, was an asset transfer, essentially, since few EEX hands were essential to the larger Newfield organization.

Trice noted that the company's 2004, $575 million acquisition of Inland Resources raced off to a great start. "We moved Gary Packer—a ten-year Newfield veteran—out to Denver to manage the Inland operations."

Just months after Newfield absorbed Inland, Trice was proud to say, "It looks a whole lot like Newfield. When you walk into Newfield's Denver office, of course you'll see our monument of core business principles and the Newfield logo. But more important, you'll observe people who act just like the people do here in our Houston headquarters. Newfield hands respond well to the culture that Joe Foster established: a bottom-up culture as opposed to a top-down driven organization; an open organization where information is meant to be shared. One of the founding Newfield principles is employee ownership; and one thing we found out in the early days is that employee owners are better employees."

Trice remembers when Joe Foster was invited to speak to employees of Royal Dutch/Shell at the giant oil company's downtown Houston headquarters on Louisiana Street. During the question and answer session following his presentation, the then-CEO of Newfield was drilled, "What would you do differently if you ran Shell?" Foster didn't hesitate with his response: "I would break the existing Shell into numerous independent divisions and have all employees invest in stock in their divisions." Foster received a standing ovation.

> "As Joe Foster puts it, we like to be on that ragged edge between chaos and order—where all creativity is generated. Along that ragged edge, if you impose too much order, you tend to stifle creativity. Conversely, if there is too much disorder and chaos, excessive creativity never matures into action." **DAVID TRICE**

TRICE'S RAGGED EDGE

Trice and his successor Boothby refuse to succumb to any organization charts for Newfield. They don't like boxes and diagrams. "The Newfield organization was really flat when it was founded and even today—a multi-billion dollar operation—it doesn't have a lot of unnecessary structure." After Joe retired, one of Trice's biggest jobs was to be the torchbearer of the Newfield culture and to make sure that, as Newfield grew, it retained all the good things its original 23 people benefited from when they started.[189]

"Back in 1989 [that] was a lot easier to do with twenty-three than it is today, with more than 1,000 professionals in multiple locations. What Joe Foster created at Newfield was a unique and high-powered "brand" that was very different from the host of other E&P companies out there. Newfield people have a certain vibrancy. They are people who work hard, but like what they do because of the way they get to do it. They are given a healthy amount of autonomy and professional responsibility necessary to do their job.[190]

"When Joe put together Newfield, he had been in business thirty-one years. He was a petroleum engineer; Joe didn't boast a Ph.D. in Management from Harvard but—far better—he had thirty years of on-the-job training." Foster designed a set of business principles for Newfield which were all based upon his observations of what had worked and what hadn't in the Tenneco conglomerate. Trice believes Newfield's founding business principles—the notion of the flat organization and multidisciplinary teams and employee ownership—are "self evident truths that Joe collected from his business life like they were ancient Roman coins."[191]

TRICE: COMMUNICATION IS KEY

During all the years Trice worked alongside Joe Foster, debate—the healthy, honest expression of an intellectual perspective—was encouraged. This environment of open communication is the only one Trice ever knew at Newfield. He feels they make better decisions because of it. Sometimes the arguments can be heated. Impassioned, emphatic debate at Newfield is part of the essential communication and information exchange that makes the company strong and resilient. "At the end of the day, if people have had their say, they are willing to climb in the boat and row their oars just as hard as if it had been their idea in the first place."

Newfield leaders meet every Monday lunch as a management team—a protocol Joe Foster initiated back in 1990, Newfield's second year. The team is focused on one clear goal: "Let's communicate the important stuff and then get after it!"[192]

Specific Newfield teams also meet to discuss their progress (or lack thereof) every Monday morning. The management group also meets every Monday, where they go through the "Short List" in great detail. There

> "Joe would always make it evident when he'd seen enough; he'd make that real clear. When the debate was over, you knew it."
> **DAVID TRICE**

are regular full staff employee meetings, and now Newfield has introduced a monthly "all hands on deck" meeting on the fourth floor, in the room dedicated as the Joe B. Foster Communication Room. Trice comments, "The Communication Room space is great—we can get the whole Houston office in that room comfortably. We can painstakingly go through the financials to make sure that everyone grasps…the message that financial results are directly tied to our operating efforts. If the Newfield outside board has held a meeting that month, we share the key 'takeaways' from the board agenda. Terry, Bill, Dave (deceased), Elliott (no longer with the company) and I join in and hand the baton back and forth for the various presentations. There might be a few highly sensitive issues that we determine shouldn't be revealed prematurely to the Newfield staff, but there are damn few because we believe that comprehensive and honest communication is so important."

"Success is assured if you make a commitment to the culture, if you are committed to free information flow, and embrace the notion that the best ideas come up from the bottom, and if you set a system in place where ideas can percolate up as opposed to being stifled, where there are not a lot of people who can shut things down with a careless 'No,' on the way up. If somebody's got a really good idea they can trumpet it to the top even if their supervisor doesn't like it. Admittedly, there are only a few 'gee whiz' ideas that make it all the way to the top, but in the executive wing at Newfield we are always on our toes, craning our necks, looking for that great new idea that does soar!" **DAVID TRICE**

THE POST-JOE ERA AND CORPORATE GOVERNANCE – DAVID TRICE INTERVIEW FROM 2005

"In our minds, we've been in the post-Joe era for the past five years—this company has been run with help from Joe and the board, but it's been run by the management team that's [been] here now since January of 2000. I admit that I was sad to see Joe leave the Newfield board in May 2005. I'll miss the ability to have him come in and look at an acquisition and ask the tough questions. And my one-man executive committee has disappeared. But we've been doing this for five years with the board, and our management team has a lot of credibility with the Newfield board of directors. I don't think anything changed after Joe Foster retired from the Newfield board. You can look at a couple of examples around the industry where the retired CEO continued to have an office and remain active on the board of directors. It just flat doesn't work. Joe and I are both believers in term limits.

"We have term limits for elected politicians and we ought to have terms limits—though I'm not sure what duration—for CEOs. When your term is over, you need to get out of the way and let the new group come in. The reason term limits exist is that every company needs fresh ideas and new blood. Since Joe stepped down as CEO, his mission over the past five years has been to be helpful and supportive but not meddlesome. That was never an issue. Look at all the fallout from Sarbanes-Oxley and all the endless drivel that came out of the NYSE blue-ribbon commission about whether there should be separate chairman and CEO posts. It can work if you have the right relationship—but there is a delicate balancing act. It worked very well with Joe and me in those roles because we had

open communication and shared values and strategies. We had years of working well together already under our belts."

It is noteworthy that so much of Newfield's executive talent today derives from the recruits assembled in 1989—"in the beginning"—with the exception of Elliott Pew, who was enlisted by Joe Foster just prior to his retirement. Trice reflects, "There are only a few founders left since Joe, Bob Waldrup, and Betty Smith retired. The only founders left are Terry Rathert, Dave Schaible, Bill Schneider, and me....Plus, there is one other great employee, Mike Sewell, who remains active in the drilling group. So, there are five little Indians out of the original 25, surrounded by the Newfield ranks of 675 other professionals here now."

BLACKBEARD AND THE LOWER TERTIARY'S PROMISE

By 2005, any oilman or oil-service hand would cite the deep shelf Treasure Island/Treasure Bay play and the Blackbeard prospect being drilled at South Timbalier Block 168 as the center of attention in the Gulf of Mexico. Newfield was in the very thick of it. To the amazement of everyone in the global oil industry, little ole' Newfield convinced the giant oils to drill a rank wildcat that will well over cost $100 million [*Author's Note:* actual cost $180 million!] Operator ExxonMobil, with partners BP and Petrobras, financed a test on the concept that extremely deep reservoirs (25,000 to 30,000 feet deep—five to six miles below the seabed) could hold commercial volumes of hydrocarbons. In oilfield parlance, Newfield was "being carried"—it shared in the potential success of Blackbeard but bore a very small portion of the costs of drilling the wildcat. Blackbeard West No. 1 represented another intriguing chapter in Newfield's history.

Trice recounts, "The concept of the deep Tertiary was developed by geophysicist Jay Menard, now at MMR; then at Newfield. Jay was working for EEX at the time when the management philosophy at EEX was elephant-hunting—if a prospect wasn't huge, they weren't interested. EEX blunted its pick, drilling deepwater wildcats, so he tried to figure out how they might find something big on the Gulf of Mexico shelf. Jay is one of those guys who is right on that ragged edge—a very creative conceptual thinker." While Menard was at EEX, he began to tell his fellow geoscientists, "We know there are some great big structures out in the deep water [greater than 1,000 feet] and we need to determine where those structures exist up on the shelf."

BP's monster discoveries in the Thunderhorse and Tahiti deepwater Gulf of Mexico projects penetrated the Lower Miocene sands. Back up to the shelf, Lower Miocene sands exist onshore South Louisiana and in the shallow West Cameron waters. Trice connects the dots: "We've got Lower Miocene here, and then again a hundred miles offshore; where are these sands in between? The answer must be that they are buried very deeply."

Menard pored over existing seismic data all the way down to 35,000 feet and began to map a structural set of prospects that had never been seen nor even really searched out. When geologists and geophysicists went back and started pursuing this play seismic-wise, they played out seismic reflections to only about six seconds. Menard insisted that the seismic data be printed out down to eleven or twelve seconds. When pursuing structural geology, explorationists are looking for bumps. In this case, it was, "There's some damn big bumps down there and they cover an enormous area." Trice knew that there is a large structural ridge that runs deeply across most of the Gulf of Mexico. "It could be part of the Cretaceous shelf. We don't know. But what we do know is that it created a structural setting with sands draped over the top, which is a great setting for hydrocarbon traps."

Menard and EEX had taken the play from nothing to conceptual status, and began to assemble a leasehold position about the time Newfield was completing its acquisition. Trice recalls, "The people at EEX were convinced that they had something that could be a really big deal, and that's why we created the Treasure Island Royalty Trust to bridge a valuation gap. Newfield has really advanced the deep Tertiary concept. EEX just didn't have the financial wherewithal to get there."

Since the EEX transaction, Newfield has expanded the play to the west and picked up a string of additional leases. "We started doing some of our own pre-stack depth imaging on these prospects to really enhance them. We had the guts, when it came to it, to throw BP out and terminate the agreement rather than doing something that was not in Newfield's best interest. Then we began to market the play among the world-class players in the industry and convince these top players in exploration, 'This is a well that ought to be drilled.'" [*Author's Note:* Newfield is not longer active in the play following the company's sale of GOM shelf assets to MMR.]

> "If the deep shelf is not the salvation of the GOM shelf, it surely represents a big blob of potential!"
> **JOE FOSTER**

THERE'S A WHOLE NEW GULF OF MEXICO

Trice comments, "The Gulf is mature, depletion is everywhere, and the domestic offshore industry is in pretty big trouble. There is either a whole other Gulf of Mexico down there or there isn't. There's only one way we know of to find out: We've got great big structures down there that must be penetrated by the drillbit; multi-trillions [of cubic feet] of natural gas could be down there."

Trice notes the parallels of the deep-shelf play with the early days of deepwater activity in the Gulf of Mexico. "In the emerging years of the deepwater play, drillability was an issue. There were very few deepwater drillships and semisubmersibles that were suitable. Could we drill and complete wells in thousands of feet of water? What was the marine environment going to be like? We have overcome an enormous number of challenges and the deepwater Gulf is a world-class hydrocarbon basin.

"With the deep shelf we have the same issues of high costs and drillability, but here the challenges are pressure and temperature. There are different challenges that we are worried about. The great thing about the deep shelf is that while well costs are the same, if we find meaningful amounts of petroleum—we are drilling in only 68 feet of water, right in the middle of existing pipeline infrastructure and reasonably close to shore—the economics of the deep shelf could be considerably better than the ultra-deepwater.

"Instead of having a $2 [billion] or $3 billion development program that takes six to eight years, the deep shelf development could be compressed considerably in time with considerably better economics. What we don't know is what the reservoir condition of the deep-shelf sands are going to be because of temperature and pressure over time. Every company involved in this well probably has a different view on the pressure and temperature challenge and each of us has done different analyses."

"Blackbeard West is the kind of well that requires the technology and stamina of the two biggest oil companies in the world. No doubt about it, Blackbeard will be a tough well to drill [*Author's Note:* Update—it was drilled and results were inconclusive], but Exxon and BP have experience from around the world, and collectively they've drilled every kind of well that can be drilled. Exxon has told us that Blackbeard is right up there with some of the most challenging wells ever designed. Fortunately, if we are successful in locating pay zones but end up with production issues, we've got the depth and breadth of BP's and Exxon's research. We could benefit from those huge resources to call on to move this play forward. That's the greatest thing about having these kinds of plays; Newfield is proud to have advanced the deep shelf and its truly cutting-edge technology."

Danny McNease of Rowan on the Blackbeard Well

In his letter to shareholders for the 2004 annual report, Rowan Companies Chairman and CEO Danny McNease highlighted the potential of deep drilling on the Gulf of Mexico's shelf. McNease's pride in Rowan's "well-trained, creative and safety-conscious employees" and leadership in equipment suitable for hostile drilling environments is evident.

"The Scooter Yeargain has spudded ExxonMobil's Blackbeard well in South Timbalier Block 168. The target depth of this well is greater than 32,000 feet— the deepest well ever drilled on the Gulf of Mexico Outer Continental Shelf (OCS). Five years ago, a well so deep was not even imaginable, much less possible. Today, with Rowan's personnel and equipment, this well is a reality. As the well depth reaches uncharted territory, it will challenge both the rig and its crew. I am confident that both will perform to a level never seen before in our industry.

"The Blackbeard well will be one of the most-watched projects in the long history of Gulf of Mexico drilling. If successful, the well will act as a technology

template for future drilling on the OCS. The Minerals Management Service has predicted that the lower Miocene structure may hold as much as 55 trillion cubic feet of gas reserves. If the Blackbeard well proves this potential, it will increase demand for two million-pound hook-load capacity rigs in the Gulf of Mexico—and Rowan owns all four of them. We see no way for our four rigs to drill all of the ultra-deep wells currently under consideration for later this year and next. Thus, our second (the Bob Keller) and third (the Hank Boswell) Tarzan Class rigs should be even more marketable when delivered in the third quarter of 2005 and late 2006, respectively. The timing for our introduction of the Tarzan Class jack-ups into the marketplace could not have been better."

[*Author's Note:* For an update on Blackbeard see Appendix C.]

THIS TOO SHALL PASS AWAY

Joe Foster recounts a parable that holds great significance for his fifty years of business experience. In an ancient Middle Eastern empire, the ruler asked his advisors for a proverb: one that would apply to all situations at all times, in no more than five words. After months of deliberation, the council came back: "This, too, shall pass away."

In his lifetime, Joe Foster has witnessed a host of bad times and distressing events that have passed away: The Great Depression, World War II, the Korean Conflict, the assassinations of the Kennedys and Martin Luther King Jr., the Viet Nam War, the collapse of the former Soviet Union, and the blatant discrimination against African Americans and women.

Foster laments the disappearance of wonderful things as well, like nickel Cokes and nine-cent movie tickets, a few energy bull markets, Tenneco Oil, and a first marriage. He also mourns the deaths of many the people he has known. Joe reflects that in these days of

"Mother Nature and the free market are filled with self-correcting mechanisms that work out the excesses and return us to a steadily improving norm. The quality of life will continue to improve in the midst of the ups and downs of the market, of business, and of our everyday lives." **JOE FOSTER**

"It is well to keep in mind that, short or long, the cycles will, in time, revert to the mean; that if we will be patient and persistent in doing our job, if we will hedge our bets on the downside and not try so hard to cream the upside, there is a very high probability things will work out just fine. I believe that with all my heart." **JOE FOSTER**

instant information and wide-open communication, there is more volatility and uncertainty in our lives than ever before. Foster concludes, "Thanks for listening to my preaching. My dad used to say, 'preaching is simply reminding others of what they already know.' I make no apologies. The really good stuff is worth saying over and over again.

"My kids, my family, my grandkids—they are my greatest accomplishment. That's the greatest legacy anyone can leave. But I put Newfield right up there. It's as close to family as a company can get."

WHY I RETIRED IN 2005 – JOE FOSTER'S SPEECH, NEWFIELD FOUNDERS' DINNER 2005

I have been asked, and some of you may wonder, why I would want to retire from the board of a company which I helped found and which is such a source of pride to me.

Well, there are three reasons.

First, I am seventy years old, which on most boards is the mandatory retirement age for directors. And I have to tell you that, now that I am seventy, I see that there's a reason for that. I'm not as quick or incisive as I used to be. As a matter of fact, I probably observed this more acutely when I was in my fifties serving on a board with a number of seventy-year-old guys.

I recognize I could probably have asked for and gotten an exception to serve longer, but I knew that, at some point, I should retire from the board and age seventy seemed like as reasonable a time as any.

Second, there has been a very good transition in the management of Newfield from me being CEO to David being CEO. The organization has been strengthened in many ways. Its performance speaks for itself.

By now, just about everybody in management and in the boardroom can anticipate what I will say about every issue and every deal. As you can tell from the introduction of the board members this evening, we have a very strong group of directors with a diversity of viewpoints and experience, fully capable of asking all the right questions and guiding the company in the right direction. If I felt otherwise, you could not pry me off this board.

Third, there are other things I want to do in the oil and gas business—not competitive with Newfield, certainly not on the scale of Newfield—which I could not or should not do if I remain on the Newfield board.

I know, and I think you know, I would never do anything that is detrimental to Newfield. But in the post-Sarbanes-Oxley world, conflicts of interest are often perceived where none exist and board service is precluded where there are simply potential conflicts of interests. I don't want to be in a position or put Newfield in a position where perceptions or potential conflicts might create even a hint of suspicion or question.

Having said all that, I want to make it clear I will not disappear from Newfield. I have told David I will come to the monthly birthday luncheons for as long as I am invited. I will continue to hold a significant amount of Newfield stock. I will keep up with what is going on. I will continue to use, when appropriate, the title, "Founder, Newfield Exploration," knowing that it is not an exclusive title, I share it. I hope to visit or have lunch with many of you on an informal basis from time to time. In fact, you may enjoy and be more comfortable going to lunch with Joe Foster, the old retired guy, than Joe Foster, the board member.

I want to close with a story I have told several times in the past at retirement parties—usually when other people were retiring.

It is about the commencement exercises at a large university. One of the graduates-to-be who will be among the last to receive his diploma notices that, as each graduate walks to the stage, the university president hands him or her his diploma, and makes a brief comment. This seems to induce a chuckle from most graduates and they hurry on across the stage. The youngster near the end of the line is curious as to what the university president might be saying or will say to him.

Finally, it is his time to cross the stage. The university president gives him a firm handshake with one hand, stuffs the diploma into the other hand, and emphatically says, "Keep on moving! Don't slow down!"

That's good advice for young graduates and it is good advice for old retirees.

That is precisely what I intend to do, to keep on moving.

This is also what I want Newfield to do, to keep on moving—up and to the right!

A YARDSTICK ON JOE B. FOSTER

Ask a dozen people, "How tall is Joe Foster?" Most will answer "Six-two or six-three." Surprisingly Joe is a perfect six feet. When gauged against a tape measure, Joe Bill Foster and my father, Arthur Norbert Smith (now 90) both are a perfect six feet tall—not less, not more.

> "I find good reason to go to my office every day, which my wife, Harriet, seems to appreciate." **JOE FOSTER**

Joe attributes the fact that he is visually superior to the reality of his vertical coordinates to his ability to maintain a lean physique. Joe monitors his caloric intake and works hard to burn off the extra energy—no easy feat when he ran Newfield day to day and was on the business breakfast, business lunch, and business dinner circuit as CEO of a NYSE-traded company. "Computers and communication will take all the time you will give them. I read the newspapers regularly and more thoroughly that I ever did while I had a full-time job."

Harriet and Joe Foster

When Joe Foster celebrated his seventy-sixth birthday in July 2010, he conceded that he had slowed down some—Mother Nature had something to do with that. But he is still involved in a host of business and charitable projects, and Foster approaches his current slate of activities the way he pursues his morning runs. "I run about ninety yards, then walk about thirty yards, over and over again, until I get in my two or three miles. I may have redefined running, but I still run."[193]

Joe notes that he has made several venture capital investments since he retired. He's discovered that wildcat drilling is a good deal less risky—and simpler, too.[194] But he says, "I have no intention of starting or leading another E&P company. I may serve on the boards of some smaller private companies where I can provide some good counsel. And I may invest in a prospect or deal that I like from time to time. I have been in the oil and gas business over fifty years, and I've never owned a working interest or an overriding royalty interest. I may rue the day I make such an investment—or I may never make one—but I want the flexibility to consider it." He chides himself on accepting the role of chairman of the audit committee for two public reporting companies—a responsibility that has grown immensely in the wake of Sarbanes-Oxley legislation.

He also finds time to sit on several not-for-profit boards in Houston, and notes that the Memorial Hermann Healthcare System offers even more complexity than the oil business. Joe continues to trek back to his alma mater in College Station while managing several small private foundations and advising two of his children on their businesses.

Joe took up golf at age sixty-five after years of playing tennis, a sport where he excelled. "I broke a score of 100 in golf once about a year ago. It baffles me that I can hit a tennis ball moving [at a mere] sixty to seventy miles per hour but I cannot successfully and consistently strike a stationary golf ball." Joe still skis the Rockies in the winter and hikes the Colorado mountains in the summer.

As I write, Joe Foster still has that fire in his belly.

CHAPTER X
NEW DIRECTIONS AT NEWFIELD

POSTSCRIPT: DAVID TRICE INTERVIEWED, 2007-08

I asked David Trice, "Since Joe formally retired from the board, what do you consider the most important 're-direction' shifts for Newfield under your watch?"

"The changes in the profile of Newfield really started in the late 1990s, many years before Joe retired. The legacy is that, from inception, Newfield was a shallow-water, exploration/acquisition/exploitation focused, Gulf of Mexico independent. After what was clearly the result of a painstaking and painful internal struggle, Joe approached me and Terry and David Schaible and proclaimed: I want you to craft an onshore South Louisiana strategy.[195]

"Onshore south Louisiana was, in Joe Foster's mind, the natural place to advance the firm, since at that time he didn't think we were big enough to sally forth into the very expensive and very long lead time blue depths of the deepwater Gulf of Mexico."

Onshore Louisiana offered the same geology that the technical staff had been working offshore for years—hence, Newfield's technical attention shifted to the northward geography south of Interstate 10 (affectionately known by energy corridor regulars as Eye-10).

The strategic underpinnings of this new initiative for Newfield lay in the knowledge that what the NFX team had done offshore with 3D seismic should be able to be replicated onshore. Trice comments, "It seemed a sure-fire bet that NFX was poised for greatness; a new treasure trove lay at our feet. Like modern Indiana Jones archaeologists, we pored over the maps of the hundreds of old onshore south Louisiana salt domes that hadn't ever been shot with 3D."

With humility, Trice admits, "We were flummoxed; that onshore 3D salt dome initiative, frankly, was not very successful." Newfield may have been practicing "state-of-the-art" geology and engineering, but many earlier pioneers had already picked over the choice cuts. With the benefit of good timing, natural selection, and chance—and perhaps some brilliant early geological calls—thousands of successful and prolific wells already had drained the best petroleum deposits. David reflects, "A legion of explorationists had already picked clean the bones. So many wells had been drilled on salt domes that, it has been said, a blind pig could have found Louisiana's equivalent to Saudi Arabia."[196]

Newfield needed a new direction and now Trice found himself without his mentor, Joe Foster. Fortunately, a catalyst for change already existed in the form of Elliott Pew; he had joined the company in January 1998 and the lion's share of his professional experience had been gained onshore. Pew immediately set out to build an onshore Gulf Coast presence. He'd been deeply involved in the development of the Lower Wilcox Play in South Texas and wanted to get Newfield involved there. Trice recalls, "That was our onshore starting point. We did a joint venture with Shell in the Provident City area. The Shell j.v. got us started—albeit… a really small start."[197]

Trice stresses that over the last decade, the Newfield management team learned that it helps tremendously to start with an acquisition—a toehold position in the basin. For example, Newfield completed the Headington acquisition in January 2000, when Newfield's CEO was changing from Foster to Trice. Trice proclaimed Headington to be the first deal of the new administration, while Joe Foster responded, "Or you could consider it the last deal of the old administration."

Trice states, "The Headington deal provided entry points to three significant plays. It put us into the Vicksburg and the coastal Frio play. Sarita, a large acquisition from Headington, was a big leap for Newfield. We stretched the price deck to a $2.30 per MMBTU gas price to justify that deal! Sarita worked for a number of reasons."[198]

These onshore acquisitions were a key ingredient of change, allowing the company to branch out from the Gulf of Mexico. Wanting more legs on its corporate strategy stool, Newfield tacked on the Tulsa-based Lariat acquisition some fifteen months later. Lariat was the result of deliberate strategic thinking. Notwithstanding its successful new beachhead onshore in South Texas, Newfield still had a very short reserve life, endemic to the shelf plays in the Gulf of Mexico. Newfield's "R/P needle" had hardly budged from a reserve life of four-and-a-half to five years.

This short reserve life caused Newfield to be penalized by investors, as prospective shareowners feared reinvestment risk. Trice notes, "And that's when Lariat popped up in 2001 and we were able to complete a deal on a negotiated basis with Randy Foutch. That put us into a new area which have really broadened and changed the profile of the company over time."[199] Trice comments wryly, "Newfield enjoyed a plethora of 'learning experiences' from that acquisition. After a decidedly slow start, Lariat didn't look like a very good deal 12 months later. Since then Lariat turned out to be a tremendous deal for us, a continuing evolution. About a year and a half later, we bought EEX, our second corporate acquisition. EEX had a significant presence onshore Texas and, while EEX was known for its [lackluster] deepwater strategy, it was these onshore assets that Newfield coveted. Prior to the EEX deal, Newfield was a canvas with only a few blobs of paint on it; EEX allowed us to color in the canvas. That important transaction provided Newfield with a position in Texas. It gave us a small position in East Texas. It gave us a position in the Panhandle. It also gave us some deepwater acreage."[200] In all those areas, Newfield has expanded. "Early on it was a question of getting a toehold; a well conceived acquisition gives you a basis, gives you land—it gives you a presence. Dave Schaible used to call it 'the value of being there.'[201] Our Gulf of Mexico operations are not getting any smaller [*Author's Note:* Newfield's Shallow Water GOM operations were divested in 2007.], but all the growth of the company is coming from layering in new areas— South Texas, Mid-Continent, Rockies."

Lee Boothby coined the term "gas mining" in 2003 to describe the activities of Newfield's

"When Newfield first started drilling in the Woodford Shale, I pumped three or four vertical Woodford wells and I was not impressed. I did not know at the time what the deal was. And we had a meeting one day at McAlester and I asked Lee Boothby just who in hell was in love with that Woodford Shale. And he just kind of smirked. And now I know why he smirked. These were test wells at the time. Everything was tight-holed. When Newfield first started drilling, everybody wanted to know where we were getting the Newfield gas, at what zones. Of course, I loved that. We had something they didn't. And I kept it to myself."

GLEN MARSHAL, WOODFORD FIELD PERSONNEL

Mid-Continent Division. The concept of gas mining at the time was immature, at best. Newfield had some stacked horizons in the Arkoma basin—not at all sexy by themselves. Trice says, "We could drill a well for a little over a million dollars, and we'd get a decent Discounted Cash Flow (DCF) back from the ability to commingle three or more zones in each well. And the main two zones we were looking at, at the time, were the Wapanucka, which is a limestone formation, and the Cromwell sandstone." Newfield had inherited about 4,000 acres in the Lariat acquisition. One Newfield geologist in the Tulsa field office came in with the revelation, "You know, there are a couple of shales right below the Cromwell, and one of those shales, Caney is the geological equivalent of the Barnett Shale, plus there is another shale below that called the Woodford Shale."[202]

Trice recalls Newfield's first key chess move in the Woodford. "We had a section of land with a working interest of 100 percent—a rare 100 percent section. We could drill a well and not have to share information with anybody. While we did not own the royalty interests and had to pay the landowners, we did not have to share the well performance results with any partners. So we drilled a vertical well and tested the Woodford formation at 1.8 MMcf per day—a healthy volume for sure. And that well switched the light on."[203]

Newfield immediately plugged back and completed in the Wapanucka and the Cromwell formations. Trice recollects, "For Lee Boothby, who was running the Mid-Continent office at that time, that well set off his lights, bells, and whistles. Boothby jumped on the next flight to Houston and blurted out, 'I need $15 million to fast-track a leasing program.' That was something Newfield had not historically done. We had not been a trend acreage developer. We had never been a widely aggressive spender in the lease sales in the Gulf. Until this moment, Newfield had prided its heretofore surgical execution of its legacy lease acquisition strategy."[204]

As a neophyte in the land grab game, and one that had never bet "all chips down" on acreage, it comes as no surprise that Newfield encountered fierce internal resistance. Trice allowed Newfield's open debate system to function. The key executives concluded that Newfield was large and well enough established to take the risk; they could visualize the potential to develop and dominate a major developing natural gas shale play. In the Arkoma Basin Newfield's undeveloped acreage portfolio went from 4,000 acres to 25,000, and today is 166,500 net acres and counting. Now Newfield and Woodford are synonymous, as the play went from drilling conventional vertical wells to drilling complicated and expensive horizontals. Trice comments with satisfaction, "As the Woodford play has continued to mature, it just gets better and better."[205]

"If you get there and opportunity beckons, and you have the right people and creative thinking, the world unfolds to receive you every day. We really did launch the new Newfield out of necessity. The acquire/exploit model was tired and competition was ferocious."[206] Trice notes that for many an acquisition, Newfield was outbid. "For deal after deal we were the proverbial day late and a dollar short!"[207] Newfield's bids—well crafted and aggressive, by all conventional measures—were summarily given the thumbs-down, at only two-thirds to three-quarters of the winning bid. Trice recalls his frustrated outburst to his colleagues: "This isn't getting us anywhere!"

Trice retraces an inspirational moment at Newfield: "We had exited yet another data room and—again despondent with our lack of success—we found solace in the insight that new creative competitors had emerged. These folks pushed us to begin thinking differently— natural gas prices had already levitated from $2 to $5. Formations that heretofore were anemic and sub-economic in a $2 world, with better completion technology and higher prices, made a lot of sense. So that was the genesis of the Woodford shale."[208]

Also important, for Newfield, is the Granite Wash play in the Texas Panhandle. "We had picked up a small field in the EEX transaction—the Stiles/Britt Ranch. Newfield applied a new concept to development of the whole series of stacked formations in the Mountain Front Wash play, including the Marmaton Cherokee, the Red Fork, and the Atoka washes. Well, the clear pay zone was the uppermost member, the Granite Wash; this had long been the primary target for most development activity."

"And, again, Lee Boothby and the team out there came back and said, 'Well, you know, there's a 3,000-foot section here. What would happen if we drilled that whole section and started commingling?' You know, going back to the concept of gas mining. So we thought that would work. We bought out our partner in that field for $9 million. Basically we owned nearly 100 percent of the working interest there. The field had reserves of about 20 Bcf at that time. It was making about 2 MMcf/d. That field has produced as high as 100 MMcf and still has proved reserves of 300 Bcf today. We've drilled a lot of wells and it's been a very successful play. Not what we started out to do, you know…when we did Lariat. And those are the two main plays that we've created. But those are resource plays—and we started those plays before the term 'resource play' was being used. They both were…vintage 2003, 2004, and really started taking off in 2005 and 2006. If you go back and think about what we looked like as a company in 1999, we had about 500 Bcf in reserves. When we acquired Lariat in early 2001, we acquired about 240 Bcf of natural gas reserves, making about 60 million a day. Today we have about two trillion cubic feet (Tcf) of reserves in the Mid-Continent region alone. So [that is] twice as big as Newfield was, four times as big as Lariat was; and our production has soared fourfold."[209]

"Again, it was a very different strategy. It was a people deal. We had Lee Boothby, who is a charger and a leader up there. He managed to assemble a team of people who were similarly creative and driven, and made a couple of plays happen."[210]

"While that play was maturing, the next big thing we did was the acquisition of Inland

Resources in the Rocky Mountains in August 2004. With due deference to Newfield's management group, strategic thinking led to that acquisition. Early in 2004, we had lost a series of bids for long life gas reserves; long-lived gas was what everybody wanted."[211]

"But [like] a bunch of kids chasing a soccer ball, we weren't getting…to the [goal] in those deals because other people were offering a lot more money. And we stepped back: 'Well, if everybody wants long-life gas reserves, maybe we ought to take a look at oil.' So we basically started out just by doing a lot of research on oil, and where we thought the price might go. You know, we don't have any inhouse capability to do that. It [took] reading John S. Herold, and Goldman Sachs, and PIRA and other people, to try to get a view. At the time, oil was $25 a barrel. Oil was an out-of-favor commodity in the U.S. It wasn't highly pursued. I can still remember to this day the PIRA Energy Group representatives coming down. I know you've seen the graph of per-capita consumption. It showed the history of the so-called Asian tigers, and how, as those countries started development, their per-capita consumption would soar."[212]

"Then Boothby started plotting China and India on top of that. The light went on, and it was, Wow! This is real. So we convinced ourselves that oil was not going to be a $25 commodity any more. We were really smart and concluded, 'Man, it's gonna trade between $30 and $35 a barrel.'[213] The futures curve had started to levitate higher—the Wall Street consensus was (at that time)…that oil would revert back to $25 a barrel or lower."

"So there was an arbitrage opportunity, plus we gained conviction that oil was, in Martha Stewart's parlance, 'A good thing.' We were beginning to look for an oil acquisition and lo and behold, I answered a call from investment banker, Jim Hansen, who was with First Albany at the time: 'How would you like to look at a really large oil acquisition?' I asked, 'Where is it?' Hansen replied, 'Utah. It's a huge waterflood that needs capital and innovation.'"[214]

Trice's first reaction was to dismiss Hansen. "Well, we're not in Utah and we don't do waterfloods." Then he agreed to evaluate the opportunity. "The reason I reconsiderd, was that it was black oil. If Hansen had called six months earlier, Newfield would have slammed down the phone: 'We're not interested in Utah. We don't do that. We don't do waterfloods.' But we'd had an epiphany and now were open to an oily acquisition. Within days, we had circled a team and dug into research on the Monument Butte field to unlock the secrets of its two billion unrecovered barrels of oil in place."[215] Monument Butte was like an untouched West Texas field; it had never been owned and engineered by a major oil company like ExxonMobil or by a focused independent like Occidental. No one had ever orchestrated a long-term strategic development plan for the field.

It was owned by Inland Resource, which was basically owned by Trust Company of the West (TCW) at the time. Inland had been through its share of ups and downs, but mostly downs—the roller coaster had been going the wrong way. So once oil turned a little bit, TCW was ready to get out. "Newfield liked what we dreamed we might do with two billion barrels of oil potential—an innovative engineering exercise. We probably didn't understand permitting in the Rockies as much as we do now, but that's turned out to be an extraordinary acquisition for us. We've doubled production. Just to have a resource like that, where you are free to be drilling thousands of wells for the next fifteen or twenty years, and continuing to have a production on the incline as opposed to decline, is huge for us."[216] In August of 2004, Newfield was really beginning to add extra legs to the stool.

Spin your leather office chair one revolution, Trice suggests, "Then add the trials the company encountered in 2005 with the evil sisters, Rita and Katrina." The hurricanes left an indelible mark on Newfield—they exposed the vulnerabilities of being heavily weighted to the Gulf of Mexico. Trice's voice moves up a decibel: "Those two storms were extraordinary, and to this day most people don't realize how extreme the damage was and how…these gigantic storms tortured the central Gulf of Mexico oil and gas infrastructure and the people who lived along its coast."[217]

Newfield had great momentum behind it in 2005 and was anticipating major volume gains in natural gas production. Trice laments, "Newfield planned to deliver 265 Bcf to its clients and customers that year. And, wham! The '05 hurricanes took 25 Bcf out of our production for the year and dinged our revenues by $200 million. We had losses in excess of our insurance capacity—all in all, a sobering experience. Looking back to post-KatRita, we said, 'Thank God Newfield reached its grasp outside of the Gulf of Mexico.' And, after those super storms, to this day the Gulf of Mexico E&P has remained in the valuation penalty box by Wall Street."[218]

Under the leadership of Joe Foster and David Trice, Newfield has never sought to court Wall Street analyst favor—or win "most beloved investor relations" trophies. That said, Trice remembers, "We had a lot of long and hard discussions and debates about whether we should divest our Shelf properties in 2005 and through 2006. We did more than kick the notion around a little bit. We didn't move quickly since we were convinced that our shelf assets were at the time worth a substantially greater value than the then-current A&D market would fetch."[219]

Then in 2007, "we jettisoned our legacy assets and—with firm conviction and a smile—sold the shelf."

For the early team (a.k.a. "the old guys") the McMoRan divestiture completed the 1998-2007 cycle. Newfield was no longer a shelf player. Their assets were ten percent international and ninety percent onshore. Fast-forward to 2010: the new nifty Newfield is dominated, production- and asset-wise, by eighty percent Rocky Mountains and the Mid-Continent, with a healthy portfolio of long-lived oil or gas reserves, offering a lot of repeatability.

Newfield benefits from strategic thinking—its management team goes on retreats twice a year to ask, "What do we need to do to adapt to change?" Trice comments, "One thing that is predictable about the oil and natural gas business: it never stays the same. You have to metamorphose constantly to survive and prosper."[220]

MONUMENT BUTTE UPDATE

The acquisition of Inland Resources and the giant Monument Butte field is one of Newfield's finest acquisitions to date. Whether the company was clairvoyant in its view that crude oil could trade in a higher future range than most believed or simply lucky in its timing, is irrelevant today. The bottom line is apparent—this is an oil resource play that any operator would covet in its portfolio of domestic assets.

Since 2004, Newfield has attacked the field on multiple fronts:

Improved recovery of oil in place – With more than two billion barrels of original oil in place, a slight improvement in ultimate recovery translates into millions of barrels… and dollars. Newfield has increased by ten-fold the amount of water injected into the reservoir. Infill drilling results from the nearly 1,000 wells the company has completed over the last six years indicate recoveries of eighteen percent to twenty percent of the oil in place.

Drilling efficiencies – At the time of the acquisition, Monument Butte wells averaged approximately eight days to drill. With optimizations from the workstation to the drilling rig floor, Newfield has reduced average "days to depth" to less than five days. In 2010, Newfield plans to complete an impressive 375 wells with a five-rig program.

Acreage expansions – Over the last several years, Newfield has added more than 70,000 net acres in the Monument Butte area. The northern expansion of the company's footprint takes the greater Monument Butte field to approximately 180,000 net acres.

A decade-long inventory – Newfield's inventory of undrilled locations in the Monument Butte field area today totals nearly 5,000 locations.

Oil growth – Since the field was acquired, Newfield has grown its Monument Butte production from approximately 7,000 BOPD gross to more than 22,000 BOPD gross (as of August 2010). The field is capable of significant oil growth over the next decade as the inventory of undrilled locations is translated into producing wells and cash flow.

Monument Butte, 2008

Perhaps as impressive as the actual results, Newfield's ability to expand beyond its original Gulf Coast roots and enter new basins deserves a mention. In 2004, Newfield had no properties in the Rockies, nor did it have experience in oil resource plays or waterflood developments.

The company's undeniable success is attributable to its founding business principles—talented people, control of operations and the use of the best technologies. Newfield's culture has been effectively "franchised" to multiple new basins and Monument Butte is a great example.

"YOU GUYS ARE OUT OF THE GULF, AREN'T YOU?"

"The deepwater Gulf of Mexico actually is very significant for us today, says Trice. "We'll be investing some $100-$200 million on our annual deepwater inventory for the next five years or more. The company exposed more money in the 2006-2008 Gulf of Mexico lease sales than we had cumulatively spent in Newfield's whole history. The lion's share was devoted to virgin blue-water leases in the deep water.[221]

"When we sold our assets on the GOM Shelf, McMoRan bought the majority of our deep Shelf plays. We retained a small interest. And we did have a small interest in Blackbeard. When McMoRan elected to re-enter and re-drill that well, we and all the other partners that were in that play—and it was a tough decision—elected not to participate in the re-drill. That's when McMoRan brought in a couple of new companies, Energy XXI and Plains Exploration, and they're re-drilling, so prior to that, Exxon had already withdrawn, BP had withdrawn. The remaining players were Petrobras, Newfield, ENI, and BHP. All of those players declined to participate in the re-drill. One of the reasons that we transferred those assets and kept an interest, [was] we thought that if anybody would rejuvenate that play, Jim Bob Moffett (chairman of McMoran) was the guy to do it, and he has. He has also shown that the well could be drilled deeper, safely…which was something that we truly believed could be done. I'm glad to see that happen and I am a big fan. So I hope [the Blackbeard redrill] works."[222]

A new producing play in the shallow water, super deep well, central fairway of the Gulf of Mexico would be good for our country. The Gulf of Mexico is getting pretty skinny these days, from the gas output perspective. The reversal is remarkable, and Newfield has seen it "up close and personal." In 1986, the shallow water fields of the Gulf of Mexico shelf were producing more than 14 Bcf a day, and by 2008, the rate had plummeted by nearly two-thirds, to four or five Bcf a day. It's an extraordinary decline and there's nothing to reverse that, unless Newfield and their colleagues can generate a great new play in the deep sections. Don't forget: super deep successful producing wells may cost $200 million a pop, so it's not a game for shallow-pocket amateurs.

THE DAVID TRICE TRANSITION

"The transition of me going from president to CEO as Joe was moving out of the head jockey seat—no other than Joe could have handled that transition better. And we won't name names, but you can think about some transitions where the founder left but never really left. It was pretty tough on the guy who tried to step into the shoes of the founder. It's something that Joe gave a lot of thought to. He was always just supportive, you know. When I retire I have the 'Joe Foster Game Book' in hand to assist in the transition process."[223]

"Joe's [new venture at] Tudor Pickering Holt looks like something that gained traction because Joe loves a challenge. Remember that Bobby Tudor was at Goldman when Joe

> "Everyone who ever joined Newfield in its early years—each and every individual—joined Newfield because of Joe Foster… [Newfield stood] on the shoulders of Joe Foster's reputation and stature."
>
> **DAVID TRICE**

took Newfield public in 1993. Then in the early years of Newfield's life as a public company, Goldman was our primary investment banker, and Bobby Tudor was our primary contact. Joe always liked to work around bright young people and feel their energy and see their ideas. And Tudor Pickering Holt certainly houses a concentration of young energetic Type-A personalities. I understand that Joe negotiated with Bobby Tudor a commitment to three days a week in the office.…However, the last time I saw Joe he was out on the streets raising money, and that's not a three-day-a-week job."[224]

"Joe has never wavered in being supportive of Newfield. He was a mentor but he never overstepped and he never intervened. He was there to help. Whenever Newfield did a big deal, we would invite him to a dress rehearsal before it was presented to the board. His views were invaluable and made us better managers. Joe always knew how to do things right—very constructive and positive. If he ever second-guessed me, I never knew it. So Joe stayed in that chairman/mentor role until 2004. Then Joe went off the board because there were other things he wanted to do, and some that he didn't want to do anymore. We respected his opinion that it was time to move on.[225]

"Over the past five years, we are always happy when Joe visits us at Newfield headquarters. We have our monthly birthday lunches here at the office and Joe often joins us. I think Joe Foster continues to be extraordinarily proud of Newfield. He continues to be an extremely close friend to me; I'll always treasure that."

A WORTHY MILESTONE – DAVID TRICE'S SPEECH, NEWFIELD FOUNDERS' DINNER 2009

For some of us who were here in the early days, it is difficult to believe that Newfield passed the milestone of its twentieth birthday on Friday, January 2, 2009. So, Happy twentieth Birthday, Newfield! We have come a long way.

We were founded by Joe Foster in January 1989, with just a handful of talented people, a handwritten business plan, and a unified desire to "create something from nothing." We are certainly more than "something" today, and as has always been the case, our best days are ahead of us.

The year 2009 kicks off our third decade as a company. Our first decade was all about creating a focused, successful Gulf of Mexico company. Our rapid growth and undeniable success in this period allowed us to diversify our asset base throughout the second decade and add exciting new plays onshore, in the deep-water, and internationally. We have an enviable portfolio of assets today and we have more plays and prospects than most of us, including me, ever thought possible. Thank you for your hard work and contribution to our success!

Twenty years is a long time in this business. Most of the companies we considered peers in 1989 are now gone—either sold, merged, or simply unable to survive the volatility that characterizes the E&P business. Our success stems from maintaining financial strength and adhering to our business principles. This road map has served us well.

I am certain that 2009 will present many challenges for Newfield and our industry. The global economy has slowed, financial markets are struggling to regain stability, and the sudden drop in commodity prices surprised us all. As for Newfield, we will be just fine. We have a strong balance sheet, valuable oil and gas hedges, and a portfolio of assets that gives us tremendous flexibility in 2009. We are in an excellent position to not only survive, but to emerge stronger, and with the assets in hand, to grow profitably as the demand for oil and gas once again increases. These "cycles" will always be a part of our business.

I look forward to celebrating our achievements in 2009 and am confident that we will continue to find creative ways to add value. I also look forward to Newfield's thirtieth birthday and to see and celebrate the success of the third decade.

LEE BOOTHBY TAKES OVER

On February 5, 2009, David Trice announced his plans to retire as CEO at Newfield's annual meeting in May. Trice stated, "I have had the privilege to serve as Newfield's CEO for more than nine years. It's time for a change. I am a firm believer in term limits. If re-elected to the board of directors at our annual meeting, I will serve as non-executive chairman for a one-year transition. Although I look forward to new challenges and more control over my time, I will miss working day to day with our board, our management team, and the talented people who make Newfield a special place. Together, we have transformed Newfield—from a small company focused in the shallow waters of the Gulf of Mexico into a larger and stronger company with a diversified portfolio and an extensive prospect inventory that will carry us into the future. I am proud of our accomplishments and confident that our new leadership team will take Newfield to the next level."[226]

AN AFTERWORD
BY LEE K. BOOTHBY

What a story! The preceding pages chronicled the early days of Newfield Exploration Company. Colorful stories told through the memories of equally colorful characters, all cast in an industry that is second to none. It makes for quite a tale and I'm confident that it made for an entertaining read for all.

As Chairman of Newfield Exploration today, I was asked by Art Smith to provide an afterword to this book. Anyone that knows Art, will understand that "no" is not an option. Let me first offer my sincere appreciation to Art for his hours of research, interviews, writing, editing and fact-checking. Without his perseverance over the last several years, the wonderful tale that is Newfield would not have been told.

I was honored to be asked to write this afterword and view serving as Newfield's chairman today as an opportunity of a lifetime. I awake each and every day knowing that I have big shoes to fill. But just as it has always been, Newfield is not a story of one or two dynamic leaders. It's a company that derives its success through what I frequently refer to as "Team Newfield." This descriptor covers all of us – from the original twenty-three founders to the nearly 1,300 men and women that work night and day around the globe for Newfield today.

Newfield has a unique culture. It existed on day one and it still thrives today. Our management team dedicates a considerable amount of time to ensuring that we preserve the attributes that made us successful. Joe Foster captured the essence of our culture succinctly in our Founding Business Principles. As any guest to our offices can attest, these Principles are "etched in stone" and prominently displayed in the lobbies of all of our offices in the U.S. and overseas. These Principles are engrained in our corporate DNA.

In this business, change is required for both success and longevity. We have certainly seen great change at Newfield! I think often about our past and how we got to where we are today. For me, it's simple to categorize our history into decades:

Decade 1 – The first decade was all about building a successful company in the shallow waters of the Gulf of Mexico. Joe Foster had a vision and there was not another company with more focus in its operations. Although the stories in this book about the early days contain great humor, getting off the ground was no easy task. Because of my Tenneco roots, I knew most of the founders and carefully followed Newfield's first decade from the outside.

The success was undeniable. The Founders truly created "something from nothing" and amassed an enviable track record of profitable production and reserve growth in the Gulf of Mexico. By the end of the first decade (1998), Newfield was well known and respected in the industry and was one of the largest independent producers in the Gulf. Its people were as well regarded as it assets.

Decade 2 – I was asked by founders David Trice, Dave Schaible, Terry Rathert, Bill Schneider and Joe Foster to join the Newfield family in 1999 – the beginning of the company's second decade. Change was underway at this time. Despite our exemplary track record in the Gulf, we recognized that the shallow Gulf was becoming more mature and that new basins outside of the Gulf would be required to grow. David Trice recognized our challenges and led us successfully into new regions in both the U.S. and overseas.

In the late 1990s, we had a limited experience onshore but were confident that the Newfield model could be successfully transported to new areas. We entered onshore areas through acquisitions in South Texas, the Mid-Continent and the Rocky Mountains. We developed new resources in China and Malaysia. But most importantly, we proved to ourselves, and our shareholders, that we could successfully franchise Newfield. At the end of the second decade, nearly ninety percent of our proved reserves were onshore and we had large, operated positions in both oil and gas plays.

Decade 3 – We recently entered our third decade and I succeeded David Trice as CEO. Today's Newfield looks quite different. Our portfolio of opportunities is deep and we have five business units, all focused on a limited number of plays and driven by the desire to control operations. We understand what has made us successful and will adhere to our roots.

Our portfolio is providing us with competitive advantages today. We have the flexibility to shift our investments to oil or gas plays, depending on commodity prices and resulting margins. Newfield is in great shape today, but we didn't get here by accident.

There are many sports fans in our company, including myself. Oftentimes, we speak with sports analogies to emphasize our key points. As I was preparing for our annual Founders' Dinner in 2010, I re-read the previous twenty-two speeches written by Foster, Trice, Schaible, Packer and a host of other leaders in our organization. One particular story stood out and as Joe is fond of saying, "good things deserve repeating."

Lee K. Boothby (left) David A. Trice (right)

FOUNDER'S DINNER
MAY 7, 1998

In his remarks, Joe Foster referenced the Boston Celtic's legendary basketball all-star Kevin McHale. He stressed how McHale's generation was motivated by all the greats who played before them.

"We are pushed by our past," Joe said. "This is why we have these dinners… one night a year we come together to honor those who got Newfield up and running and to reflect upon how far we've come. We are here tonight to be pushed by the past."

That quote resonated with me. All of us that comprise Team Newfield today are pushed by our past. We work to uphold our operational excellence and maintain the intergrity earned by all of our people, past and present.

I used this story in my 2010 Founders' Dinner remarks, and closed my talk that evening by saying:

"Tomorrow, we will be pulled by our future."

I believe that the full story on Newfield is far from finished. These early chapters chronicle the development of a lasting culture, the assembly of top-notch employees and the creation of an enviable asset base. Because of this, we will always be "pushed by our past." It's imperative that we remember where we came from and acknowledge the vital elements that attributed to our success.

Today, we are all pulled by our future.

APPENDIX A
FOSTER'S PHILOSOPHIES

YOU CAN'T WIN IF YOU'RE NOT AT THE TABLE

Joe Foster learned this truth from shooting craps, not from geology or engineering: whether it's exploration or acquisition, "You can't win if you're not at the table." Joe notes that legendary golfer Ben Hogan nailed it with his wry observation, "I've noticed that the luckiest golfers are the ones who practice the most."

"One of the secrets of being lucky is to give yourself enough chances to be lucky, to roll the dice, or flip the coin, enough times to avoid gambler's ruin. To be successful in exploration, you cannot stay on the sidelines and evaluate. You have to be in the middle of the fray, drilling holes and testing ideas. You have to be willing to be wrong a lot to be right every now and then. You have to be willing to expend a lot of time and effort on prospects that never get drilled and on wells that are dry when drilled."

Foster reflects on the inspirational words of the poet Randall Jarrell: "A good poet is one who, in a lifetime of standing out in thunderstorms, manages to get struck by lightning [i.e., with the inspiration to write a great poem] four or five times."

"To a greater extent than we'd like to admit, that's what we do in exploration: stand out in thunderstorms, managing—with the geological and geophysical tools we have, as best we can—to get struck by lightning. Exploration is somewhere between shooting craps and poetry."

As a bedrock business principle, Newfield looks at every potential acquisition that is reasonably available within its geographical focus areas. "At the minimum, we may learn something new or meet some people who can help us on the next acquisition. And, frequently, we learn something new and different."[172] Newfield has humility and recognizes that by no means does it have a patent on all the good ideas.

> "Joe was familiar with all of Tenneco's far-flung operations—from shipbuilding, automotive parts, packaging, to fruits and nuts and farming. What Joe concluded, and shared with us at Newfield, was…that anything at Tenneco that was successful had some notion of focus about it, whether it was a product line where they were dominant, or a geographic area where they were better than everybody else. Some notion of focus was instrumental to success." **DAVID TRICE**

"A lot of managers go through their business lives and never stop to record their key observations – to separate the business wheat from the chaff. Joe remains a great observer and teacher. I didn't know what a flat organization was until Joe told me, and that basically meant Joe was here and everybody else was here. From the outset of Newfield, Joe always preached the gospel of focus—very few people talked about focus as a business principle in 1989." **DAVID TRICE**

FOCUS WORKS!

During his years at Tenneco, Foster observed that the one thing the successful business units all had in common was focus. On the granite tablet that graces Newfield's headquarters (as well as all of its regional offices), "Focus" is prominent among the company's seven famed Founding Business Principles. Foster singles out focus as being critically important to business success. "The focus may be in a market segment or a product line or geographic area or geologic province, but every successful business has some strong and identifiable area of focus about it."[173]

Reflecting on the many great oil finders he has known, Joe Foster describes an explorationist who embodies the essence of focus: William Kreps, a geologist Joe worked with early on. Kreps later left Tenneco and spent the rest of his working life in Lincoln County, Oklahoma. "Bill knew every well, every lease, every log in the county, and what he did not have in his file, he had in his head." Foster believes that such an intense focus stimulates creativity and inspires geological interpretation. "This focus let Bill see things others did not see because he knew things others did not know."[174]

According to Foster, the company's success in property acquisitions and generating compelling economics is due to focus areas that Newfield "knows like the back of our hand" and which benefit from the continuity of its people and their efforts. Conversely, NFX's setbacks and failures have been in areas where the company lacked local knowledge—and "management didn't have the good sense—and lack of hubris—to go out and hire it or buy it."

Foster notes the frustration of being focused on getting a deal done but finding that an important counterparty is more interested in knocking a few strokes off his handicap. In such business transactions, progress can be excruciatingly slow. Newfield fights calendar drag as if it were a threatening dragon blocking passage to the fair maiden in the castle—constantly pushing for closure, pressing to break the forward calendar and beat externally-imposed mileposts or deadlines. Newfield seeks out that inspired individual—the counterparty champion who sees the venture as a win-win deal and is just as eager as Newfield to celebrate achievement at the long-awaited dinner that celebrates closure.

"Pushing for closure is just one element of focus. I can assure you that whether we are talking about generating a prospect or evaluating an opportunity—or getting a deal done—focus works."

"Joe would recite his core business principles—the ones that we have carved in stone in the reception area of every Newfield office. Key among those principles is focus and the notion that we were not in this for a quick buck. Newfield was built on bedrock—to create something…create value, create jobs, and have lasting value. That sounded great in 1989, and I'm sure there were skeptics back then when we didn't have anything. But the record speaks for itself—it all eventually turned out to be absolutely true." **DAVID TRICE**

FAILURE IS NEVER FATAL

One of Foster's strongest and most persistent characteristics as an oilman is his stoic acceptance of failures and setbacks. Success often follows failure, and Foster has long viewed drilling dry holes as Babe Ruth did strikeouts. Like the Babe, Foster has no fear of setting "whiff" records of failure in the pursuit of home-run successes.

This anonymous quote is a favorite of Foster's: "Failure is *never* fatal and success is *never* final." Foster recalls the fate of Eastern Airlines, whose slogan was, "We earn our wings every day." Only Eastern's bleached bones remain—in the form of aircraft sold to other survivors and a few collectible decks of blue playing cards now found on eBay. In Joe's words, "Eastern's management and employees forgot to earn their wings on a daily basis, and the company died when Eastern's vision was lost."

THE DISCIPLINE OF DEBT

On Wall Street, a company's ratio of long-term debt to permanent equity is termed "leverage;" in UK vernacular it is "gearing." The oil and gas industry loves debt and the historical record attests to many abuses of the privilege of borrowing. Joe's experience at Tenneco left an indelible imprint on his business philosophy and on the Newfield of today.

Joe felt Tenneco had sold a true value-adding organization because it had too much debt, and its oil company offered the only salvation for that debt sinkhole. Too much debt has caused heartache for many people, companies, and, as was seen in Houston, whole communities.[175]

In a few short months, Tenneco disappeared as a household name in Houston because its chairman and board of directors made some big bets on non-energy businesses—mainly

"A little debt is healthy and necessary. Too much is debilitating—and deadly. Bankers will always loan you more money than is healthy. Take Mr. Micawber's advice to David Copperfield: 'Annual income twenty pounds, annual expenditure nineteen nineteen and six, result happiness. Annual income twenty pounds, annual expenditure twenty pounds ought and six, result misery. The blossom is blighted, the leaf is withered, the god of day goes down upon the dreary scene, and—and in short, you are forever floored.'" **JOE FOSTER**

farm equipment—using the debt capacity created by its energy subsidiaries.

Bankers make much larger fees from their distressed clients than they ever do from solvent companies. Economists like New York University's Edward Altman and Roy Smith stress that there is an inflection point in financial leverage at which a company becomes exposed to distress costs. When a company breaks loan covenants, banks charge ever-higher interest and fees, and agency costs from increased costs of compliance and legal expenses can quickly drain an organization's lifeblood.

TWO PERCENT BETTER THAN THE COMPETITION

Early in his career at Tennessee Gas, Joe Foster and his colleagues went through an exercise that helped to drive home the value of modest incremental improvement. Foster sums it up: "To succeed in the E&P business, you don't have to be a lot better than the competition—to thrive, you just have to be a little bit better, across the board."

The Tenneco upstream executives asked themselves: What would happen…

…if our explorationists managed risk such that our success ratio on wildcats was just two percent higher than industry average?

…if our drillers kept drilling and completion costs were just two percent below industry average for both wildcat and development wells?

…if we could reduce the time from discovery to the date of first production by just two percent?

…if production engineers held lifting costs two percent below industry average and got two percent more production, due to less downtime or higher rates?

…if reservoir engineers managed reservoir and production behavior to obtain a two percent higher recovery efficiency?

…if we could achieve a two percent higher success rate on development wells?

And, finally, what would happen if we could obtain oil prices that are two percent higher than the industry average? By intelligent use of forward markets, even a company as small and non-integrated as Newfield has the potential to realize better-than-average prices.

It doesn't seem a Herculean task to obtain a mere two percent improvement in any of the above steps.

But two percent better at every step in the E&P process begets a miracle: enhancement to net present value of 30 percent or more, depending on the production profile of the property. In short-life Gulf of Mexico fields, net present value can be dramatically enhanced with a two percent improvement at each step in the value chain!

This approach to cost control goes a long way toward enhancing acquisition economics—both when making the bid and then, after you succeed, in making it work.

Such attention to detail in cost control cannot be over-emphasized; Foster stresses that there is a lot of blocking and tackling involved in a successful acquisition effort. Newfield engineers are often accused of overworking the reserve analysis and going into infinite detail. "We look behind the seller's estimates and generally at the underlying data to come up with our own estimates. We make a comprehensive upside study. We get operations people involved to chase down potential cost savings. We scrutinize abandonment liabilities. We develop strategies to manage the price risk. We don't bet on unevaluated upside. We don't value statistical reserves. We don't make a price bet that we don't at least partially hedge. We do pay for upside we see. And we do assign option value to properties that lead us somewhere. We are aware that detailed evaluations sometimes—maybe often—result in losing bids. In any event, we have a firm opinion of what the value is and what our bid should be. I never view Newfield as being overly conservative, even though we were probably overly detailed."

Newfield heeds the investment advice of Berkshire Hathaway's Warren Buffett: "It is better to buy wonderful properties at a fair price than to buy fair properties at a wonderful price."

DEALS ARE LIKE STREETCARS

Joe Foster and the legendary H.L. Hunt share a common perspective: "Deals are like streetcars. There is always another one coming along." Pressured to buy a hot deal, Hunt reportedly responded, "That's OK. We'll pass on that one. In my experience, the money always runs out before the great deals do."

Foster stresses the necessity of patience and reason. For Newfield, there is no acquisition or prospect that "we *have* to attain." Foster recounts, "I went to the 'last big Gulf of Mexico Lease Sale' in 1970. As it turns out, there was another 'Last Great Sale' in 1972. Then, lo and behold, the oil industry witnessed a whole series of 'Final Best Sales' in the 1980s, as area-wide leasing was introduced by the Minerals Management Service. When less than 300-foot depth shelf prospects were becoming increasingly competitive, along came deepwater leasing in the 1990s. Then we turned to the exceptional opportunities existing in the ultra-deep leases now available in the twenty-first century." Go to New Orleans for the next MMS lease sale and listen to the sealed-bids reading—no doubt, Newfield Exploration will be among the leaading competitors.

Joe is skeptical when told, "This is our last opportunity. We really need to press here, because we'll never get this chance again." He responds, "Maybe. But we'll get other chances just as good, and at a price we like. Our motto at Newfield has always been, 'Bid what we think it's worth and let the chips fall where they may.'"

OPERATE ON THE "RAGGED EDGE"

It's clear that Joe Foster has an aversion to debt. Joe's Tenneco experience with an overleveraged balance sheet left an indelible and ugly imprint. A good oil and gas company was destroyed to rescue an also-ran farm equipment (J. I. Case) and automobile parts (Monroe and Walker brands) and packaging conglomerate. A great oil and gas company was sold because it was profitable and because it was salable. Foster's view is that Tenneco was victim to the Three Ds: 1) Debt (too much); 2) Dog(gy assets that weren't divested); and 3) Dividends (that sapped operating cash flow for reinvestment).

Beyond his strict aversion to excessive debt, Joe is conservative at heart and worries a lot about the downside. However, there is a point beyond which Joe fights his natural conservative inclination—say, once the trousers are buttoned, the belt is buckled, and the suspenders are secured. Foster stresses, "To be a success in any business, you must operate ninety percent of the time at the ragged edge between chaos and order, between too little and too much, between comfort and anxiety, if not outright fear."

The oil and gas business is complex, always challenging the rapid transition from order to chaos. Foster looks to life on the boundary between them. "Stay too far back on the order side, and no progress is made. Get too far on the chaos side, and all is lost." Joe is a fan of Suzanne Farrell, the great ballerina. Farrell commented after a virtuoso performance that she was "always off balance, yet always secure."

Foster reminisces, "When I was happiest and when Newfield made the most progress [we were] walking—running—down that ragged edge: the borderline between comfort and confusion."

NO APOLOGIES – BUSINESSES MUST MAKE A PROFIT!

Borrowing from the game book of all great capitalists—from Ben Franklin to John D. Rockefeller to Warren Buffett—Joe reminds us all that the ultimate role of any business is to make a reasonable profit: "We should never forget [that] and we should never apologize."

Oil and gas companies do not win many "most loved and admired" awards from J.D. Power & Associates. The oil industry continues to suffer from the imperious public relations of such stalwarts as Unocal's Fred Hartley and Exxon's Larry Rawl.

After a major offshore oil spill in 1969 at a Unocal platform in California's picturesque Santa Barbara channel, Hartley asked memorably, "What's all the buzz over a few dead seagulls?"

And after the notorious Exxon Valdez spill of March 24, 1989, Larry Rawl and his legion of imperial executives sat immobile in the majestic Exxon headquarters on Manhattan's Avenue of the Americas. It took two weeks for a ranking Exxon officer to get off his duff and fly to Prince William Sound to see firsthand what was going on. After the damage was done, no amount of Madison Avenue hoopla could ever atone for Exxon's stone-faced inaction. (Total cost to Exxon for the Valdez spill, cleanup, and legal morass: $2.5 billion—$9,542 per barrel spilled, or $227 per gallon. Some 260,000 barrels—eleven million gallons—of ANS (Alaska North Slope) crude was lost. The Exxon Valdez clean-up procedure involved 1,400 vessels, eighty aircraft, and more than 11,000 people at the peak of activity during the summer of 1989.)

Joe reminds us that with every well drilled, there are risks of oil spills and gas leaks. Oil and gas companies exist to find and produce new resources of petroleum, striving to make a profit. Whether a profit is ever recorded, exploration and production companies like Newfield invest in land (lease payments and delay rentals), in "Geological and Geophysical activities" (seismic), and in "General and Administrative." A prospect is created, drilling contractors are hired, and drilling commences after proper site preparation.

Anyone who has ever invested in drilling a wildcat well knows the meaning of the term "completion point." A crucial point is reached when the exploration well has plumbed its total depth objective and a series of wireline logs have been run. Promising wells that have encountered oil or natural gas "shows" during the drilling process, or that have encouraging logs, are "completed" through a process whereby a long string of metal casing is inserted into the well in preparation for a production test (and ultimately for the well to be put on production). Completing a well adds 30 to 40 percent to its final cost. Therefore, many unencouraging wells are plugged prior to the expense of completion. Of course, in such "non-complete decision points," the operator and investors may never know whether an exceptional producing zone has been overlooked. There are great examples of uncompleted wells that were re-entered and tested—and some of these turned out to be extraordinary discoveries.

Foster makes his case for the key role that the oil and gas industry plays in the success of the U.S. economy and its citizens. "In the day-to-day struggle to find, develop, and produce hydrocarbons, taxes are paid by oil and gas companies and their employees. Charitable contributions are made. Auxiliary businesses are established. A lot of mouths get fed. A lot of kids get educated. Tens of millions of vehicles get filled with gasoline. And millions of homes get heated and cooled. Let's not forget that what we do is important to society. And we can only do it if we make a profit."

THERE'S NO INSULT TO YOUR OFFER

While Newfield will regularly decline to evaluate properties that obviously "don't fit its geographic focus," the company frequently bids on select oil or natural gas assets where success, its executives realistically concede, is a remote possibility. "Early on in Newfield, I would not approve a bid on a property because I thought that our valuation (and the odds for success) was so low that it would insult the seller," Joe reminisces.[137]

Bottom line: David Schaible convinced Joe there was little downside to an insult. "We made the bid, we were at the table, we won. As luck would have it, this great new acquisition provided the impetus for Newfield Exploration's initial public offering."

Over the years, Newfield has turned to acquisitions to provide about a third of its reserve additions and these new reserve purchases have been consistent. In its early history (1990-94) Newfield began to recognize the maturity of the shallow water Gulf of Mexico. The company set out to diversify its asset base. The first logical step was onshore Louisiana; the geology was the same: water replaced by sand and rocks. Then in 1995, the company initiated onshore activities on the Gulf Coast of Texas. In 1997, the company acquired a meaningful thirty-five percent interest in an exploration venture in Bohai Bay, offshore China. International activity was stepped up in 1999 when the company acquired two producing oil fields offshore Australia and agreed to drill six high-potential wildcats. A sizable $140 million package of gas properties in South Texas was brought into the Newfield fold in 2000.

Then in 2001, Newfield acquired privately held Lariat Petroleum for $333 million, bringing a new core producing area and 256 Bcfe of proved natural gas reserves in the MidContinent Basin. The Lariat deal was followed by the company's largest (at that time its largest to date) acquisition of a publicly traded E&P company, EEX Corporation, for $650 million. EEX brought a major stakehold in South Texas gas and a portfolio of deepwater GOM assets.

In August 2004, Newfield acquired Inland Resources, a private independent producer, adding 326 Bcfe of proved oil reserves. More important, the $575 million transaction brought potential reserves of more than 1 trillion cubic feet of gas equivalent (Tcfe) into Newfield's fold. That one mega-deal increased the company's reserve life to seven years, from five, and upgraded the blended assets to thirty percent oil. Newfield now had a meaningful oil business in the Rocky Mountains.

> In 1999, only five percent of Newfield's reserves were located outside of the Gulf of Mexico. A decade later, as December 31, 2009, eighty percent of the company's reserves are onshore in longer-lived basins.

WHAT HAVE YOU DONE FOR NEWFIELD LATELY?

Newfield's challenge today is no longer survival, but sustainable profitable growth. Joe Foster never has been able to rest and Newfield doesn't rest today: the Newfield team is obsessed with innovating, learning, and creatively working to perform better.

The great oil and gas fields discovered from 1920 to 1970, the halcyon years of the oil industry, remain the anchor of domestic petroleum today. These behemoths—Elk Hills, Yates, Midway Sunset, Hugoton, Kelley Snyder, East Texas, Seminole, Wasson—continue to provide significant oil and gas supplies to the cheap-energy addicts of North America. But these fields are old and tired, and relentless annual production declines are inevitable and insurmountable. Even Alaska's gem, the North Slope Prudhoe Bay field, has fallen to less than twenty percent of the peak production it attained in 1988.

Today, newly discovered oil and natural gas fields may be depleted (eighty percent of ultimate recovery) in only three to five years, thanks to continuing advancements in oilfield technology. These advances are partly due to the dynamic leadership of the oil service industry by the likes of Baker Hughes, Halliburton, and Schlumberger. It takes a continual stream of new prospects and opportunities wedded to new technological advances to keep oil and gas companies going and going.

Joe believes strong company leadership is a serious responsibility. When he left Newfield in 2001, he left it in the hands of David Trice, Terry Rathert, David Schaible, Bill Schneider, et al. He also adamantly believes that every employee has a reciprocal responsibility to deliver his best each and every day. Managers should be able to ask, "What have you done for the company lately?" and expect a good answer.[176]

> "To be a good businessman, you must aspire to be a good businessman. Never rest on your laurels…to qualify to be on other companies' lists for farmouts and acquisitions, you must be a solid, reasonable, and ethical person—someone people want to deal with—every day." **JOE FOSTER**

> "We all sit around the table just as we did as a company fifteen years ago and look at each other; and when somebody is falling behind, everybody around the table is thinking 'Hey, you need to get this done.' Every team has its own targets, its own goals. The same accountability that we had as an organization fifteen years ago exists healthily within Newfield today." **DAVID SCHAIBLE**

TEAMWORK AND DIVERSITY

Joe B. Foster built Newfield with a strong foundation of independent thinkers who had academic training and experience in multiple disciplines. He felt the best prospects were generated by geologists, geophysicists, and engineers working together, applying different mindsets and different technologies. Even the gifted oil finder—maybe especially the gifted oil finder—is more effective when he works with a team.[183] The teams were valuable not just in exploration but in the Mergers & Acquisitions & Divestitures (M&A&D) business as well. The best acquisition evaluation efforts were naturally created by teams. And the exploitation plans that become reality once the properties are acquired were always team efforts.

From the beginning of Newfield, Foster believed that as a risk management tool, it was important to bring in other people's money. To achieve higher levels of technical analysis, Newfield still finds it helpful to work with partners and vendors. The traditional behavior in the U.S. upstream business is that prospects and leases have divided interests, and Newfield usually must work with others. Landmen—the professionals who negotiate leasing arrangements with everyone from the U.S. Government's MMS to rural mom-and-pop farmers and ranchers—are the lubricants and facilitators of grassroots exploration. They bridge the idea people and the commercial people, the landowners and the land developers, and the companies that should partner together on a prospect or transaction.

> "If you are smart, you get the geologists and engineers out of the 'potential trade transactions' early and don't let the lawyers in too soon. You make sure management really understands what the deal is, what the sticking points are, and get their support. You also make sure all the appropriate people in both organizations are aware of the full array of alternative opportunities out there. The exploration and production industry is a unique business: our companies are competitors, but we are just as often partners. We have much to gain by working together. Once the lease sales and property auctions are held, most of the things we do in this business involving others are not zero-sum games." **JOE B. FOSTER**

Betty Smith has done very well as an investor in Newfield over the years. To this day, she is nagged by friends who whine, "I can't believe you didn't tell us to invest in Newfield back then. You should have forced us to buy some shares." Betty has a standard response: "I'm not Warren Buffett, but I think they put you in jail for that [hard-sell stock-broking]." A friend from Tenneco called Betty the other day and said, "You know, I could have kicked myself when Newfield hit [the equivalent of] $160 per share. Nonetheless, it's nice to have a rich friend."

NEWFIELD'S CONTRIBUTIONS TO HIGHER EDUCATION

Significant economic value accrued at Newfield Exploration as a public company under Joe B. Foster's watch. In the six years he served as CEO from year-end 1993 (the company went public in late 1993), some $505 million of true value was created at Newfield. Consider this simple math: the original value of the company's proved reserves was $159 million. Six years later in a flat oil-pricing environment it was $913 million. Newfield's $408 million of net investment was the residual capital plowed into upstream capital projects over the 1994-1999 time period that was not funded by operations-generated cash.

> "It is irrefutable that 'Little old Newfield' has done a lot more for higher education than many well-known benefactors." **JOE FOSTER**

> "We have to give Joe all the credit for the foundation built at Newfield; that's what makes it work." **DAVID TRICE**

Also consider Newfield's stock price performance from its original IPO. It is impressive that with few setbacks, the company has managed to strongly grow its per-share Appraised Net Worth. Also, the stock market appreciation of the company's shares has been exceptional, closely tracking gains in Appraised Net Worth.

The long-term record shows that the biggest winning investors in Newfield have been the endowment funds of the University of Texas, Yale, Duke, Dartmouth, and private equity investors Warburg Pincus. These entities have realized and unrealized gains of many hundreds of millions on the early seed capital investment in Newfield. At year-end 2008, the Warburg Pincus Group still owned 4.8 million NFX shares, worth more than $200 million.

[*Author's Note:* Please see the table on pages 212 and 213; it documents growth from 1989 to 2009]

APPENDIX B
DALE ZAND'S REFLECTIONS ON FOSTER AND NEWFIELD

DALE ZAND – STRATEGY CONSULTANT, INVESTOR, AND NFX BOARD MEMBER

Dale Ezra Zand trained as an electrical engineer prior to his service in the Navy during World War II. He joined a small industrial firm after completing an MBA at New York University in Manhattan. Zand excelled in business academics, sold his share in the industrial company, received his doctorate and joined the faculty of the prestigious NYU business school, then located in the heart of Wall Street.

Zand gravitated to microeconomics, business strategy, organization design and leadership behavior and the nascent field of strategic consulting. "Initially, I consulted to the brokerage and banking industries and then branched into consulting with chemical, paper and food companies. I worked with senior executives to clarify goals, strategy, and structure to improve a firm's strategic position and operational performance."

Zand began a long association with Tenneco's E&P company through the recommendation of a former Union Carbide executive who worked at Tenneco. After top Tenneco E&P

JOE'S PROBLEM-SOLVING TALENT

From Dale Zand's standpoint, one of Joe Foster's key managerial attributes is his great talent for problem solving. Zand says, "I think that Foster would agree that he becomes energized when confronting problems. Foster handles stress well, deliberates creatively, comfortably enlists the help of others, persists and does not hesitate to make decisions when he runs into difficult situations." Zand recalls the dark days when Joe had the Tennessee Gas Transmission natural gas pipeline in his portfolio. It was an inherited problem: the trunkline faced a daunting overhang of "take or pay" financial obligations that ran to several billion dollars. "We spent many sessions talking about how Tennessee Gas could deal with the 'take or pay' nightmare. Then there were periods when commodity prices were down, and E&P was not really doing well. But Joe's a creative, persistent realist. We all face periods when seemingly insurmountable business problems roll in like a huge tidal wave; but Joe Foster manages to ride the wave and reach the beach with good solutions." **DALE ZAND**

executives interviewed a number of well known national consulting firms, they chose executive coach, lone operator Dale Zand. While at first reluctant to tackle the required New York/Houston commute, he immediately hit it off with the team at E&P. "I got to know Joe Foster when he was president of Tenneco E&P; Joe B. was clearly an unusually competent problem solver and an extremely effective, respected leader." Zand also recalls his first meeting with Phil Oxley, EVP, who told Joe, "You know, it's like being on a psychiatrist's couch with this fellow, Zand. I would feel comfortable telling him anything, business or personal."

Some E&P executives were concerned about the complex structure of the large offshore division, which generated half of the company's revenues. It had additional layers of management and specialists in contrast to the smaller, nimble onshore divisions. Other executives said the division was efficient, leave it alone—'It ain't broke, so don't fix it.' Although E&P executives understood that offshore and onshore activities might require different strategies, structures and performance measures, they had strong, unresolved differences about the right structure for the offshore division. Zand elaborates, "To net it down, however, we eventually discovered that offshore had become extremely production-oriented and needed to pay more attention to exploration, which ultimately was the key driver of success and future growth of the business."

When Zand was initially engaged, he learned that key E&P executives wanted to restructure offshore into two or three smaller, separate divisions. He challenged the executives: "What's magic about dividing Offshore into two or three divisions? To determine what an organization's structure should be, we need to understand how well its strategy fits its likely future environment; the key is to uncover and analyze conditions of poor future fit and then build a sound relationship between the strategy, the structure and the expected environment." [*Author's Note:* Zand later authored a noteworthy article on strategic and structural change in an E&P company - that is; "Strategic Renewal: How an Organization Realigned Structure with Strategy," STRATEGY & LEADERSHIP, VOL. 37 NO. 3 2009, pp. 23-28, Q Emerald Group Publishing Limited, ISSN 1087-8572 j Reference DOI 10.1108/10878570910954619].

As a solo consultant working alone, Zand explained that E&P would have to actively participate in all aspects of the relationship—designing the study, gathering data, analyzing findings, generating solutions and implementing change. Also, E&P would have to provide all needed resources as he was not bringing a team of young MBAs and was not interested

JOE IS BEDROCK TRUSTWORTHY

"Joe is a remarkably supportive individual who encourages the professional growth of people. He has an uncanny knack for making people feel comfortable in the most difficult situations; Foster can confront and discuss difficult things without being punitive or vindictive, or making other people feel unworthy. Joe is just bedrock trustworthy—the kind of guy who can stand on a corner in downtown Houston, and people who know him will come up and say, "Joe, here's several hundred thousand dollars. Take it and invest it in whatever you want. Someday, when you have time, let me know what you did with it." **DALE ZAND**

RATHERT/SCHAIBLE/TRICE – A TON OF TALENT

"Terry Rathert went through a wonderful process of growing with the company. He was a sharp economic planner at Tenneco and grew into a key financial and corporate executive at Newfield. Joe Foster has an incredible gift for finding talented people. People say, 'I don't know how Joe does it, but he seems to be able to identify talent.' David Schaible, a young petroleum engineer at Tenneco E&P, was thinking of going to the Harvard Business School program when Newfield was being founded. Joe recruited Dave by explaining 'You will learn more and have more opportunity with Newfield than you will get out of the Harvard Business School program.' And he was right. Dave rose to the challenge and became a superb executive who grew with the job and the company. That's the marvelous thing about Newfield people. They enter at the early stage of a startup and adapt to the demands of the organization as it gets larger and more structured and faces new problems at each stage of growth. Generally, however, the E&P business tends to attract strong, independent, entrepreneurial people. As their organization grows and requires more interdependence, structure, new skills and delegation, many often resist fiercely. Their independent personality doesn't allow them to adapt. Newfield, remarkably, recruits and retains competent people who don't have a problem adapting to growth."

"The loss of Dave Schaible (to cancer) was a tragedy. Dave had a knack for finding deals, farms-ins, farm-outs, and so on. He was destined for the top ranks of Newfield. It's hard to avoid singing the praises of Newfield people. Joe was also very astute in identifying David Trice. Part of Joe's talent is to be positive and receptive. Although Dave Trice left Newfield to head an overseas-focused oil and gas company, Joe thought so highly of him that he welcomed him back—a boomerang hand so to speak—and Trice hit the ground running and eventually succeeded Joe as CEO." **DALE ZAND**

"Bob Waldrup is a very competent production manager—in the tradition of hands-on command and control, expert knowledge, close supervision, feeling personally responsible for any foul up, and reluctance to delegate. When the company was small and he could monitor and regularly visit the platforms and handle the production decisions, he made a great contribution to Newfield. But as the organization grew there was increasing concern about the development of people below Bob. What if, so to speak, Bob was 'hit by a truck when he stepped off the curb,' were people sufficiently developed and aware of what was going on to be able to carry on the myriad challenges of the production function? Newfield has great respect for Bob and his contribution—as someone competent and enthusiastically dedicated to the production function. But the issue of developing others and delegating decisions had to be resolved, and, I believe, ultimately it was an important factor in Bob separating from Newfield." **DALE ZAND**

in endless "analysis paralysis"—that is, doing work that would require more and more work, as some consulting firms do to maintain revenues.

Phil Oxley remarked, "You're making us do all the work." "You are right," Zand replied. "I'll provide guidance about what to look for and how to look, but E&P people will do most of the work. That way you will understand everything that's happening and there will be full commitment to implementing any change. If I do all the work and write a report, you'll spend your time arguing about the report and you'll still be in the same stalemate as today." Zand's liaison to E&P was Larry Augsburger, director of human resources, a fellow Zand describes as "serious, dedicated and highly respected. He smoothed the way through the whole consulting process."

The strategic restructuring of Tenneco E&P Offshore launched Zand's relationship with Tenneco and Joe B. Foster; additional assignments followed with E&P and Joe as he moved up to become EVP of Tenneco and a member of the corporate board of directors. To resolve a debt crisis of the parent Tenneco Company, CEO James Ketelsen, and the board sold the energy upstream and downstream businesses in 1988. Professor Zand was not involved in that decision, however, he wrote an insightful analysis of the breakup of Tenneco in an article titled, "Managing Enterprise Risk: Why a Giant Failed." (Reference: STRATEGY & LEADERSHIP, VOL. 37 NO. 1 2009, pp. 12-19, Q Emerald Group Publishing Limited, ISSN 1087-8572 DOI 10.1108/10878570910926016.)

Zand recalls, "My consulting relationship was with Joe Foster and the energy business. I had met Ketelsen and the CFO of Tenneco, but had no consulting relationship with them. Joe, as EVP of Tenneco, was the head of corporate planning in addition to the energy business. Zand also had relationships with two very competent executives, Steve Chesebro and Chuck Shultz, who, as part of their development, did a rotation in corporate planning. Both Chesebro and Shultz went on to very successful careers after Tenneco E&P. Chesebro rose to run Pennzenergy (the E&P division of Pennzoil) before it was acquired by Devon Energy in 1999. Shultz became CEO of Gulf Canada (acquired by Conoco in 2001) and later served on the Newfield board.

Interviews with many executives, including Foster, Chesebro, and Shultz, and analysis of decades of company data, provided information for Zand's article on Tenneco ("Why a Giant Failed"). He credits those executives plus contacts with several Tenneco outside directors for providing background on the various options considered by the holding company board. Zand reflects, "It ultimately boiled down to one feasible, realistic financial option—sell the only fungible asset sufficient to deal with the crushing debt overhang— Tenneco E&P. Ultimately it was a decision born out of necessity and desperation."

Dale Zand invested in the original Newfield Exploration startup, and again during the difficult period leading up to going public in late 1993. There was a bumpy stretch when capital was very tight and although Newfield was not distressed, it was definitely struggling. "I invested in both the first and second round of private equity finance," Zand says, "and have kept practically all of my original NFX stock, which has done very well."

Dale Zand joined the Newfield Exploration board of directors in 1995, two years after NFX stock made its public debut. Zand notes, "Prior to joining the NFX board, I did some consulting with the start-up company 1989-1994; my inputs, however, were hardly earthshaking. After I was elected to the board, I concluded that serving as a consultant while also a director, was a conflict of interest and potentially confusing to NFX people. I was wearing two hats—would Newfield managers feel comfortable telling me, as a consultant, about problems and issues? They would wonder what might be done with that information when I put on my hat as a director. I decided to clarify the relationship by withdrawing from consulting with the company. I don't think Joe was pleased, but I felt that the situation was too ambiguous and the Newfield director role should take priority." When Zand joined Foster and former Tenneco hand Chuck Shultz on the Newfield board, also active were Thomas Ricks representing the University of Texas and original co-investor Charles Duncan. Zand recalls, "Duncan was very astute, tuned in to what was going on, with substantial, helpful government and public company experience from his activities with American Express and other boards. Representing Wall Street private equity was Howard Newman of Warburg Pincus. He was an effective shadow CEO monitoring and reviewing almost every detail of company operations and actively advising Joe about decisions." Zand served on the NFX board until 1998 when he reached age 72 and the company celebrated its 10th anniversary.

THEN THERE'S JOE TIME

"One other thing, one of the people at Tenneco said to me, 'There's Joe time, and there's ordinary time.' I asked, 'What do you mean?' He said, 'Joe can see and understand a problem a hundred times faster than anyone else,' he continued, 'When you're just beginning to understand what's happening, he's a hundred steps ahead of you with the solution.' Although he has this remarkable ability, Joe Foster is a very decent, thoughtful human being who will patiently guide and encourage people to find and solve problems themselves. That's the great thing about him."
DALE ZAND

APPENDIX C
WHAT HAPPENED TO BLACKBEARD?

For the notorious pirate active in the Atlantic and the Caribbean in the eighteenth century, the history books are clear: Blackbeard the pirate was slain and beheaded in a swashbuckling encounter that would make Jack Sparrow proud. Blackbeard, a.k.a. Edward Teach, finally met his match in a fierce schooner battle with bounty hunter Lieutenant Robert Maynard off the North Carolina Outer Banks (Ocracoke Island) circa 1718.

Why did Newfield name their exploration prospect Blackbeard? Oil and gas geologists have a long tradition of naming offshore exploratory prospects—and later if commercial hydrocarbons are found—producing fields. For example, Cognac, Mars, Tahiti, Mad Dog and Thunder Horse are among the deepwater Gulf of Mexico's most celebrated oil and natural gas prospects/fields. Attaching mystical or fanciful nomenclature to a barren 5000-acre tract of water hundreds of miles offshore adds allure to the drilling of a "wildcat" well.

Referencing the UK and Norwegian sectors of the North Sea, oil executives can easily recite a litany of giant offshore petroleum field discoveries made over the past fifty years with exotic names like Ekofisk, Forties, Brent, Brae, Statfjord and Troll. Oilman Boone Pickens once paid his (then second of four) wife Beatrice a huge and unique compliment naming a Mesa Petroleum oil discovery in the North Sea after her. Boone, being the ultimate trader, then divested Mesa's Beatrice field to Kerr McGee in the 1980s (presaging, perhaps, Beatrice and Boone divesting themselves in an expensive and acrimonious divorce. In oilfield parlance, the Beatrice Carr/Boone Pickens marriage was eventually plugged and abandoned in the 1990s.)

WHERE IS BLACKBEARD NOW? BLACKBEARD LIVES WITH DAVY JONES!

The original Blackbeard West exploration well attracted worldwide interest, no doubt because of hydrocarbon reservoir targets ranging downhole to 38,000 feet, just shy of the world record of around 40,000 feet, established years ago by Russian scientists studying the world's geological depths.

It has been more than five years since I interviewed David Trice about the promise of the ultra-deep Gulf of Mexico and Blackbeard. There have been many downs and ups over that half decade; very recent exploratory results at the prospect Davy Jones have significantly revived interest. Let's trace key developments:

Blackbeard West #1 Well – South Timbalier 168

Water depth: Seventy feet

Spudded early February 2005 – Abandoned August 2006

Rowan "Scooter Yeargain" Tarzan-class JackUp Rig

Drilling time: Eighteen months Estimated cost: $180 Million Total Depth: 30,067 feet

Objective: 32,000 to 38,000 feet

Partners: Exxon Mobil (25%) and operator, BP (20%), Petrobras Americas (20%), Newfield Exploration (23%), Dominion Exploration & Production (7%) and BHP Billiton Petroleum (Deepwater) (5 %). Finally a 1.25 percent overriding royalty interest is held by the Treasure Island Royalty Trust.

WHAT HAPPENED?

In late May 2005, Newfield's CEO Trice was quoted "The industry basically is like a bunch of birds on a wire watching the Blackbeard well go down.…(However) I think people want to see how long does it take, how much does it cost, and did you find anything."

Trice called it! When the Blackbeard West first attempt was spudded he noted with caution that certain drilling equipment problems could be encountered down hole where intense pressures (15,000 psi) exist and temperatures hit extremes of from 400 to 600 degrees Fahrenheit.

The initial heart-pounding excitement among oil explorationists surrounding the exploratory test faded to ennui as the original well on South Timbalier Block 168 encountered one mechanical difficulty after another. While the well was quickly brought to a depth of 13,000 feet by the end of May 2005 (roughly 3,250 feet per month) drilling progress slowed to a crawl thereafter. Between June 2005 and the August 2006 abandonment date, Blackbeard West drilling snailed along at less than 1,250 feet per month or roughly forty feet per day.

But during the year and a half drilling continued at Blackbeard West, promises of more ultra-deep wells to come were rampant. In March 2005, Rowan was telling industry analysts that ExxonMobil wanted to drill more ultra-deep wells in the region, even if Blackbeard came up dry. In May 2005, Newfield said it was discussing with third parties about the possibility of drilling more ultra-deep wildcats on prospects located near Blackbeard West, including Blackbeard East.

However, Newfield later acknowledged that many companies originally interested in participating in ultra-deep drilling had decided to wait it out on the sidelines until results from Blackbeard came in. Then came the bad news and all talk of another ultra-deep well on the scope of Blackbeard evaporated. ExxonMobil and its partners opted to abandon the Blackbeard West well due to "higher-than-expected" pressures and temperatures downhole after reaching a measured depth of 30,067 feet and scant hydrocarbon potential was encountered.

Nonetheless, Newfield remained somewhat encouraged and noted that the Blackbeard West #1 penetrated a thin gas-bearing sand below 30,000 feet. The Blackbeard West structure was believed to extend over several Gulf of Mexico blocks and hold reserve potential of one to five trillion cubic feet.

Trice commented, "Although disappointed that we were unable to test our primary objectives, we have learned a great deal about drilling ultra-deep wells. This has been a challenging well to test a true frontier play."

ENTER MCMORAN, PLAINS EXPLORATION AND ENERGY XXI

By 2007 Newfield's focus had shifted to the development of onshore natural gas resource plays, such as the Woodford, and the company changed its strategic course and divested its Gulf of Mexico shelf properties to McMoRan Exploration, based in New Orleans.

The Newfield properties acquired by McMoRan included 125 fields on 146 offshore blocks currently producing (at the time) 270 million cubic feet of natural gas equivalents per day. Proved reserves were estimated to be 327 billion cubic feet of natural gas equivalents. Offshore leases included in the purchase agreement totaled 1.3 million gross acres. McMoRan also acquired a fifty-percent stake in Newfield's non-producing exploration leases on the shelf including the Treasure Island ultra-deep prospect inventory. Moreover, McMoRan retained the technical and operating personnel and contractors that supported Newfield's ultra-deep exploration initiative

McMoRan had the courage to seek a new depth target at Blackbeard West of 33,000 feet, adding that "drilling results (from the original test)…confirmed the geological model and thesis that was led to the prospect being tested." However, by this time it was known that such optimism was not shared by ExxonMobil and any of the other former Blackbeard partners, including Newfield, BP, Petrobras and BHP Billiton; all declined to participate in the re-drill.

"It's our intention to deepen this well to allow it to test its primary target," McMoRan co-chairman Richard Adkerson stated. McMoRan elected to hire a beefed up drilling rig, explaining that the Yeargain was capable of going deeper than 30,000 feet but lacked a suitable tree and blowout preventer, one of the reasons why the well was abandoned. "(When) we can get everybody together and get the rig situation (worked out), we…(will test the deeper zones.") added legendary explorationist and co-chairman Jim Bob Moffett.

Joining McMoRan for the next round of drilling at Blackbeard (and further tests) were Plains Exploration and Energy XXI, headed by notable wildcatters Jim Flores and John Schiller, respectively.

"Blackbeard is an exciting, opportunistic addition to our drilling program, offering multiple trillions of cubic feet of natural gas potential," said Energy XXI CEO John Schiller. "We reserve a portion of our drilling budget for swing-for-the-fences projects such as this…we are pleased to team up with McMoRan again. Adding Blackbeard to the portfolio significantly increases the potential to grow the company through near-term exploration."

In an interview we held in 2009 with Winston Talbert, CFO of Plains Exploration, he was more circumspect than Energy XXI. Talbert quoted his boss Flores as describing the ultra-deep Treasure Island exploration play as "…a huge science project."

Blackbeard West #1 Well Re-entry – South Timbalier 168

Water depth: Seventy feet

Re-entered March 2008 – Drilling completed and well temporarily abandoned August 2008

Current Status: Partners are evaluating geophysical results toward a "Go" or "No Go" development plan.

Rowan Gorilla IV JackUp Rig

Drilling time: Five months. Estimated cost: $37 Million Total Depth: 32,997 feet

Partners: McMoran Exploration (32.3%) and operator, Plains Exploration (35%), Energy XXI (20%).

BLACKBEARD WEST RE-TEST IS INCONCLUSIVE

The deepening of the Blackbeard West was considerably less time consuming and measurably less costly than the original well—but, nonetheless, results were inconclusive. For nearly two years, the partners in the wildcat prospect have been evaluating results and, at this time, no development plan has been formulated.

On a positive note, as Newfield and EEX had originally postulated McMoRan confirmed that Blackbeard's geology was similar to plays in the deepwater Gulf of Mexico that had resulted in major hydrocarbon discoveries. "Geologically, it's tied into the Miocene plays in the deepwater that we see in Mississippi Canyon," McMoRan's Adkerson said. He added that with an understanding of sand deposition and McMoRan's deep-gas experience, "we can find very attractive, potentially prolific prospects to drill in that area. Then, lying below that, in the middle Miocene and lower Miocene and older aged sands is the exploration that has been done in the deepwater, and which we now have the opportunity to pursue on the shelf through the ultra-deep plays that we have acquired."

Peter Ricchiuti, research director for the Burkenroad Reports, Tulane University's acclaimed equity analysis program for business students, was quoted in the *New Orleans Times-Picayune* "The mega-deep well, located just off the mouth of the Mississippi River, could end up producing the equivalent of four billion barrels of oil." Ricchiuti noted that "(the Blackbeard West re-entry)…has the potential to be a game changer for the industry."

DAVY JONES—HAS THE REAL GAME CHANGER BEEN DISCOVERED?
Davy Jones Prospect – South Marsh Island 230

Water depth: Nineteen feet

Spudded: July 1, 2009

Re-entry of Stone Energy/McMoRan Exploration well that was plugged and abandoned at 19,958 feet

Drilling Status at January 20, 2010: Drilled to 28,603 feet of 29,000-foot objective, logged 200 feet of net pay in several sand intervals

Current Status: Logging in preparation for flow tests

Rowan Mississippi JackUp Rig

Drilling time: Seven months

Estimated cost: $30 Million; Total Depth: 28,603 feet

Partners: McMoRan Exploration (32.7%) and operator, Plains Exploration (27.7%), Energy XXI (5.8%), Nippon Oil (12.0%), W. A. "Tex" Moncrief, Jr. (8.8%) and a private investor (3%).

PAYDIRT!
In early January 2010, McMoran Exploration ignited a fierce rally in its shares (MMR) and those of partners Energy XXI (EXXI) and Plains Exploration (PXP) when it issued the press release which follows below. The MMR and EXXI shares surged fifty percent and forty percent, trading on January 11th.

NEW ORLEANS, LA, January 11, 2010 – McMoRan Exploration Co. (NYSE: MMR) announced today a discovery on its Davy Jones ultra-deep prospect. The well has been drilled to a measured depth of 28,263 feet and has been logged with pipe-conveyed wireline logs to 28,134 feet. The wireline log results indicated a total of 135 net feet of hydrocarbon bearing sands in four zones in the Wilcox section of the Eocene/Paleocene. All of the zones were full to base with two of the zones containing a combined ninety net feet. The Eocene/Paleocene (Wilcox) suite of sands logged below 27,300 feet appears to be of exceptional quality. Flow testing will be required to confirm the ultimate hydrocarbon flow rates from the four separate zones. The resistivity log obtained on January 10th was the last data needed to confirm hydrocarbons in South Marsh Island Block 230.

McMoRan's Co-Chairman, James R. Moffett, said, "Davy Jones log results confirm our geologic model and indicate that the previously identified sands in the Wilcox section on this large ultra-deep structure encompassing four OCS lease blocks (20,000 acres) provides significant additional development potential which, upon confirmation development drilling, could make Davy Jones one of the largest discoveries on the Shelf of the Gulf of Mexico. The geologic results from this well are important and are redefining the subsurface geologic landscape below 20,000 feet on the shelf of the Gulf of Mexico. The results from this well will be incorporated into our models as we continue to define the potential of this promising new exploration frontier."

McMoRan plans to deepen the well to 29,000 feet to test additional objectives.

Joining the McMoRan consortium for the Davy Jones re-entry were Nippon Oil of Japan and legendary Fort Worth oilman, W.A "Tex" Moncrief. Moncrief, 89, was reportedly awakened at 3:30 am on January 9th with initial news of the Davy Jones discovery. *Forbes* magazine added, "After learning of the discovery…Moncrief went back to sleep. In the morning, at breakfast, in keeping with the pirate theme denoted by the Davy Jones name, 'my grandson brought a bottle of that Captain Morgan's spiced rum. I haven't had a taste yet,' Tex noted. 'But I have it sitting right in the breakfast room where if I need it I can reach over and grab it.'"

On January 20th, McMoRan issued an additional press release:

NEW ORLEANS – (BUSINESS WIRE) – McMoRan Exploration Co. (NYSE: MMR –News) announced today that the Davy Jones ultra-deep well has been drilled from 28,263 feet to 28,603 feet and the well has been logged with pipe-conveyed wireline logs to 28,530 feet. The wireline log results indicated a new hydrocarbon-bearing sand that totaled sixty-five net feet. A porosity (neutron/density) log will be necessary to quantify the porosity in this new sand member. The new sand interval combined with the 135 feet of net pay announced on January 11, 2010 brings the total possible productive net sands to 200 feet in the Davy Jones well. Flow testing will be required to confirm the ultimate hydrocarbon flow rates from the well.

As this book goes to press, McMoRan's offset appraised well was setting casing at 12,000 feet. The well was sited two-and-a-half miles southwest of the discovery well on South Marsh Island Block 234. Meanwhile, McMoRan is procuring long-lead time equipment with plans to complete and flow test the discovery well in SMI Block 230 in the third quarter of 2011. A number of questions remain to be answered about the Davy Jones discovery:

What is the areal extent of the reservoir? (The prospect is said to potentially cover four offshore lease blocks or 20,000 acres).

Can development wells be drilled that overcome the extreme pressures and temperatures?

How will wells perform over time given the hostile ultra-deep environment?

Will the development economics ($100 million platforms and $50 million wells) work?

Does the play extend to other shallow-water shelf leases?

These questions are not simple or easily answered. But that's what makes the oil and gas business so complex and exciting!

JOE B. FOSTER TIME LINE

1934	Born in Arp, Texas, July 25
1952	Graduates Greenville, Texas H.S., May
	Texas A&M; Corps of Cadets; 1952-57; B.S. Petroleum Engineering; B.B.A. General Business
1957	Junior Petroleum Engineer, Tenneco
1962	District Petroleum Engineer, Offshore Louisiana
1966	Staff Engineer, International
1968	Chief, Economic Planning & Analysis
1970	Manager, Vice President—Exploration
1974	Senior Vice President, North American E&P
1976	Executive Vice President, E&P Operations
1978	President, Tenneco Oil E&P
1981	Executive Vice President, Tenneco Inc., Chairman, Tenneco Oil
1983	Director, Executive Vice President, Tenneco Inc.; Chairman, Tenneco Oil; Chairman, Tennessee Gas Transmission
1988	Head of LBO effort during Tenneco Oil Sale
1989	Founded Newfield Explorations, Chairman, President, CEO
2000	Non-executive Chairman, Newfield Exploration, 1/28/00
	Interim Chairman, President & CEO, Baker Hughes, February–August
2001	Trustee, Texaco Alliance Trust
2004	Retired as non-executive Chairman, Newfield Exploration, 9/30/04
2005	Retired from board of Newfield Exploration
2008	Joins Tudor Pickering Holt & Co. as Chairman of private equity investment business, TPH Partners, L.L.C.

TENNECO

NEWFIELD

AWARDS RECEIVED   Houston Entrepreneur of the Year, Energy Sector, 1994

Distinguished Alumnus Texas A&M, 1997

Spindletop Service Award, 2000

Mays COllege of Business Outstanding Alumnus, 2001

Joe B. Foster Chair in Business Leadership, Mays Business School, 2004

Texas Business Hall of Fame, 2006

BOARD OF DIRECTORS

Corporate:	**Industry**:
Tenneco Inc.	IPAA
McDermott International	API
Baker Hughes (11)	Chairman, National Petroleum Council, 1997-99
Newfield Exploration	All American Wildcatter
New Jersey Resources	
Valero Energy	
Dual Drilling Corp.	

COMMUNITY SERVICE   Chairman, Greater Houston YMCA, 1989–91

Chairman, Houston Museum of Natural Science, 1991

Chairman, Houston A+ Challenge, 2009-10

Director, Memorial Hermann Healthcare System, 1999-2006

Director, Houston Hospice

Texas A&M Foundation, Trustee, 1988-96; Chairman, 1993

NEWFIELD TIME LINE

EARLY NOVEMBER 1988 Following the failed LBO attempt to purchase properties from Tenneco, Foster settles on the notion of a Gulf of Mexico start-up as his next career step and begins discussing the notion with key managers in Tenneco's Lafayette offshore divisions, including Al Wilkinson, Bob Taylor, Bob Waldrup, and Bill Schneider.

MID NOVEMBER 1988 Foster has individual meetings with working level Tenneco technical employees identified by the offshore Division managers as strong candidates for the new company. This takes place in Room 711 in the Hilton Hotel in Lafayette.

NOVEMBER 20, 1988 Foster meets with Charles Duncan and other members of his private investment firm to discuss the business concept and seek equity capital. Presents memo for oil & gas start-up company.

DECEMBER 8, 1988 Foster incorporates 4D Exploration Company. (Nobody else likes the name.)

DECEMBER 1988 Offers are made to employees, office space is found in Lafayette and Houston, with Foster and Charles Duncan's firm funding the activity.

JANUARY 2, 1989 Offices are open for business with Joe Foster and Betty Smith in Houston and remainder in Lafayette. Fundraising is the number-one priority in Houston, and getting organized to generate prospects is number-one priority in Lafayette.

JANUARY 1989 Committed to purchase $2 million of seismic data for Central Gulf of Mexico and an $180,000 3D work station.

JANUARY 1989 Foster introduced to University of Texas Endowment Fund by Ed Randall and John Duncan of the Duncan Firm to discuss possible investment in the new company.

FEBRUARY 1989 Select the new name Newfield Exploration Company.

MARCH 1989 Went to first offshore lease sale. Acquired five of eight blocks bid on for about $700,000.

APRIL 1, 1989 Initial funding closed with $9 million of equity - $3 million from Foster and the employees, $3 million from the Duncan Firm, and $3 million from the University of Texas Endowment (UTIMCO or University of Texas Investment Corporation).

APRIL 14, 1989 First Newfield Founders Dinner in Lafayette, Louisiana.

APRIL 1989 David Trice joins company as chief financial officer and Terry Rathert joins as manager of planning and analysis. (Terry had continuing duties at Tenneco which precluded him joining the company sooner.) David was referred to Joe by Clyde Metz, a former associate of David's at Huffco.

AUGUST 1989 Drilled first Newfield exploratory well at South Timbalier 103. Dry Hole.

FOURTH QUARTER 1989 Two additional dry holes drilled: South Marsh Island # 102 and Vermilion 373 #2

APRIL 1989 – MAY 1990 Trice was on the road seeking participants to join Newfield in its drilling program. These parties joined Newfield as working interest owners, subject to a small ORRI for the employee bonus pool and a back-in after payout. Participants included Resource Investors Management Company (RIMCO), Continental Land and Fur, MDU Resources, and the Princeton University Endowment through a private Houston-based investor relationship.

FEBRUARY 1990	Rig at Eugene Island 10 collapsed. It was a turnkey well so NFX did not owe any money because the contractor did not complete the well.
APRIL 1990	Made first discovery at West Delta 20 with reserves in excess of 20 Bcfe. This discovery well was logged on Memorial Day 1990. Received letter of intent on Chevron property acquisition, of Eugene Island 172 Field.
APRIL – MAY 1990	Second private placement adds a total of $37 million of funding for the company. New shareholders included Warburg Pincus Investors LP, Yale University, Duke University, and Dartmouth College. Some initial investors, including UTIMCO, made additional investments.
MAY 1990	Closed first acquisition of producing properties at Eugene Island 172 from Chevron and took over operations. Several wells were drilled during this timeframe, including the Breton Sound 44 #1 dry hole in May.
JUNE 1990	W. Cameron 401 #1 gas well in June.
MID 1990	Less than $100,000 in the bank. Five employees had departed the company since late 1989. (3 departed Feb-April, 2 others left in June.)
JULY 1990	As a result of the resignations and exploration dry holes, the Lafayette office is reorganized with Bob Waldrup being responsible for Operations and Engineering and Bill Schneider responsible for Exploration.
AUGUST 1990	Ship Shoal 157#1, which TD'd on August 29th and was the first operated discovery in a 6 well drilling program.
SEPTEMBER 1990	The decision is made to move the Lafayette office to Houston to be "under one roof", effective in January 1991.
OCTOBER 1990	Dry Holes: Ship Shoal 197 #A-1, Ship Shoal 186 #8
NOVEMBER 1990	A modest gas discovery at W. Cameron 415 #1
1990	Exited the year with 4.5 Mcfe/day net production and 23 Bcfe reserves, and was profitable in its second year of existence.
JANUARY 1991	NFX offices relocated at 363 N. Sam Houston Parkway E, Houston, Texas to have employees "under one roof." Key managers include:

        Joe B. Foster, Chief Executive Officer
        David Trice, Vice President-Finance
        Bob Waldrup, Manager Production & Operations
        Bill Schneider, Technical Co-ordinator
        Terry Rathert, Manager Planning & Analysis

MAY – OCTOBER 1991	Drilled A-3 and A-4/A-4 ST.
MAY – JUNE 1991	Made significant gas discovery at South Timbalier 193 & 194. Development drilling included Ship Shoal 157.

Dry holes in 1991 included: South Marsh Island 71; South Timbalier 80; Eugene Island 177 and Ship Shoal 298.

Exited the year with 78 Bcfe reserves and production of 16.3 mmcfe/day. This year, West Cameron 109 was acquired from Chevron. Drilled A-2 and A-4/A-4ST in May-October with first production in January 1992.

NOVEMBER 1991

Third private placement adds $20 million of funding for the company and Iowa Illinois Gas & Electric becomes both an equity stakeholder and a drilling program participant.

David Trice returns to Huffco International to become its CEO. Exited the year with 78 bcfe reserves and production of 16.3 mmcfe/day.

1992

Continued Gulf of Mexico focus. Acquired Eugene Island 181/182 from Exxon. Resulted in seven well drilling program and increasing production from minimal to 65 mmcfe per day from that field.

This year there were 9 exploration dry holes

Development drilling occurred on Vermilion 287.

George Dunn joins Newfield.

In 1992, Terry Rathert was promoted to CFO and Dave Schaible was promoted to manager of acquisitions and development.

DECEMBER 1992

Exited the year with 55 mmcfe/day production and 97 bcfe reserves. Bill Schneider appointed exploration manager.

1993

Eugene Island 251/262 acquired from Exxon.

This year, there were redevelopment programs on Eugene Island 182; Ship Shoal 322 and East Cameron 330. Numerous step-outs and new fault block tests made possible by acquiring or reprocessing 3D surveys to create superior subsea imaging. Exploration success at South Timbalier 111 and West Delta 20.

NOVEMBER 12, 1993

Initial public offering under symbol of "NFX" at a split adjusted price of $4.38 per share, brings in net proceeds of $57.3 million.

DECEMBER 1993

Exited the year with 77 mmcfe/day production and 141 bcfe reserves.

MID-1994

South Timbalier 148 acquired farm-in position and began a drilling program. Eugene Island 251/252 also was acquired this year. Eugene Island 262 "B" platform development; redevelopment at High Island A-537 and Ship Shoal 145

Exploration successes at Vermilion 355 and West Delta 1B.

1995

South Timbalier 148 "D" and "E" platforms with continued exploration success in progressively older (deeper) sands. Additional developments around South Timbalier 111 and South Timbalier 193/194 discoveries.

Onshore Gulf Coast initiative launched in South Louisiana.

West Delta 152 and Ewing 947 – drilling.

1997

A key program this year was East Cameron 286 where Newfield had identified prospects. David Trice returns to Newfield.

JANUARY 1998

Elliott Pew – ex-Tenneco; Leaves Louis Dreyfus/American Exploration to join Newfield as vice president-exploration.

	Bill Schneider named vice president-international.
MAY 6, 1999	David Trice named president and COO. Foster remains as chairman and CEO
JULY 1999	Lee Boothby – ex-Tenneco; Supporter of Foster's LBO group joins NFX, immediately moves to Australia to run Newfield subsidiary.
1999	Offshore Australia – two oil fields on production.
	Steve Campbell joins Newfield from Anadarko.
JANUARY 2000	Foster retires as Newfield CEO to become Interim CEO at Baker Hughes (where he served as a director), while it searched for a new CEO. He became non-executive chairman of Newfield.
	Headington onshore South Texas Sarita Field properties are acquired by Newfield; Leads to strong emphasis on South Texas Onshore.
FEBRUARY 1, 2000	Trice becomes president and CEO of Newfield
2001	Lee Boothby moves to Tulsa to manage Mid-Continent Office. Early this year, Newfield completes its largest acquisition – Lariat Petroleum ($333 million) in Oklahoma. Discoveries in West Cameron 294 and Eugene Island 251 "C" platform stepout.
2002	Newfield acquires EEX Corporation for $650 million.
SEPTEMBER 16, 2002	Bob Waldrup retires from Newfield Exploration.
2003	Boothby launches Woodford Shale resource land grab. First well was in 2003…Leasing was 2004, 2005, 2006.
2004	Newfield acquires Inland Resources for $575 million. Denver regional office opens with Gary Packer as lead executive.
MAY 2005	Foster retires from the Newfield board. Trice named chairman.
MAY 2007	Newfield announced the $578 million acquisition of assets in the Rocky Mountains.
JULY 2007	Newfield divests Gulf of Mexico Shelf assets to McMoRan Exploration for $1.1 billion.
OCTOBER 2007	Newfield retires its first tranche of public debt issued in 1997. David Schaible, president and COO of NFX, dies at age 46.
MAY 2009	Trice retires as CEO and assumes non-executive chairman role; Lee Boothby takes over as president and CEO.
	Newfield entered new operating area of the Marcellus Shale in Pennsylvania. This year, the company commenced oil development in the Pearl River Mouth Basin in China.
MAY 2010	Trice does not stand for re-election and leaves NFX board. Boothby named to additional role of chairman.
DECEMBER 2010	Newfield shares added to S&P 500 Index

YEAR	ANNUAL PRODUCTION			
	OIL & COND. MBBLS	GAS MMCF	EQUIVALENTS MMCFE	OIL & COND. MBBLPD
1989	–	–	–	–
1990	25	812	964	0.07
1991	105	5,334	5,963	0.29
1992	662	16,091	20,066	1.81
1993	901	22,540	27,946	2.47
1994	1,394	24,267	32,631	3.82
1995	2,071	33,719	46,145	5.67
1996	2,558	41,323	56,671	7.01
1997	3,424	53,505	74,049	9.38
1998	3,643	66,600	88,458	9.98
1999	4,354	87,400	113,524	11.93
2000	5,764	105,400	139,984	15.79
2001	6,998	133,200	175,188	19.17
2002	6,575	144,700	184,150	18.01
2003[1]	6,054	184,200	220,524	16.59
2004	7,565	198,200	243,590	20.73
2005	8,446	191,000	241,676	23.14
2006	7,315	198,700	242,590	20.04
2007[2]	8,759	192,800	245,354	24.00
2008	10,575	172,900	236,350	28.97
2009	13,179	174,300	253,374	36.11

Note: First discovery and producing acquisition took place in May 1990
[1]   Australia was sold in 2003.
[2]   UK was sold in 2007.

AVERAGE DAILY PRODUCTION		RESERVES AT 12/31		
GAS MMCFPD	EQUIVALENTS MMCFEPD	OIL & COND. MBBLS	GAS MMCF	EQUIVALENTS MMCFE
–	–	–	–	–
2.22	2.64	939	17,428	23,062
14.61	16.34	2,636	62,023	77,839
44.08	54.98	4,443	70,375	97,033
61.75	76.56	6,414	102,261	140,745
66.48	89.40	8,610	153,967	205,627
92.38	126.42	9,633	203,580	261,378
113.21	155.26	13,659	241,385	323,339
146.59	202.87	16,307	337,481	435,323
182.47	242.35	15,171	422,277	513,304
239.45	311.02	25,770	440,173	594,790
288.77	383.52	27,934	519,723	687,327
364.93	479.97	36,342	718,312	936,364
396.44	504.52	38,125	977,115	1,205,865
504.66	604.18	37,774	1,090,140	1,316,786
543.01	667.37	90,500	1,241,000	1,784,000
523.29	662.13	101,600	1,391,000	2,000,900
544.38	664.63	114,000	1,586,000	2,272,000
528.22	672.20	114,000	1,810,000	2,496,000
473.70	647.53	140,000	2,110,000	2,950,000
477.53	694.18	169,000	2,605,000	3,616,000

INDEX

JOINED		DATE OF KEY POSITION
1989	Terry W. Rathert, Exec. VP and CFO	5/7/2009
1989	William D. Schneider, VP Onshore Gulf Coast and Int.	10/1/2007
1992	George T. Dunn, VP Mid-Continent	10/1/2007
1993	Brian L. Rickmers, Controller and Assistant Secretary	12/8/1993
1995	James J. Metcalf, VP Drilling	3/1/2004
1995	Gary D. Packer, Exec. VP and COO	5/7/2009
1996	Daryll T. Howard, VP Rocky Mountains	5/7/2009
1997	Susan G. Riggs, Treasurer	5/16/2007
1997	James T. Zernell, VP Production	3/7/1997
1999	Lee K. Boothby, Chairman, President and CEO	5/7/2009
1999	Stephen C. Campbell, VP Investor Relations	9/7/1999
2000	John H. Jasek, VP Gulf of Mexico	1/24/2000
2001	W. Mark Blumenshine, VP Land	9/19/2001
2003	John D. Marziotti, General Counsel and Secretary	11/17/2003
2004	Samuel E. Langford, VP Corporate Development	5/7/2009
2006	Michael D. Van Horn, VP Geoscience	5/16/2009
1989	Robert W. Waldrup, Manager Production and Operations	Retired 9/16/2002
1998	Elliot Pew, Senior VP Exploration	Left company on 12/31/2006

FOOTNOTES

1-4	Joe B. Foster interview, February 2007
5	Joe B. Foster – Life Story
6-21	Joe B. Foster interview
22	John S. Herold, Inc.'s Petroleum Outlook, June 1988
23-28	Joe B. Foster interview
29-30	David Trice interview
31	Howard Newman interview
32	David Trice interview
33-35	Bob Waldrup interview
35a	Records from Merlin Prosper and Larry Oliver
36-56	Robert W. Waldrup interview
57	David Schaible interview
58-63	Bob Waldrup interview 3
64-77	Schneider interview
78-87	Betty Smith interview, circa 2006
88-104	David Trice interview
105-115	Terry Rathert interview, March 2009
116-118	David Schaible interview
119-123	Terry Rathert interview, March 2009
124	Joe B. Foster interview
125	Howard Newman interview
126	Joe B. Foster interview
127-129	Betty Smith interview
130-131	Joe B. Foster interview
132	David Trice interview
133	Howard Newman
134	Joe B. Foster interview
135	Bobby Tudor
136-137	Joe B. Foster interview
138-140	Steve Campbell interview
141-142	George Dunn interview
143-150	Gary Packer interview
151-164	Elliott Pew interview
165-176	Joe B. Foster interview
177	Schaible passed away in 2007
178-182	D. Schaible interview
183	Joe B. Foster interview
184-192	David Trice interview
193-194	Joe B. Foster interview
195-225	David Trice second interview
226	David Trice Newfield Exploration Company 2008 Annual Report